THE WAY
OF THE
STRANGERS

THE WAY
OF THE
STRANGERS

ENCOUNTERS
WITH THE
ISLAMIC STATE

GRAEME WOOD

RANDOM HOUSE
NEW YORK

Published in the United States by Random House, an imprint and division of Penguin Random House LLC, New York.

RANDOM HOUSE and the HOUSE colophon are registered trademarks of Penguin Random House LLC.

Portions of this work were originally published in different form in *The Atlantic* and *The New Republic*.

Hardback ISBN 978-0-8129-8875-8
Ebook ISBN 978-0-8129-8876-5

Printed in the United States of America on acid-free paper

randomhousebooks.com

2   4   6   8   9   7   5   3   1

First Edition

Book design by Christopher M. Zucker

Abu Huraira reported: The Messenger of God, peace and blessings be upon him, said, "Islam began as something strange and it will return to being strange, so blessed are the strangers."

—Sahih Muslim 1/130

They were brought up in houses like his own. They were raised by parents like him. And so many were girls, girls whose political identity was total, who were no less aggressive and militant, no less drawn to "armed action" than the boys. There is something terrifyingly pure about their violence and the thirst for self-transformation. They renounce their roots to take as their models the revolutionaries whose conviction is enacted most ruthlessly. They manufacture like unstoppable machines the abhorrence that propels their steely idealism. Their rage is combustible. They are willing to do anything they can imagine to make history change. . . .

This was his daughter, and she was unknowable. This murderer is mine.

—Philip Roth, *American Pastoral*

THE ISLAMIC STATE VIEW OF HUMANITY

MUSLIMS

Jesus

**Muslims pledged
to the Islamic State**
Boko Haram
and other groups

Abu Bakr
al Baghdadi

Quraysh
The Prophet Muhammad

The Mahdi

Abdullah II
of Jordan

Mohammed VI
of Morocco

Shia
Alawites
(e.g., Bashar al Assad);
governments of
Iran, Iraq

**"Sunni"
enemies of IS**
Supporters of kings,
democracy, and secular
government (e.g., Muslim
Brotherhood, Hamas);
most Sufis; leaders of
Taliban, Al Qaida

APOSTATES

INFIDELS

The Anti-Christ

**Eligible to
be enslaved**
Hindus, Buddhists,
Yazidis, secular
humanists, etc.

**Eligible to
pay *jizya****
Jews
Christians

*tax levied on
subjugated non-Muslim
residents of the Islamic State,
in exchange for safety

—

CONTENTS

A NOTE ON TERMINOLOGY

The war against the Islamic State is not primarily a war of words, though it is sometimes treated as one. To discredit and annoy the Islamic State, its enemies often insist on calling it "ISIS," "the so-called 'Islamic State,'" "Daesh," or "the un-Islamic State." This name-calling has yet to show any palpable effect. "We're happy to have you discussing whether to call us 'Daesh,' 'ISIL,' or 'ISIS,'" one supporter of the Islamic State told me. "As long as you're talking about that," he said—and not about theology, politics, or military operations—"we know you're not taking us seriously."

Throughout this book, I refer to "the Islamic State." Some readers will recoil at my decision to use the name the Islamic State calls itself. No writer has yet discovered neutral terms to describe the Islamic State or its beliefs, and my choice is not an endorsement. By calling it "the Islamic State," I am no more supporting it than I am implying divine favor for Hizbullah when I use its name, which means "the Party of God."

The Islamic State has many names, all of which describe the same entity:

- The Islamic State in Iraq and the Levant (ISIL)
- The Islamic State in Iraq and Sham (ISIS)
- Daesh or Daʿesh
- The Islamic State

Sham is an Arabic name for the Levant, the geographic area roughly encompassing modern Syria and Lebanon, and possibly the West Bank and Jordan.[1] The acronyms "ISIL" and "ISIS" differ only in that "ISIL" uses the English word for the Levant, and "ISIS" uses the Arabic word for the Levant and English for the rest.

The Arabic equivalent of "the Islamic State in Iraq and Sham" is *al Dawlah al Islamiyya fi-l ʿIraq wa-l Sham*. Arabic-speaking opponents of the group prefer the acronym "Daʿesh" because it sounds similar to words ranging in meaning from "trample" to "uncouth."[2] The *a* in "Daʿesh" stands for the Arabic word for "Islamic," and the *d* stands for "State" (*d*awlah). The letter ʿ is the Arabic letter *ʿayn* (ع), which represents a sound rarely made by English-speakers. (My first Arabic teacher taught me to practice it by singing along to the Rolling Stones' song "Angie." The fourth time Mick Jagger sings the name "Angie," he produces a perfect *ʿayn*.)

Calling the entity "Daʿesh" in no way denies its claim to be an Islamic state. The term does, however, annoy the Islamic State's partisans. Their preferred label is "the Islamic State," and they have whipped people and threatened to cut out their tongues for saying "Daʿesh." Also acceptable to the Islamic State are **al Dawlah** ("the State") and **al Khilafah** ("the Caliphate," led by a **khalifah** [caliph]). They say that the entity known as "ISIS" or "ISIL" dissolved upon its declaration of a caliphate in June 2014 and became the Islamic State.

The Islamic State maintains its own armory of insults and praise. As an extreme Sunni group, it reserves the word "Muslim" for a small group of fellow Sunnis, and it has strong negative views of Shia theology. Other self-described Muslims are not considered Muslims at all. They have nullified their Islam by act or belief, and they must repent or be killed.

First among these are the Shia. The Islamic State considers them *ex*-Muslims—that is, apostates, people who have left the faith. The Sunni-Shia split began over the question of who should succeed Muhammad as leader of the Muslims after his death in 632. The Shia wanted to follow members of Muhammad's family, and the Sunni chose leaders from the community of Muslims as a whole, without preference for the Prophet's line. The Islamic State claims that the Shia have, up to the present day, "refused" the legitimate leadership; it calls them **rawafidh** or **rafidha** [refusers]. On these points, the Islamic State's propaganda is clear:

> The scholars also called [the Shia] so because the *Rāfidah* rejected the *imāmah* [leadership] of [the first Sunni caliphs] Abū Bakr, 'Umar, and 'Uthmān, because they rejected the *Sahābah* [companions of the Prophet], because they rejected the Sunna [example of the Prophet], and because they essentially rejected the Qur'ān and the religion of Islam.[3]

In refusing the Koran, the Shia *left* Islam, and so every Shia is a **murtadd** [apostate] and must be killed.

Most of those the Islamic State considers apostates consider themselves Muslim. To claim or imply that the Prophet Muhammad and the Holy Koran are imperfect, or that their commands are optional or in need of revision or reinterpretation, are all potential acts of apostasy and would likely incur the death penalty in the Islamic State. Since the Islamic State believes that many actions and beliefs constitute apostasy, when its followers use the term "Muslim" they do so in a highly restricted sense, to which the vast majority of self-identified Muslims would strenuously object.

Any so-called Muslim ruler who rules contrary to God's will (for instance, by holding elections, legalizing consumption of pork or alcohol, or not stoning adulterers) is an apostate. This harsh standard yields counterintuitive results, since the Islamic State considers even most well-known Islamists (including the leaders of Hamas and the Muslim Brotherhood, and Recep Tayyip Erdoğan of Turkey) apostates. Because they replace God's law with their own, they are guilty of *shirk* [elevating someone other than God to God's status; literally, assigning a "partner" to God] and therefore are *mushrikin* [polytheists; sing. *mushrik*].

The Islamic State calls the strongmen in Arab countries *tawaghit* [tyrants; sing. *taghut*]. The clergy who serve the tyrants are apostates if they flaunt their error and *munafiqun* [hypocrites; sing. *munafiq*] if they preach the truth but do not practice it. They, too, are cast out of Islam. The Islamic State calls Saudi royals and their supporters *al Salul*. The name is a reference to ʿAbdullah Ibn Ubayy (d. 631), known as Ibn Salul, a Medinan leader who pledged loyalty to Muhammad but later betrayed him. He is the original *munafiq*. The slur against the Saudis implies that they preach the right things but do not believe them.

Most religiously literate Muslims in history have been **Sufis** (mystics who seek oneness with God through meditation, poetry, dance, and wine) or followers of theological schools (chiefly **Maturidis** or **Ashʿarites**) that the Islamic State and its predecessors have opposed. The Islamic State insists on literal reading of the Koran, with minimal figurative or allegorical interpretation. (When the Koran says "the hand of God" [*yadu llahi*], most Muslims interpret "hand" [*yadu*] to mean "power." The Islamic State interprets it to mean "hand."[4]) They revile the Sufis for venerating the graves and shrines of saints and holy people. These practices are *shirk* or idolatry, the Islamic State says, and nullify one's Islam.

This book contains as little Arabic as possible. But discussion of the Islamic State is impossible without occasional resort to the Arabic terms above. Many non-Arab supporters of the Islamic State spice their conversation with Arabic, even when the Arabic words—such as *Allah* [God] and *dawlah* [state]—have exact equivalents in their native languages. To reduce the burden on non-Arabic-speaking readers and to keep the flow of the original quotes, I have kept the Arabic and provided bracketed translations.

PROLOGUE

In November 2004, I took a job with a courier company in Iraq and moved to a patch of gravel next to the airport in Mosul. Two small, temporary buildings served as office and living quarters. I shared them with two homesick Nepalese Gurkhas and a retired British soldier. Our planes flew in from Bahrain, and the four of us worked with a team of five Iraqis to unload and deliver their cargo. U.S. soldiers received care packages from family and equipment from far-off bases. Iraqis came to collect diesel engines, X-ray machines for the local hospital, and crate upon crate of untaxed Jordanian cigarettes for resale. At night, the Gurkhas ran up massive bills calling Nepal on our satellite phone, and the Brit watched movies, drank whiskey, and cleaned his boots and his gun.

The occupation of Iraq, by then over a year old, was not yet at its most dangerous, and the insurgents' attacks were still journeyman efforts, not the masterpieces of mayhem they would become over the next three years. The U.S. military could secure the airport but not the city around it. Insurgents regularly lobbed mortars and rockets, and the distant *CRUNK!* of incoming fire served as a five-second warning to dive into the small concrete bunker adjacent to my office and wait for the blast. A volley of inbound mortars could last seconds or an hour, and I sometimes heard helicopters buzzing off toward the authors of the attack and, with a rip of machine-gun fire, killing them. By the third attack, I had begun prepping the bunker with a book and a flashlight, so I'd never get caught dead or alive without reading material.

During those long cold evenings, huddled with the Gurkhas on a camp cot beneath six inches of concrete, I wondered about the man trying to kill us. He was probably my age, twenty-five, or younger. Was he Iraqi, or a foreign adventurer like me? If the latter, how did he get here, and why? I hardly knew why I had come to Mosul—better jobs beckoned closer to home—so how could I expect to understand the motivations of this man I had never met? Did he also have better options? As he waited for the right time to drop a mortar into its tube, was he also cradling a paperback?

This book grew out of curiosity about him.

On December 21, 2004, a suicide bomber infiltrated one of the airport's two cafeterias and blew up twenty-two Iraqis and Americans. I was eating lunch in the other cafeteria at the time. I was saved because my stomach grumbled in front of one mess tent and not another. When I learned the details of the attack—the bomber had weighed himself down with bolts and screws to multiply the shrapnel—my powers of empathy were taxed. I could imagine myself angry, even violent. But in imagining the physical sensation of murder—a vest heavy with a whole hardware store's worth of metal— I reached a limit and resigned myself to bafflement.

Over the next decade, the insurgents changed, and so did I. I returned to Iraq as a journalist. The Gurkhas moved to Bahrain, and the Brit now guards the life of an ambassador in London. The last U.S. soldiers left Mosul in late 2011. My Iraqi friends say the Iraqi soldiers who replaced them stole and sold a large amount of the equipment the Americans left behind.

With the Americans gone, the insurgents emerged from the shadows. A few years after the cafeteria bombing, members of the group responsible pledged fealty to the Islamic State of Iraq (ISI), the forerunner of the Islamic State in Iraq and Sham (ISIS). When I last visited Mosul, in August 2012, the city was nominally under the control of the Iraqi government, but people lived in fear of ISI, which they still called "Al Qaida" (a name the group itself hadn't used since 2006). ISI/Al Qaida extorted shopkeepers. They killed and kidnapped. When we drove around, my friend Yasir asked me to slouch in my seat and remove my military-looking sunglasses, because the streets had again become dangerous enough that I could be mistaken for a U.S. soldier or mercenary and kidnapped by Al Qaida, or shot dead while we waited in traffic.

On June 10, 2014, Al Qaida—now called ISIS—conquered Mosul with a force of between five hundred and a thousand men. The Iraqi Army barely resisted. Mosul's population, mostly Sunni Arab and disdainful of the Shia-dominated government in Baghdad, greeted ISIS's Sunni fighters with trepidation, then terrified acquiescence. ISIS imposed Shariah law, and it ruled Mosul uncontested until the Iraqi Army began its assault to retake the city in October 2016. The man I first imagined in 2004 was now in charge.

To observe the conquest of Mosul by ISIS was to witness something both familiar and novel. A decade of continuous war had passed since the city's fall to the Americans, and the appearance of yet another truck-borne gang of gunmen hardly counted as revolutionary.

Also familiar were former elements of Saddam Hussein's regime among ISIS's leadership. Few insurgencies in Iraq, secular or religious, arose without Baathist influence, and some Baathists switched with remarkable ease to religious conservatism. Once mustachioed like Saddam, they now grew out full beards and enforced Islamic codes of law, dress, and behavior. Abu Muslim al Turkmani, a former army officer, became the group's chief of operations in Iraq. Izzat Ibrahim al Duri, the ginger Baathist who commanded the largest contingent of fugitive Saddamists, praised the group and allied with it. For some outside observers, the fingerprints of Baathists were reassurance that nothing had changed and the enemy was no one new.

But dedicated scholars of jihad, who watched ISIS carefully and haunted the online forums of its fighters and propagandists, detected something worrying. Jihadists did not regard the seizure of Mosul as a local victory, let alone as one whose main beneficiaries were Saddam's henchmen. Instead, first as a murmur and soon as a roar, they insisted that ISIS's ascent was an event of world-historical import. Indeed, to call it world-historical would diminish it, because the entire cosmos was in play. They suggested that ISIS was fulfilling prophecy; that it was resurrecting laws and forms of government dormant for more than a thousand years; and that it would continue to vanquish the enemies of Islam until Jesus himself returned as a Muslim warrior to slay the Anti-Christ.

Both the excavation of a distant, imagined past and the projections into the future were calculated to exploit a familiar narrative. Among Muslims, and among non-Muslims, the word "caliphate" (a territory ruled by a successor of the Prophet, the establishment of which ISIS had identified as its goal) conjures a collective memory of an imagined Islamic past—the courts of Baghdad, the Arabian Nights, scientific and philosophical triumphs like the invention of algebra and the first theories of optics. Children have gone to bed at night with visions of palaces and flying carpets. Many Muslim children have asked to keep the night light on after bedtime-tales of clashes between Muslim armies and the Anti-Christ, and the tribulations at the end of the world. ISIS invoked this narrative. To all who joined it, it promised glory and virtue, and the honor of participating in nothing less than the grand finale of the universe itself.

Every generation of Christians and Muslims yields up its crop of madmen and howlers at the moon, and they always spook the rationalists of their eras. A previous generation noted with concern the Iranian revolution's rhetoric of apocalypse. More than half of American evangelicals believe, or profess to believe, in imminent doomsday.[1] Luckily, most apocalyptic movements sputter out, soften their tone, or turn out to be bluffing. Many of the Iranian revolutionaries who thought the Ayatollah Khomeini would reveal himself as the Mahdi—a messianic figure said by most Shia to have been in hiding since 941—now deny they ever believed such a thing. The ruling mullahs are at least as interested in trade agreements as in nuclear weapons. As for American evangelicals, they claim to believe they live in the end times, but they still contribute to their retirement accounts. There is similar reassurance in the belief that when a jihadist tells you he wants to kill you and billions of others to bring about the end of the world, he is just speaking for effect.

What worried me about the new overlords of Mosul was the mounting evidence that they—and a growing society of supporters from distant corners of the planet—meant what they said. Instead of talking about imminent death but planning for long life, they talked about imminent death and sought it avidly. By midsummer 2014, fighters for ISIS had long since been Instagramming and tweeting ghastly images—baskets of heads, piles of corpses, looped videos of executions. As for their steps to self-slaughter, discussion of the longing for battlefield martyrdom intensified, and recruits rushed to emigrate to the worst war zone on the planet. By then ISIS had made northeast Syria its stronghold. According to U.S. military sources, about twenty thousand people had traveled there to fight by that time, and twenty thousand more have defied their home governments and dodged police and border patrols to do so since.

Many who immigrated—or, in Islamic State parlance, "made *hijrah*"—quickly died in combat. To die was the point. But many others lived on and encouraged their friends to join them. Some warned of hardship and expressed regret—imperiling their own lives in the process, since the Islamic State kills defectors. But no propaganda effort could conceal the uncomfortable fact that for immigrants to the Islamic State, the killing was a source of profound fulfillment.

The letters they send home combine quiet dignity with complete moral insanity. In May 2015, twelve members of the Mannan family of Luton, England, traveled together to Raqqah, Syria, the de facto capital of the Islamic State. They ranged in age from one to seventy-five, and an open letter from the family rebuked anyone who suspected they had been tricked into going. "Don't be shocked when we say that none of us were forced against our will," they wrote. "It is outrageous to think that an entire family could be kidnapped and made to migrate like this." They had made their journey "by the command of the Khalifah [caliph] of the Muslims." And they found what they wanted—"a land that has established the Shariah, in which a Muslim doesn't feel oppression [. . .], in which a parent doesn't feel the worry of losing their child to the immorality of society [. . .], in which the sick and elderly do not wait in agony."[2]

In June 2015, an Australian doctor, Tareq Kamleh, appeared in an Islamic State video extolling the health system in Raqqah, Syria. The Islamic State, like any other government, had to administer its territory and population, and was busy building bureaucracies for taxation, health, education, and other official functions. Australian media investigated Kamleh's past and found evidence that he had adopted piety late in life. He was, they said, a "playboy" who collected photos of the "hot girls" he dated.[3] The Australian Health Practitioner Regulation Agency wrote him suggesting that his service to the Islamic State constituted an ethical breach that voided his medical license. He replied:

> I made a very well educated and calculated decision to come here, it did not involve any brainwashing. Since being here I have seen that it is in no way as described by the colorful Australian politicians "murdering and raping everyone in their way" . . . [a] "death cult." The only death that I have had to deal with since being here has been from either pathology or coalition drone strikes. Running the pediatric component of the casualties, my favorite time was telling the mum of a 6 year old girl that the fact that her brains were on her face meant that she was dead [. . .] Good work "Team Australia"!! From what I've seen you have more blood on your hands than ISIS has on their knives . . .
>
> Is it not my humanitarian duty to help these children also?! . . . or only kids with white skin and blue passports?! I formally deny that I have ever taken part in unprofessional conduct which would have jeopardized my doctor-patient relationship.
>
> I never intend to return to Australia, I have finally returned home.[4]

The breadth of the appeal of the Islamic State was as shocking as its depth. Three generations of conservative Muslims from outside London, a skirt-chasing bachelor from South Australia, and tens of thousands of others had all drunk their inspiration from the same fountains. In addition to the physical caliphate, with its territory and war and economy to run, there was a caliphate of the imagination to which all these people had already emigrated long before they slipped across the Turkish border. They believed the state that awaited them would purify their lives by forbidding vice and promoting virtue. Its leader, Abu Bakr al Baghdadi, would unify the world's Muslims, restore their honor, and allow them to reside in the only truly just society. Its Muslim citizens would enjoy perfect equality, free of the iniquities they had suffered due to differences of race, wealth, or nationality in the countries of their birth.

To realize this dream, they had joined a fascist, expansionist movement of global reach. They rejected the values by which they had previously lived, and instead embraced practices such as slavery, mutilation, and extreme violence against non-Muslims and many self-described Muslims. They had been persuaded by the same propaganda and, in many cases, the same people.

I started looking for these seducers. Some had, for one reason or another, not yet emigrated themselves, and therefore were within the reach of an infidel journalist. Many loved the attention. I kept my questions naïve: What do you want? Who are you? Why, among all the versions of Islam, did this most ruthless one attract you?

In December 2014, on a warm afternoon in Melbourne, Australia, I began to get answers. One of the most prolific of the Islamic State's defenders is Musa Cerantonio, a thirty-two-year-old convert from Catholicism then living under state surveillance in the Melbourne suburb of Footscray. His lectures, essays, and translations litter the jihadi Internet, and by mid-2014, terrorism analysts counted him as one of the key online influences on Islamic State supporters. Authorities tracked him to the southern Philippines, then deported him back to Melbourne and stripped him of his passport. The Australian tabloids liked having a jihadist in their midst—a bearded face to go with screeching banner headlines about terror at home—and when he returned to Melbourne, the media scrum resembled the parading of an enemy captive for purposes of shame and humiliation. In mid-

2014, Facebook canceled his personal page, which had maxed out at about 12,000 devotees, and he stayed quiet for a few months.

When I met him, he was ready to talk. Indeed, he was so eager to answer my questions that he bought me lunch, plates of lamb and okra at a modest Sudanese joint. I recognized in him a familiar form of missionary zeal: by telling me about his religion, he was binding me to it, removing ignorance from the list of excuses I could use before God on Judgment Day. Through me, he would bind my readers, too. In that conversation—the first of many—he outlined the duty of Muslims to appoint and obey a caliph, a successor to the Prophet himself. He explained how the Islamic State had done exactly this, and so fulfilled an obligation many previous generations had ignored, at peril to their own souls. "I would go so far as to say that Islam has been reestablished," he said.

Before long, he said, will come the final days prophesied by Muhammad. The earth will suffer drought—a third of the planet will go without rain one year, and two-thirds the next. We will live in an age of miracles, both counterfeit and real; of inconceivable suffering, bloodshed, and tribulation; of global war waged with tools ranging from sabers to thermonuclear weapons. Those who survive—Muslim and not—will wish for death.

He related this dispassionately while I listened and chewed my lamb. With each minute, my food lost its flavor. Next to final battles and apocalypse, who cares about food? Who cares about anything? The quotidian concerns I had brought to my meeting (was my recorder working? Was I sure I had locked my hotel room?) receded in importance. For a moment, I could feel the riptide of belief, and could imagine why someone might renounce the dull world I inhabited in favor of Musa's enchanted one.

"The sun will rise in the West," he said, "and from then on, Allah will accept no repentance, and the final hour will be upon us." He paused. At first, I thought he stopped because I looked distracted, preoccupied by the widening emotional and imaginative distance between our respective universes. Then I realized that he had stopped because his apocalyptic narrative had ended, and with it the universe itself.

We eyed each other in silence for a few seconds—not aggressively, but to assess whether further discussion would be worthwhile. He had imparted these prophecies as the most humdrum facts, as if he were recounting his toothbrushing routine or a recipe for flan. To me, they may as well have been science fiction, or a retelling of Götterdämmerung, an apocalyptic cosmology reduced—some might say elevated, but at any rate desacralized—to the status of literature. But Musa was inviting me to join him in considering these events as realities no less concrete than the table and plates of food sitting in front of us. *Here,* he was saying, *is what the Islamic State is going to do, and how the world will end. And no one can stop it.*

This was big talk for an unemployed Aussie licking grease off his fingers. And if he were a lone voice of apocalypse, I would have paid him no further attention. But in dozens of interviews with him and his comrades on four continents over the past two years, I came to think of them as the visible surface of a cause that was stirring the emotions and convictions of tens of millions of others, and that would continue to inspire them for decades to come, even if it lost its core territory in Syria and Iraq. These men and women were not psychopathic automata—indeed, they were often smart, at times even gentle and well-mannered. They adhered to more than a system of belief. It was a way of thinking and living, of sharing joy and pity; it was a culture unto itself.

The cognitive dissonance still jars me: these are intelligent people with the most wicked beliefs. It's tempting to try to resolve that tension by doubting their sincerity—surely they don't want genocide, surely they don't want me dead. But I have looked for signs of a con, and if there is one, they are its victims and not its perpetrators. When someone says something too evil to believe, one response is not to doubt their sincerity but to expand one's capacity to imagine what otherwise decent people can desire. That, I have concluded, is the proper response to the Islamic State. Listening to its voices, and seeing its endless portfolio of stonings, immolations, and bullets to the head, has felt to me like one of those peculiarly terrifying nightmares whose vividness turns out to be its own undoing. Eventually, the horror becomes so intense that you snap awake. But this nightmare has grown only more real, without return to waking life, and its expansion of our intimacy with evil has not yet concluded.

Some will continue to see the Islamic State's supporters as maniacs and doubt the value of analyzing the madness, let alone the sickening propaganda, in any detail. What is the benefit in reading the rantings of crazy people, even if they quote the Koran correctly? I am reminded of a story the late film critic Roger Ebert told about his days as a cub reporter, when he interviewed a carnival barker.

> His star was a geek, who bit off the heads of live chickens and drank their blood.
> "He's the best geek in the business," this man assured me.
> "What is the difference between a good geek and a bad geek?" I asked.
> "You wanna examine the chickens?"[5]

Much of this book consists of examining the chickens. It is not pretty, but it is more rewarding than the Islamic State's detractors might think. For years now, the Islamic State and its supporters have been producing essays, fatwas (religious rulings), films, and tweets at an industrial pace. In studying them we see a coherent view of the world rooted in a minority interpretation of Islamic scripture that has existed, in various forms, for almost as long as the religion itself. This version of Islam bears only passing resemblance to the Islam practiced or espoused by most Muslims. Mainstream Muslims resent that the Islamic State claims exclusive access to the truth about their religion, and in solidarity with their revulsion, many non-Muslims have averted their eyes and willfully ignored the particulars of the Islamic State's religious claims. This studied ignorance has been a costly mistake. Our enemy has invited us to know more about it, and we have been so repulsed that we have declined the offer.

The Islamic State's followers revel in their minority status. They see it as evidence of the majority's error, not their own, and they note that the early Muslims whom they so ostentatiously seek to emulate were also a persecuted minority that triumphed and remade the world. And Islamic State supporters' confidence in their own righteousness gets stronger when they are told—often by enemies who have never bothered to examine their claims—that they know nothing of their religion, when they often know a great deal (often more than their critics) about scripture, law, and theology, if not about the basic humane virtues that most Muslims consider central to their faith. They just prefer their violent interpretation over their critics' peaceful one.

In portraying a view of the world, this book is also a portrait of the people who have adopted that view. They have, in all cases, made disastrous decisions for themselves and for others, and at no point in my interviews have I concealed my disagreement with them. But I have also tried to present their views in a manner they would recognize. They have spoken to me in full knowledge that I oppose them. But their confidence keeps them talking—even when they think talking to me means aiding an enemy. As one wrote to me after we spoke:

> What stands out to me that others don't seem to discuss much, is how the Islamic State, Osama [bin Laden] and others are operating as if they are reading from a script that was written 1,400 years ago. They not only follow these prophecies, but plan ahead based upon them. One

would therefore assume that the enemies of Islam would note this and prepare adequately, but [it's] almost as if they feel that playing along would mean that they believe in the prophecies too, and so they ignore them and go about things their own way. . . . [The] enemies of the Muslims may be aware of what the Muslims are planning, but it won't benefit them at all as they prefer to either keep their heads in the sand, or to fight their imaginary war based upon rational freedom-loving democrats vs. irrational evil terrorist madmen. . . . We know that those in charge will ignore [you] and screw things up anyway.[6]

My correspondent and many of his colleagues are, as Matthew Arnold wrote, "wandering between two worlds, one dead, / The other powerless to be born." This impasse, already fatal to too many, will have grave consequences for decades.

THE WAY
OF THE
STRANGERS

THE CHOSEN SECT

Man at last will begin to harmonize himself in earnest. He will make it his business to achieve beauty by giving the movement of his own limbs the utmost precision, purposefulness and economy in his work, his walk and his play. He will try to master first the semiconscious and then the subconscious processes in his own organism, such as breathing, the circulation of the blood, digestion, [and] reproduction. . . . The human species, the coagulated *Homo sapiens,* will once more enter into a state of radical transformation.

—Leon Trotsky, *Literature and Revolution* (1924)

The Islamic State's war for the end of the world began for me the same way it has for many others: with a lesson in etiquette.

In October 2011, two and a half years before the declaration of the caliphate of Abu Bakr al Baghdadi, I came to Cairo, the capital of Egypt and the largest city in the Arab world. That Cairo is also the most ill-mannered city in the Arab world is not in doubt; whether one loves it or reviles it for its discourtesy is a matter of taste. Short-term visitors are cheated by cab drivers or browbeaten by tourist guides, and they board their flights home denouncing Cairo as a city of rogues. But Cairo's disobedience often breeds cleverness—artistic, social, literary—of a productive and admirable sort. Nine months before, it had made Cairo a crucible of political renewal, when the Tahrir Square revolution ousted Hosni Mubarak and put in his place a provisional government led by the Muslim Brotherhood, and therefore far friendlier to religious politics. Now the country faced an uncertain fate, and all factions were plotting, with varying competence, to press their advantages.

At twilight, after the sun is down and before the shop lights and street lamps switch on, Cairo becomes a city lit by headlights, and the dust and grit from the day's traffic hang visibly in the air. One such evening, at a political rally near Tahrir Square, I met Hesham Elashry, then in his early fifties, and accepted his invitation to a meal and a stroll. Hesham was a politically engaged Muslim. At the time, there was not yet an Islamic State to support, but he associated with other people and groups with clear jihadist leanings.[1] He did not conceal his motive in talking to me: he wanted me to become a Muslim.

We were downtown, in an area near several government ministries and offices. Traffic interrupted our dialogue now and then. But occasionally we'd pass close to a sensitive building, and security checkpoints would stop most cars from entering, so that we'd have a few minutes of pedestrian peace. Hesham filled the silences. His instruction began with bearing, poise, and dress. I had been hopping around to avoid tripping on chasms in the broken pavement. Hesham approved of my pace and noted that the Prophet Muhammad walked quickly as well. "The Prophet walked fast," he said, "as if he was jogging." He corrected me, politely, with literally every step. When the cars came back, they passed close, their slipstream tickling the hairs on my forearm and dusting us with carbon. "Walk this way," he said, taking my left arm with his right arm and putting himself, chivalrously, between me and the traffic. "The Prophet said to touch other people with your right hand, to keep what is good on your right." He explained the virtue of elegant footsteps, particularly for women; of hair kept short on certain parts of the face and body and allowed to grow jungly elsewhere; of gentle language, for both men and women, and abstention from guttersnipe dialects of Arabic in favor of the baroque and complex language of classical Arabic and the Koran.

I felt myself straightening my back and tongue under his tutelage. He could be kind and insulting in the same sentence. "With Islam, there is a way for everything," he told me—a way to pick one's teeth (with a *miswak,* a gingery-tasting stick), a way to dress (in loose trousers that stop mid-calf, exposing the ankles), a way to eat and drink. "Without Islam, you are like an animal," just making decisions based on instinct, and ruled by base pleasures. ("Worse than an animal," another jihadist later told me. "An animal has to obey Allah. It has no soul, no will. You can disobey. You can be worse.") Hesham assured me that God would be patient. "If you become a Muslim tonight," he said, "you will be a baby Muslim." Just as a child learns to walk by pulling himself up, staggering and tumbling, I would be expected to falter and misstep at first. But he promised I would soon glide through the world with righteous aplomb. I would float three inches above the filth of the sidewalks and the decay of the mortal world—in it, but no longer of it.

The Sheikh Henry Higgins routine, offering an extreme makeover of my soul, had a political purpose as well as a personal one. When the Islamic State's predecessors in Iraq began recruiting globally over the next few years, they stressed a theme of metamorphosis through Islam. And I recognized from my experience with Hesham, which did not end with that gritty stroll, that he had been recruiting me to join more than his religion. He was recruiting me to a polity that didn't yet exist, an Islamic state that might resemble, ultimately, *the* Islamic State to come.

One of the illusions surrounding the Islamic State is that it arose from nowhere, that it drew itself into being on a blank slate. But it could never have achieved so much, so fast, if there had not been millions of people already hungry for what the Islamic State promised. And in Hesham's proselytizing I detected a voracious appetite.

Both Hesham and the Islamic State adhere to a broad category of

Islamic interpretation and practice known as Salafism.[2] The term "Salafi" comes from the Arabic *al salaf al salih* [the pious forefathers], which refers to the first three generations of Muslims. Sunni Muslims all profess to adore these early Muslims and to take them, after the Prophet himself, as models of behavior.[3] The reason for this veneration is a saying of the Prophet: "The best of my community are my generation, the ones who follow them, and the ones who follow them."[4] Salafis take the Koran, the example of the Prophet, and the actions and beliefs of these men and women as their primary sources of religious authority, and they reject the opinions of many Muslims who came later.

In reviving the ways of the Salaf, they tend to view the present world as a fallen one, and the majority of Muslims—who are not Salafi—as misguided for modifying or modernizing the faith from its perfect beginnings. Salafis reserve particular scorn for Sufis and Shia. Both Sufis and Shia, Salafis contend, are guilty of idolatry [*shirk*] for their innovative practices, particularly the veneration of saints and building shrines. Salafis' first order of business is to expiate sin by ridding the world of these innovations. Some Salafis have been willing to use force to do so. Most household-name violent jihadists, including Osama bin Laden and the Islamic State's Abu Bakr al Baghdadi, have been jihadi-Salafis. Since the Prophet and his followers lived in a period of military conquest, their historical example offers modern jihadists ample precedent for violence.

But to model oneself after the Prophet and his followers is not necessarily to embrace violence, and to fight in the name of Islam is not to be Salafi. (In Chechnya and Libya, to name two recent venues, Sufis have wreaked havoc on infidel armies.) And most Salafis are political quietists who eschew political violence and concentrate on personal piety. Salafism, in a form evangelized by Muhammad ibn ʿAbd al Wahhab (1703–1792), is the state religion of Saudi Arabia, and that country's political establishment views Salafism as a way to keep its population acquiescent to the existing order.

Well-behaved Salafis seldom make history, however, and neither Hesham nor Abu Bakr al Baghdadi has been among the more couth of their kind. They believe it is a virtue and an obligation to resist, violently, an infidel political order. The name of that resistance is jihad. Those who think the ideology of the Islamic State emerged Athena-like, suddenly and fully formed, from the head of Abu Bakr al Baghdadi would see their illusion dispelled by observing the transformation of Hesham, and the rise of jihadi Salafism as a whole.

For years the Islamic State's predecessor movements were seemingly dormant. They woke from a period of suspended animation at the same time as many other ideologies—socialism, pan-Arabism, Nasserism—during the Tahrir Square revolution. In Mubarak's thirtieth year in power, activists took over the main square in Cairo to protest authoritarian rule. The square was a zoo of political action, and the jihadists were only a small part of its fauna. The diversity accounted at least in part for its broad appeal. Everyone from committed Islamists to Occupy-style secularists could find heroes on the barricades.

But the square had a circadian cycle that favored different groups at different times of day or night. Young, secular, democratic activists did their planning in little powwows on the grass late into the evening. But after midnight, while the youngsters slept or went home, the square thinned out, and its inhabitants aged by twenty years. Gray-bearded Salafis emerged like werewolves—too old to man the barricades themselves, but not too old to watch the developments with interest and a personal stake in the outcome.

Members of the older generation sat alone or in small groups, and many talked freely to me about lives spent evading the security services of Hosni Mubarak and his predecessors, Nasser and Sadat. After the 1981 assassination of Sadat by Khalid al Islambuli, a young army officer from the Middle Egyptian town of Mallawi, Mubarak ordered the rounding up of these pious and unusual suspects. More than one of the old men in the square claimed to have known Ayman al Zawahiri, Osama bin Laden's then deputy and now successor as head of Al Qaida. Many had been jailed and tortured. The others were forced underground, and through the 1980s and 1990s, when they poked up their heads, the government hunted them like prairie dogs.

During that period, Egyptian Islamists split into two broad groups. The first operated under the banner of the Muslim Brotherhood, whose members had flirted with violence since its founding in 1928 but were now mostly nonviolent. The second consisted of others, far more obsessively persecuted by the Mubarak government, who favored violence. The most prominent of these latter groups were Islamic Jihad and the Gama'a Islamiyya (Islamic Group), both of which had been implicated in Sadat's assassination and were marked by Salafi puritanism. The Muslim Brotherhood's nonviolence, which took the form of community-based activism and, later, democratic campaigning, won deeper popular support, and its success in other countries suggested that its strategy might pay off. In Turkey, Recep Tayyip Erdoğan's Justice and Development Party—a necktie-wearing version of the Brotherhood—won control of Turkey in an election in 2002, and Hamas, a suicide-belt-wearing group tied to the Brotherhood, has ruled Gaza since defeating the comparatively secular Fatah party in January 2006.

The Salafis in the square regarded the ballot-box Islamists of the Muslim Brotherhood with suspicion. They worried that the Brotherhood would emerge as the prime beneficiary of the revolution, thereby ending any chance at violent overthrow. Nothing in scripture or the history of the *salaf* supported the idea that Muhammad wanted his community to be ruled by all people—pious and impious, scholarly and lay—each with a vote of equal weight. The Brotherhood accepted a modern notion of the state, with politics forged in compromise and borders and relations agreed upon with non-Muslim countries. The most extreme of the Salafis dismissed those compromises and limitations outright, preferring a constant process of forcible Islamic expansion—jihadism *sans frontières*. Also alarming, in the aftermath of the revolution, was the development of a category of Salafi democrats, a category that some previously would have considered oxymoronic. The temptations of democracy threatened to undercut an authoritarian model that many jihadists had long worked to establish.[5]

The Salafis hated Mubarak, though, and many were willing to wait to see whether the Brotherhood would govern, if it managed to take power, in a strict Islamic fashion. Seventeen days after the protests started, at the moment when Vice President Omar Suleiman announced Mubarak's resignation, I was standing near an older man, a few yards from the Egyptian Museum, the pink neoclassical landmark that holds the golden mask of King Tut. The man unfurled a banner with a slogan likening the president to the desiccated corpse of a pharaoh. The comparison echoes both recent and ancient history. "Pharaoh" [*fir'awn*]—mentioned seventy-four times in the Koran—is, for Muslims as for Jews, the archetypal oppressor. When the assassin Islambuli blew apart Sadat's body with round after round from his AK-47, he shouted, "I have killed the pharaoh!"

A decade of political stagnation under Mubarak had made even me, a non-Egyptian, antsy for change, and reluctant to imagine that change might bring curses as well as blessings. The first foreboding came one evening as I walked past Simón Bolívar Square and encountered a small, nonviolent protest opposite the U.S. Embassy.

Men held banners in Arabic and English, along with crudely reproduced images of the head of a man with a white beard and large, dark sunglasses. In many of the pictures, he wore the red-and-white headgear (a *tarbush*) of a religious scholar or sheikh. The cluster of disembodied heads gave the impression of a rally on behalf of a Sunni version of the American gospel group the Blind Boys of Alabama.

In fact, I had stumbled upon a vigil for the preeminent living Egyptian theorist of jihad, ʿUmar ʿAbd al Rahman, the spiritual capo of the movements that had inspired Sadat's assassin. Born in Daqahliyya, north of Cairo, in 1938, ʿAbd al Rahman lost his sight to diabetes before his first birthday—hence his all-but-official nickname, "the Blind Sheikh." He trained in theology at Cairo University and Al Azhar University, Egypt's center of religious learning, but fell out with the religious establishment after prohibiting his followers from praying at the tomb of president Gamal ʿAbd al Nasser.

By the 1980s, all of Egypt knew ʿAbd al Rahman as the theological force behind the Gamaʿa Islamiyya and, to a slightly lesser extent, Egyptian Islamic Jihad, the country's premier jihadi-Salafi groups. He stood trial for encouraging the killing of Sadat but avoided conviction on major charges. In the Blind Sheikh's writings before imprisonment, he outlined the legal program that an Islamic government must implement. And at his 1984 trial, he outlined the fate of any ruler who deviated from that program:

> "Is it lawful to shed the blood of a ruler who does not rule according to God's ordinances?" one of the judges asked, as Sheikh Omar stood before the bench.
>
> "Is this a theoretical question?" the sheikh responded.
>
> He was told that it was, and he responded that it was lawful to shed such blood.
>
> "What of Sadat?" the judge went on. "Had he crossed the line into infidelity?"
>
> Sheikh Omar hesitated, and refused to respond.[6]

His non-reply was characteristic of Salafis when cornered: sketch out a logical path to a conclusion and let the listener take the last step by himself. It is a tactic made famous by Ahmad ibn Hanbal (780–855), a towering figure in Sunni scholarship and a major theological influence on Salafis. According to folklore, Ibn Hanbal argued that the Koran is eternal and uncreated, and that anyone who says otherwise is an infidel. The caliph at the time, al Ma'mun (786–833), said that the Koran was created by God. When pestered by his followers, Ibn Hanbal said, "Whoever says the Koran is created is an infidel." He spelled out the beginning of the syllogism, then left its last step to the imagination of his followers. His opinion was plain to all, though he refused to excommunicate al Ma'mun by name.[7]

The Blind Sheikh recovered his tongue when offered the chance to speak to the court:

> O Chief Justice of the Supreme Court, the proof has been established and the truth has become visible, as clear as daylight for the one who has eyes; it is your duty to rule with Shariah of God, and to implement the laws of God; if you do not do so, then you are an infidel, an oppressor, and an evildoer, for the words of God will have proven true concerning you: Whoever does not judge by that which God has revealed: they are disbelievers.

During the trial, he sat chummily with Khaled El Islambuli, the man who killed the Pharaoh. Now he warned those who sat in judgment of them that a guilty verdict—or even the decision to judge him according to a man-made rule—would constitute clear disbelief and nullify their Islam.[8]

Over the next several years, the Blind Sheikh toured Pakistan and Sudan, lending moral support to jihadist movements. In the early 1990s, he lived and preached in New Jersey. In 1993, using recordings made by an informant, U.S. prosecutors convicted him of conspiring to overthrow the U.S. government by blowing up buildings, bridges, and tunnels in New York. He now resides in the Butner Federal Correctional Complex outside Durham, North Carolina, along-side fellow long-term guest Bernie Madoff.

This was the man whose supporters near Tahrir Square had con-vened what first appeared to be a gospel-themed sit-in. They had laid blankets and mats on the pavement, and the presence of extension cords and teakettles hinted that they had already been there for months. They slept and ate there peacefully, and on most days, even the American diplomats found their presence unthreatening. (One consular official told me she tiptoed around them in the morning on her way to work because she didn't want to wake them.) Tonight, they had all the familiar tools of Egyptian protest: banners, a table, and an amplifier cranked up beyond its ability to carry a comprehen-sible signal. They mentioned the sheikh's age, his failing health, and the barbarity of long-term solitary confinement of a sightless old man.

Aside from the eardrums of those present, this protest hurt no one. In using peaceful means, it followed a public reform led by the Gama'a Islamiyya's leaders, who renounced violence starting in 1997, when the Mubarak government allowed them to meet in prison and formally change their movement's credo. In the early 2000s, they were released from prison, and in 2012 their political party competed in elections. Whether the Blind Sheikh, who never occupied an offi-cial role in the group, has joined them in their peaceful turn is un-known. Many of his followers confessed to me that they had not.

At a later rally near the embassy, I met 'Abdullah 'Abd al Rahman, eldest son of Sheikh 'Umar. (Among 'Umar's other sons are Muham-mad, who has spent time in U.S. secret prisons on suspicion of ter-rorism, and Ahmed, who died in a drone strike in Afghanistan in 2011.) After a brief conversation, 'Abdullah passed me off to Hesham Elashry, who would later that evening guide me on my theological promenade through downtown Cairo.

A skilled tailor, Hesham had spent years in New York making Western suits. He then returned to Egypt and opened a shop downtown. He spoke fluent English and as a result had become an unofficial spokesman for the sheikh. When we first met, I wondered whether Hesham had mistaken me for someone else. He spent at least the first five minutes of our encounter beaming at me as we spoke—or beaming *up* at me, since he is short and I am tall. We exchanged biographical details and bonded over familiar subway stops in Brooklyn. He asked my religion; I told him I attended Christian schools, and before I could elaborate and say I owed my atheism to that education, he said, "Good, so you are Christian," and moved the conversation forward. "Will you come eat with me?" he asked, grinning so energetically that I turned around to see if he was looking past my left ear at something more interesting, perhaps a woman half-naked at her window in the hotel behind me. His eagerness was flattering but alarming, and when he templed his fingers he reminded me of a spider staring at a fly.

After the demonstration ended, we ate there at the encampment. The reverb from the amplifiers was still bouncing off the buildings around us, and the Blind Sheikh's people milled about. They served us a humble meal: sliced onions; a stew of tomatoes and other vegetables; the coarse flatbread that Egyptians call 'aish, from the word "life." I was content to drink the tea everyone else was having, but Hesham sent a boy to get an orange soda just for me.

In the meantime, I sipped tea while Hesham told his story. Born in Cairo in 1959, he emigrated to New York City in the early 1980s as a spindly kid in search of a job. He found one at Three Star Tailors near the United Nations building, and he also worked with mixed success as an importer, moving back and forth between Egypt and the United States for the next twenty-five years. During most of that period, he was not religious. He wore typical Western clothes and, in the photos from the period he later showed me, resembled any other immigrant on the make in New York—posing in front of tourist monuments, working hard, clowning with friends on the streets of Midtown. If he felt shame about this time in his life, he didn't reveal it to me. He sounded, instead, as if he were talking about another person, a molt or husk he had shuffled off and left behind.

His "conversion"—he winced when I put it like that, but admitted the term might be accurate[9]—came in the late 1990s, when he met pious colleagues in Egypt who showed little interest in the race for money that had consumed his life up until then. "They were not as rich as me, but that didn't matter," he said. "They had found Islam." He began listening to the Blind Sheikh's sermons and became a follower.

Hesham's timing was significant. It was the 1990s. 'Abd al Rahman had already been implicated, if not convicted, in the Sadat assassination, and before and after his U.S. trial in 1995, his followers were slaughtering foreign tourists. In a forty-five-minute rampage that killed sixty-two people at the Temple of Hatshepsut in Luxor in 1997, the assassins cut up their victims and pinned notes to them. Most Egyptians recoiled at the bloodshed. In time, Mubarak's security services noticed Hesham's devotion, and after jailing and torturing him in 2000, they offered him a choice: exile or death.

He chose Brooklyn. And he liked it: no one minded when he fished for converts, and he could pray when and how he pleased. He worked as a master tailor, making $5,000 suits for wealthy clients, including Paul Newman. ("Jewish," Hesham sniffed. "He gave all his money to Israel.") When Newman entered the shop for measurements, Hesham was the only employee who did not leap to his feet to attend to him, although he did grudgingly accept a free packet of Fig Newmans, the Newman's Own brand fig cake.

Hesham became a specialist at winning converts. In 2009, Homeland Security expelled him for immigration violations, and he was forced back to Cairo with his wife and two children. While waiting for his final deportation order in a Manhattan holding center, he told me, he converted six other detainees and a guard.

By the time we met in Cairo, Hesham had a tailor shop and was supporting himself with men's and women's fashion. But his passion remained Islam. The sheikh, he said, was a great man, and what's more, an innocent one. And if he were guilty, the crimes were not crimes. "He preached Islam—and was that not his right, if the United States was serious about freedom of religion?" As a frail, old scholar, the sheikh could not have hurt anyone, disagreeable though his opinions might be. Indeed, Hesham maintained that America was imprisoning the sheikh not for sedition but for revealing the lies at the heart of the country's dealings with the Muslim world. The Blind Sheikh had had great success "waking up" the Muslim world to its religion and the religion's political consequences, and the United States government could not permit that slumber to be disturbed. "Inshallah he will wake you up, too," Hesham told me.

At the time, I lived just a few minutes from Butner penitentiary, and I told Hesham I wanted to meet the sheikh. Few journalists had spoken to him during his incarceration, and I wanted to know his thoughts on the Tahrir revolution. Hesham prayed aloud that I would have my wish. "Inshallah you will take *shahadah*"—that is, recite the Arabic sentence that signals conversion—"when you meet him."

Until that moment, Hesham and his friends would be my tutors and rescue me from my squalid disbelief. I didn't remember asking for rescue, but I went along anyway and endured many hours of interrogation and indoctrination. These hours had some effect. My tutors spoke arrogantly about the fate of my soul, and they invited me to question my role in the universe and the pain that might await me if I declined their invitation to Islam. That very discomfort meant that doubt had been sown—which was the point. As a secular person, I wasn't used to contemplating cosmic uncertainty in this way.

And there was a soft sell, too. The hospitality he and his friends extended made me feel indebted. Sharing the bread and stew with Hesham and his friends at the protest felt like an obligation to endure more of their company. Picking a tomato seed from my teeth and swallowing it, I thought of Greek myth, and the six pomegranate pips fed to Persephone by Hades: for every one she consumed, a month in Hell every year. Each bite obligated me to another hour of conversation, which coincidentally was often about Hell.

Later that evening, we took our first walk, Hesham's hands clasped behind his back and his ankles gathering dirt. Along the way, he preyed on doubts I never knew I had and initiated me into secret knowledge about subjects that I had not cared about before. I had no strong opinions at all about how long one's pants should be. To hear about his standards for dress was like reading one of those *Esquire* lists of fashion dos and don'ts: what was once left to chance now required attention and intention. As we walked past the coffee shops, driving schools, and falafel joints of downtown, arriving finally at his shop near Muhammad Farid Square, it became clear that he lived in a state of peace and self-assurance that many would envy. As someone with family, friends, and love in my life, I didn't feel a great gap in my soul (or wardrobe) that Salafism could answer. But I would soon meet others less blessed and more at sea in this world, seeking precisely the solid ground of certainty he was offering.

I returned to his shop several times over the coming days, weeks, and months. Hesham always welcomed me, and for the next year, I was his special project. When I entered his studio—a spartan, walk-up space with bolts of cloth piled in a corner—he would put down his needles and thread, and no more work would be done—or rather, the work to be done was me. Eventually, we achieved an unconventional friendship. "I hate you," he told me with a smile in August 2012, nine months after we first met. "I hate all Jews and Christians, anyone who is not a Muslim."

We each enjoyed our conversations, but for different reasons. I just wanted to talk about religion and Egyptian politics. All Hesham wanted was one more chance to flip me from a woolly Christian to a Salafi. He liked to tell me about the penalty phase of the afterlife. He described in grotesque detail the fate of sinners in the Hereafter. Our skin would thicken with endless soft, thin, tender layers, each more sensitive than the last. The accumulated layers would be miles deep. God would then burn them off individually, until he reached flesh. Then he would restore them, like Prometheus's liver, so he could blister and rip them away, again and again, for eternity.[10]

"Do you feel that?" Hesham asked me once, handing me a hot glass of Lipton, straight from a whistling kettle. He never missed a chance to illustrate a point. My fingertips burned, and I recoiled a little, losing a splash of the tea. "You feel why Allah chooses heat," he said. "Because it's the worst torture there is." *If you think this tea is hot, you should try Hell!* Hesham himself hadn't recoiled when he passed me the teacup. His fingers were padded with calluses from fine needlework, or from handling too many scorching teacups. The message was conveyed: follow my lead, and the flames of Hell will spare you. Winning a soul for Islam confers immense reward on a Muslim in the afterlife, and given the ecstatic expression on Hesham's face when he told me about the immigration detainees he bagged for the faith, psychological reward in this life too.

Among the special challenges for Salafi recruiters is the danger of accidentally recruiting someone for another form of Islam instead. They need to welcome the recruit into the religion without exposing him to deviant traditions like Sufism, scholasticism [kalam] or Neoplatonism [falsafa], and much else that Salafis deride as reprehensible innovation [bida']. What most Muslims perceive as progress, Salafis consider disbelief. Hesham had to usher me past these attractions like a parent trying to drag a kid past candy at a supermarket checkout. The siren song of Sufism, some Salafis say, is so seductive that Sufi shrines should be dynamited or bulldozed at the earliest opportunity. Tolerance is a danger to men's souls. Since most Muslims do not identify as Salafi, they react to this intolerance as a personal affront, and tantamount to discarding Islam itself. Most Muslims are comfortable with reading ancient texts allegorically, and most Muslims today are pleased with the past millennium of Islamic culture and achievement and feel no particular urge to prune it back to the ninth century, before the poetry of Rumi and Hafez; the Taj Mahal; the music of Nusrat Fateh Ali Khan and Umm Kulthum; the left-foot volleys of Zinedine Zidane; a philosophical and literary tradition that includes everyone from Ibn 'Arabi to Taha Hussein. To them, these are not the works of Satan but the glories of Islamic civilization.

Critics of Salafism say it denies interpretation and debate and defiles the tradition it claims to be purifying. They say the Prophet preferred unity among his followers, rather than Salafi-style intolerance. Muslims were supposed to live together and avoid splitting the community. To dismiss a huge range of behavior as disbelief [*kufr*], according to this line of critique, and to urge violence against *kufr*-practicing Muslims—as some Salafis do—is to disobey that clear command. Moreover, the backward-looking legal interpretation of the Salafis leads them to advocate what their critics consider superannuated practices, such as slavery and corporal punishment as practiced in the seventh century.

Salafis offer three key replies. The first is contained in a hadith that Hesham quoted to me several times: "This community [*ummah*] will divide into seventy-three sects, all of which save one will go to Hell: the one that followed what I and my Companions are doing." Salafis take themselves to be the chosen sect [*al firqah al najiyyah*], and they do not mind that their putative coreligionists detest their eccentricities.

The second reply appeals to historical fact. The Salafis reply that their interpretation of early Islamic history is simply *correct* when they say that the earliest Muslims—the ones all Muslims are commanded to emulate—kept sex slaves, chopped off thieves' hands, beheaded apostates, and stoned adulterers. These practices may be rejected by mainstream Muslim scholars today, but for most of Islamic history, it barely occurred to Muslims to doubt that their religion permitted them. Muslim societies have, in the past, beheaded apostates with less alacrity than the Islamic State does today. But to doubt that apostasy has ever been a capital crime is a misreading of scripture and history. To muddy things further, many of the Muslim laymen who despise Salafis have weak knowledge of their own scriptures and the scriptural debates of their traditions. Salafis have no monopoly on historical truth, let alone on interpretation. But they read the Koran attentively, and on certain matters they occupy ground at least as solid as that of their opponents.

The Islamic State's practice of slavery illustrates this disparity. In September 2014, dozens of Islamic clerics condemned the Islamic State, asserting that "no scholar of Islam disputes that one of Islam's aims is to *abolish* slavery [. . .]. For over a century, Muslims, and indeed the entire world, have been united in the prohibition and criminalization of slavery, which was a milestone in human history when it was finally achieved." The same document claims that slavery was "abolished by universal consensus."[11] Any serious scholar of Islam would instantly recognize these arguments as misleading or factually incorrect. Slavery has been practiced by Muslims for most of Islamic history, and it was practiced without apology by Muhammad and his Companions, who owned slaves and had sex with them. At least two of Muhammad's sex slaves, Safiyya and Juwayriyya, were prisoners of war. Muhammad later freed and married both. (He is not the only Abrahamic prophet with experience in this area. Abraham had sex with Hagar the slave girl, and David and Solomon took literally hundreds of concubines.) Muslims stress that the Prophet demanded that slaves be treated well—other than their enslavement and forced

intercourse—and repeatedly reminded his followers of the rewards
for those who free slaves. (The Islamic State informs its fighters that
freeing a slave is among the most meritorious acts.[12]) He never abolished slavery, however, and practiced it himself to his death.

In the premodern period, there is scarcely a text on Islamic laws of
war that neglects to mention the rules concerning enslavement of
women and children [*saby*]. Classical jurists listed four permissible
fates [*al mubahat al arba'a*] for prisoners of war: execution, freedom,
ransom, or enslavement. Today, far from agreeing that Islam abol-
ishes slavery, major scholars such as Taqi al 'Uthmani (b. 1943) and
Yusuf al Qaradawi (b. 1926) affirm that the leader of a validly constituted Muslim state may enslave wartime captives at his discretion.
'Uthmani defends his position against scholars (chiefly the Indian
Chiragh Ali) who say that Islam permitted slavery originally but has
since abolished it. This argument, 'Uthmani contends, is so preposterous "that it would make a bereaved mother laugh."[13] No major
Muslim state practices slavery, but it was outlawed in Saudi Arabia
only in 1962 (not "over a century" ago), and in Mauritania, where it
was formally outlawed in 1981, by most accounts, it is still practiced
today. When the dissenting clerics condemn the Islamic State, the
Islamic State is fully prepared to adduce historical evidence and clas-
sically grounded argument for its positions.

The fact of slavery's strong precedent in Islamic history does not
in itself force Muslims to approve of the practice in the present.
'Uthmani and Qaradawi are towering figures, but they do not have
the last word. Their positions, however, do show why those who
claim that slavery is by "universal consensus" contrary to Islam have
yet to convince their opponents—and why Salafis often seem so
self-satisfied about their superior knowledge of Islamic law and history. I doubt even one of the original signers of the petition quoted
above was actually ignorant of the basic historical and legal facts of
slavery in Islamic history. But they are often reluctant to speak about
slavery, or do so elliptically, with embarrassment and at times pre-

varication.[14] To some extent, one can attribute this posture to fear of giving Muslims—a beleaguered minority in some of those scholars' societies—a bad name. The scholars also often hope to avoid treating bygone institutions like slavery as important present-day subjects, when most Muslims do not live in slavery-practicing societies, and do not wish to. Pro-slavery Salafis seize the silences in these conversations, and they like how others squirm when confronted with the historical fact of embarrassing practices.

Still less capable of confronting Salafi counterarguments are secular-minded non-Salafi Muslim laymen. The average lay Muslim is like the average layman of any faith: largely ignorant and prone to believe a sanitized version of it. The Princeton scholar Bernard Haykel has called this a "cotton-candy view of the religion," and notes that the view dissolves, with occasionally catastrophic psychological consequences, upon contact with the moral ambiguity of reality. Part of the task of Salafis who proselytize to fellow Muslims is to reach them at this stage of cognitive dissonance—torn between modern sensibilities and realization that slavery is part of the history and present of Islam—and convince them that the modern sensibilities must go. Some Salafis even go so far as to say they must cultivate *love* of slavery and other antique practices to remain Muslim.

Many Muslims do not take news of the existence of slavery in their tradition well. I have received stacks of correspondence from Muslims outraged because I referred in print to the fact that Muhammad owned slaves. They argue that the Prophet treated his supposed "slaves" well, or better than other slave owners in history; or that they were servants, not slaves. The first retort is not a denial that the Prophet owned slaves, only that he cleared the low bar of treating slaves better than antebellum American Southerners. The second is unconvincing: by any definition of "slavery," these "servants" were slaves, and historically, few Muslims have protested when they are referred to as such. The "slaves" were, to use David Brion Davis's criteria, "the property of another man [...] subject to his owner's authority," and forced to work; "his condition is hereditary and ownership in his person is alienable," capable of being "bought, sold, traded, leased, bequested, presented as a gift, pledged for a debt, [or] included in a dowry."[15] Muslims can—and do—deny on sophisticated grounds that slavery is permissible today, but as a matter of history, the Salafis have a point. It is the interpretation of that history, not the historical fact itself, that is up for debate.

A third Salafi reply confronts the accusation of divisiveness. Salafis *appear* to be a small minority of Muslims—probably fewer than ten percent globally—but they claim to represent a silent majority. They say the most fundamental understanding of what it means to be Muslim is the Salafi way: read the Koran, learn about the Prophet, and do what he says. That, Salafis claim, is what Muslims all believe, until they have the bad fortune to be convinced otherwise. For most of history, nearly all people, including Muslims, were illiterate, and if they knew anything of religious doctrine, they were submissive to a scholarly elite. Those illiterate masses were the lucky ones. Since most scholars have been non-Salafi, Salafis view scholars as having led the masses astray. But the great unlettered majority of Muslims were never beguiled from their simple wisdom and correct, basic understanding of Islam. The Koran itself has mixed feelings about overthinking things. It warns that disbelief and cleverness are related, and that the imperfect human response to unwelcome facts is to manufacture excuses for rejecting them.[16] Salafi scholars object to modern readings of the Koran, which they say search for hidden meanings to justify annulling corporal punishment, slavery, and jihad. Under the Salafi interpretation, a great danger is excessive cunning. God commands us to use our brains, and yet our brains trick us into discarding Islam. The proposed solution is humility: stick to the texts and traditions, and emulate the early Muslims' behavior even when it conflicts with modern norms. So the debate between Salafis and those open to influence by modernity continues.

Because Salafis are so hostile to mainstream Muslims, to increase their numbers they must woo outsiders who have no preexisting Islamic theology to offend. A 2009 jihadi-Salafi recruiting manual ranks types of people by how likely they are to convert. It puts the *non*-religious first and the deeply religious—especially "memorizers of the Koran"—last. (The author also suggests that jihadi recruiters "take the recruit on a picnic," which seems like nice advice, and which Hesham followed in my case.[17]) Maajid Nawaz, the founder of the anti-radicalization Quilliam Foundation in London, makes a similar point. "Islamist recruitment in general tends to focus overwhelmingly on non-religious Muslims," he says. "Coming from a less religiously informed background, it is that much easier to overwhelm such recruits by making them feel they are so very ignorant of their religion, thus creating a 'born-again' kind of mindset."[18]

By that standard, I qualified as a promising recruit. I had lived long enough in Muslim-majority countries to be able to detect the peculiarities of Hesham's behavior, dress, and disengagement from popular culture. But I wasn't Muslim, and although I wasn't ignorant of Islam, I also had no commitment to any particular version of it, and therefore would not feel the guilt of betrayal if I were to agree with Hesham that my Muslim friends and family were doomed to hellfire.

Still, for a man so obsessed with scripture, it is worth noting that Hesham played fast and loose with the facts when it suited him to do so. His commitment to historical and textual fidelity faltered or lowered its standards, for example, when talking about the afterlife. He did not mind lying or exaggerating to get me to convert. An Islamic State supporter later told me that the specifics of the eternal punishments Hesham described have "no basis in revelation." Most sources describe the process of being burned to expurgate sins as applying to Muslims only, and not to an infidel like me. (I should be so lucky: unbelief is a sin not dischargeable through fire.) Islamic texts do offer ghastly descriptions of punishment and reward, including eternally regenerated and burnt skin: "As often as their skins are consumed, we shall exchange them for fresh skins that they may taste the torment."[19]

But the part about getting fattened up is not strictly in the text. It appears in secondary, non-canonical literature only, and the enlargement of the physical body is meant to increase the intensity of *all* physical sensation, not just punishment. In Paradise, Muslims will feel larger pleasures with their larger bodies. In general, the emphasis on bodily pleasures and punishment is greater than in the Christian tradition, where glorifying the Creator is the greatest reward.

Our sessions continued, lubricated by the hot tea. I kept coming back because for all his bullying, Hesham was still an idealist. Democrats, Muslim Brothers, and everyone else became dispirited now and then. The Salafis did not, and I wanted to know where their reality-resistant worldview came from.

We spoke not only of religion. Hesham told me about his tailoring business, and he taught me how to distinguish a bespoke wool suit—his specialty, still thousands of dollars apiece—from a Chinese knockoff. But the conversation always returned to theology. In time, I began to notice that Hesham was doing prepared material. He had a shtick, a sales routine, a ready supply of missionary rhetoric. When he asked me to defend the doctrine of the Trinity in Christianity, I readily conceded that it didn't make sense. Detecting (correctly) my weakness in Christian apologetics, he launched into about fifteen minutes of shopworn Muslim critique, honed over more than a thousand years. The Trinity is incoherent on its own terms since one cannot be three; it attributes human traits to God, and human traits entail imperfection. The Koran supersedes the Bible in style and coherence. And so on.

I saw no point in defending a doctrine that wasn't my own, so I asked why he relished discussing the most gruesome parts of his religion—the lopping off of heads and hands, the eternal burning—instead of the parts about kindness and mercy. Again, a robotic response: "God made Islam to be easy on you, not to be hard," he said.

The punishments deter misbehavior, nudging us toward happiness. "He wants you to marry, because marriage is best. So when he says there is punishment for fornication, that punishment is for the good of the fornicator, to stop him from fornicating." The whipping is an expression of love. "If you have a child, and he goes into the street and almost gets hit by cars, do you just suggest that he not do this anymore?" he asked. "No, you make sure he doesn't do it," with stern words and a paddling.

But surely not by burning him alive, I said. He replied that the punishment must fit the crime. No crime is greater than rejection of God; no punishment should be more severe—especially since he made the burden of accepting Islam ridiculously light. All I had to do was utter a few words that many others had successfully spoken.

This became the rhythm of our dialogue. He probed me for questions. I asked. He answered, answered, and continued answering, smothering me with answers. After a while, the experience felt like a mental assault. I have an immense capacity to listen to rants—this is part of my job as a journalist—but his company grew tiresome. I could take only so much monomaniacal zeal, his idiotic tales of encounters with New York Jewry, and tips on haute couture. I fidgeted with my teacup and invented excuses to leave.

He was ready. "You need to go to Alexandria. Alexandria is the world capital of Salafis," Hesham said, tinkering with his phone. "Cairo is not the best place to learn about Islam." It was secular, modern, filled with worldly distractions. "If you go to our brothers in Alexandria, they will help you." Before I could decide whether I was up for being tag-teamed by another Salafi conversion squad, his "brothers" had texted him back to say that I'd be expected in two days, at Friday prayers in Alexandria.

The next day, when my second-class train slowed down approaching Alexandria, my nostrils began registering the distinct scent of the

Mediterranean and the overlapping cultures of Egypt, Turkey, Sicily, and the Maghreb that encircle it. The aroma reminded me of the irony of Hesham's claim about Alexandria's status as a world capital of Salafism: historically and culturally, Alexandria has rivaled Cairo as a city of openness and cosmopolitanism. Centuries before Islam, Buddhist missionaries came ashore and proselytized there. As a major port, Alexandria was also once a world-class city of vice. The Greek poet Cavafy could leer from his balcony at prostitutes and young men, and hard liquor—consumed in plenty of Cairo homes, but not often available on the street—was sold openly.

Now, Hesham had told me, parts of Alexandria have been reclaimed for Islam. Converts from all over the world have gravitated there, he said. Much in the same way Anabaptists have carved out settlements for themselves in rural Pennsylvania and Manitoba, or Orthodox Jews have in parts of Brooklyn, the Salafis have taken over neighborhoods. Hesham gave me the name of a contact—Ahmad—who would meet me at a mosque in a neighborhood called Medinat al Zuhur, or City of Flowers.

Arriving in time for noon prayers, I found a mosque with elegant calligraphy on its facade. Within seconds of entering, though, I got a call from one of Hesham's agents, who said I was in the wrong mosque and sounded peeved that I would mistake it for their own. He directed me to walk a couple of blocks in from the road. There I found a neighborhood devoid of flowers or any other physical beauty. Less than a mile away from a Sheraton, with beach restaurants and surf, the streets here were dirty and the blocky, featureless buildings looked as if they had been designed by their architect during a cigarette break.

Ahmad intercepted me. He was in his twenties and wore a maroon Polo shirt with long sleeves, as well as black track pants with the telltale pant cuffs, rolled up in the Salafi style. He spoke little English and lacked Hesham's chatty graces, but he made up for these deficits with directness. "You are a new Muslim," he informed me. "Come with me." He led me into a building and up into a nearly bare apartment for a diagnostic session before prayers. "You were Christian? And you are American?" he asked. "We have Americans here. One Dutch man. Others—coming to live as Muslims." He handed me a cold glass of thick, sugary orange nectar and watched me while I sucked it down.

The spareness of his apartment was in part a function of poverty: Ahmad was a religious student, his studies presumably financed by his fellow mosque-goers. Like Hesham, he was indifferent to money, not so much resigned to it as beyond it. "Did you ever reach into your pocket," Hesham once asked, "and think that there was a coin there— only to discover that it was gone?" When God fire-blasts away our skin, Hesham said, he will take into account all our worldly suffer- ings, no matter how small, even the passing disappointment at a quarter missing from our pocket. "A poor man will not face the same pain [in the afterlife] as a rich man," Hesham said. In the end, all are punished, and all equally. Only once the sick and poor can stand on even footing with the healthy and rich will God undertake the final sorting, based on who has believed in him, and who has lived accord- ing to his commands.

When the orange soup in my cup was gone, we went downstairs to the mosque. It was as spare as the apartment. We had passed it ear- lier, and I hadn't noticed it. It turned out to be hardly a building but more of a medium-sized shed. Light came through gaps in the wall and from a few cheap, curly fluorescent bulbs that hung down from the trussed roof and reminded me, blasphemously, of the tails of pigs. This austerity likely reflected the poverty of the worshippers, as well as a Salafi version of a Sunni aesthetic, rejecting excess adornment. I thought of the blank interiors of churches in sixteenth-century Hol- land, after Salafi-like fanaticism possessed the Protestants to strip them of the decoration, reliquaries, and art of the Catholic Church.

Perhaps the Dutchman whom Ahmad mentioned earlier would feel at home here.[20]

The Dutchman arrived a few minutes later but declined to talk to me. Ahmad deposited me in a corner, in a plastic lawn chair, where I sat as the other worshippers filed in. The ethnic and national diversity took me by surprise. A few sub-Saharan Africans were there, and several other Europeans. A faded flyer on the door advertised авиабилеты, airline tickets, in Russian.

During prayers, I sat awkwardly in my chair, which by virtue of being the only furniture in the mosque felt as grand as a throne. Afterward, while Ahmad traded greetings and farewells with fellow worshippers, a few others surrounded me to examine me further. Leading the diagnosis was Sherif, an engineer from New Jersey. They were uncertain about how to handle me. I wasn't a convert, and didn't present myself as one. But I had asked only reasonable questions so far, and it would be uncharitable to send me away. They didn't know the extent of my Arabic, so for some time I could listen in on their deliberations.

Sherif, who lived part-time in the United States, led the conversation when it switched into English. They broached the usual topics: the unity of God, the shortcomings of Christian theology, my knowledge of Islam. I decided to provoke them on the last point. I told them I was educating myself about Islam, and the day before had stopped on the way to Alexandria to visit the shrine of Sayyid Ahmad al Badawi (596–675), a Sufi saint. The mention of a Sufi shrine elicited a low, grave whistle, as if to say, *This case is worse than we thought.* They conferred more in Arabic, in less friendly tones. "He is questioning the unity of God," one fumed. "Polytheism," said another. Finally, they decided I could not be trusted to walk the path to conversion by myself.

"Listen," Sherif said in English. "Where are you staying?" I named a neighborhood downtown, convenient to a KFC and several good hotels. He suggested that I might be better off remaining in the City of Flowers. I stood firm and said I had already paid for a room and left my luggage there. Someone asked Sherif to translate. He replied, in frustrated Arabic, "He's staying among the infidels."

"Infidels" is a fighting word when applied to Muslims. And Sherif was calling a community of Muslims one of disbelief. This practice of declaring self-described Muslims to be infidels is called *takfir* [excommunication], and historically Muslims have refrained from it. Those who leave Islam are theoretically subject to the death penalty. It is therefore a serious accusation. Muslim authorities have nearly always applied safeguards to avoid implementing it. These safeguards include an interrogation of the accused's true beliefs, to ensure that he really does intend to deny Islam; rounds of education by scholars, to correct the apostate and offer an opportunity to return to the right path; and a psychiatric assessment, to ensure that the accused is not mad. The accused must also be confronted with the consequences of his apostasy. First he is shown a dagger. If showing the dagger doesn't elicit repentance, the dagger is held to his breast. If that isn't enough, the dagger is placed against his throat. If he repents at any stage, he faces no punishment at all.

Since there is no single Muslim religious authority, any Muslim can excommunicate any other Muslim. Because of the obvious social discord wanton *takfir* would cause, excommunication carries risks for the accuser as well. A well-known saying of the Prophet warns that if one Muslim accuses another of disbelief, then (at least) one of them is a disbeliever.[21] Two Muslims enter, one Muslim leaves: a false accusation invalidates the belief of the accuser. "Labeling people 'unbelievers' is a serious matter," wrote the eleventh-century philosopher Ghazali. "Remaining silent, on the other hand, entails no liability at all."[22] Little wonder, then, that most Muslims have preferred not to risk it.

Whether Sherif would have accused *individuals* of disbelief, and hazarded his soul on the accuracy of the accusation, I couldn't tell. But his words took me aback. Maybe they shouldn't have. Hesham, too, said "disbelief" prevailed in Egyptian society. Many opinion polls would disagree: Egyptians, on average, outdo the American Bible Belt in the importance they assign to religion in their lives. But Hesham said much of their religion is false. "The Prophet Muhammad, peace be upon him, said that not one in a thousand of his followers would join him in Paradise."

If there is a single intellectual father of the idea of casual *takfir*— a practice that the Islamic State has taken to extremes and defended at length—he is Taqi al Din ibn Taymiyyah (1263–1328), a favorite scholar not only of the Islamic State, but also of Al Qaida and the Wahhabis of Saudi Arabia. The attraction Ibn Taymiyyah's thought would hold for a violent and puritanical movement is plain to see, although rampant takfirism is just one interpretation of his work.

Ibn Taymiyyah's first appearance in the public record involved the case of a Christian man, ʿAssaf al Nasrani, who had been accused of blasphemy for insulting Muhammad. Ibn Taymiyyah titled his first major work "The Sharp [Sword] Drawn Against the Reviler of the Prophet," and came out firmly on the side of the sword.[23] Among other reasons for cheering on the man's execution, Ibn Taymiyyah adduced the fact that Muhammad was dead and so could not be asked for forgiveness. This opinion and others put him at odds with the Mamluk leaders in Damascus and Cairo, and Ibn Taymiyyah went to prison six times for his dissent. His hard-line views, expressed at great personal cost, impressed many scholars, both Muslim and infidel. A theme in his writing is inflexibility. "He probably would have been a nicer guy if he had gotten married," one scholar told me. A graduate student at Harvard struggled for the right theological term to describe Ibn Taymiyyah's place in Islamic thought. "Brilliant guy," he concluded. "But kind of a dick."[24]

Some have attributed his dickishness at least partially to having lived in unsettled times. In 1258, a few years before his birth, the Mongols sacked Baghdad and killed as many as a million Muslims in a single week, including the last Abbasid caliph, al Musta'sim Billah. When Ibn Taymiyyah was six, the Mongols overran his native town of Harran and sent him and his family into exile—a personal calamity he never fully got over.

One can find a harsh or uncompromising opinion from Ibn Taymiyyah on virtually any issue. Regarding treaties with infidels, he said none could be made unless they were non-binding or temporary; permanent peace was impermissible. He showed little sense of collegiality with other Muslim scholars and accused followers of the Andalusian mystic Ibn 'Arabi not only of error but also of advocating incest.[25] He argued that government should take as its primary goal the imposition of religious order, by forbidding wrong and commanding right. His personal actions confirm an ornery or humorless disposition. According to one contemporary admirer of Ibn Taymiyyah, he

> is said to have, among other things, shaved children's heads, led an anti-debauchery campaign in brothels and taverns, struck an atheist with his hand before his public execution, destroyed a supposedly sacred rock in a mosque, conducted attacks on astrologers, and obliged deviant Sufi shaykhs to make public acts of contrition.[26]

Politically, he found his greatest enemy in the Mongols, who had conquered his hometown. The Mongol chief Ghazan adopted Islam, or at least claimed to, in 1295—but not before his people had sacked Islam's greatest cities and extinguished its last great caliphal dynasty. Compounding the indignity, the Mongols ruled not according to Islam, but instead followed Yassa, a traditional form of martial law they had inherited from Genghis Khan. Over time, they added elements of Islamic law, but their ongoing rapacity left room for doubt about their sincerity. Ibn Taymiyyah therefore found himself pressed by circumstance to delineate the boundary between legitimate and illegitimate "Muslim" rulership.

Ibn Taymiyyah condemned the Mongols. "Everyone who is with the Mongols in the state over which they rule has to be regarded as the most evil class of men," he wrote. "He is either an atheist and hypocrite [. . .] or he belongs to that worst class of all people, who are the people of religious innovation [*bida*']."[27] He called for his fellow Syrians to resist. "Any group of people that rebels against any single prescript of the clear and reliably transmitted prescripts of Islam has to be fought [. . .] even if the members of this group pronounce the Islamic confession of faith." In previous eras, as well as in eras since, Muslims had mostly agreed that obedience—even to a sinful Muslim ruler—was obligatory. Ibn Taymiyyah argued that Mongol rulers' disbelief removed them from Islam. Most dangerously, he adopted the language of excommunication and openly wrote of the Mongols' disbelief [*kufr*] as a reason individual Muslims—particularly the Mamluk leaders he served—should fight against them.

By opening the gates to *takfir*, he became a darling of murderers.[28] 'Abd al Salam Faraj, an Egyptian jihadist who founded Islamic Jihad in 1979, cited Ibn Taymiyyah's fatwas to justify the assassination of Sadat. Virtually every jihadist group of the modern era has claimed support and inspiration from Ibn Taymiyyah, usually in a familiar three-step pattern. First: Declare that a Muslim leader has failed to rule according to Islam. Second: Argue that failure to govern according to Islam constitutes departure from Islam, i.e., apostasy. Third: Declare war. Faraj, in three-stepping toward the assassination of Sadat, compared him unfavorably to the Mongols—since at least their tribal law contained a smattering of Islamic, Jewish, and Christian law. "There is no doubt that the Mongol Yassa was less of a sin than the laws which the West has imposed [on countries like Egypt],"

Faraj wrote, "and which have no connection with Islam or any other revealed religion."[29]

Sadat had made peace with Israel, which according to Faraj and his generation of jihadists ranked first in the list of apostatizing acts. In many ways, by assassinating him, the jihadists were beginning with one of the harder cases. Sadat was a religious Muslim: he called himself Egypt's "Believer President," and his forehead showed the dark callus (a *zabibah,* literally "raisin") of a man who regularly bowed to the floor in prayer.[30] In the next three decades, those jihadists would also target Shia, members of the Syrian mystical sect known as Alawis, and overtly secular political leaders. The case for excommunicating, opposing, and killing each of them only got easier and more familiar. By the time the Islamic State arrived, jihadis could dance the *takfir* three-step backward and in heels.

Meanwhile in Alexandria, the hard work of conversion proceeded apace. The men from the mosque continued to press me—and to treat me with stifling hospitality. Ahmad took me to lunch at a chicken restaurant where we ate well and he, over my objection, paid the bill out of his student stipend. He corrected my Arabic over and over, studiously transposing the street dialect that came most easily to me with the high register favored by Salafis. Chicken was not *firakh,* but *dajaj.* Any time I pronounced the letter *jim* with a hard *g,* in the Egyptian way, he corrected it to the more classical *j* as in "Juliet": "Jamal," not "Gamal," was the name of the dead Egyptian strongman Nasser. The letter *qaf,* instead of vanishing without a trace as in normal Egyptian speech, had to be pronounced deep in the throat, where the soft palate meets the tongue: *qalam* [pen], not *alam.* My language was getting purer, word by word and bite by bite.[31]

Their conversion efforts could still be described, for all their intolerance and hate, as a mission of love. They wanted to spare me hellfire, to share the ecstasies of Paradise. If at times their answers became curt, or their lessons unshaded with nuance, what drove the gruffness was urgency, not spite. They were fishers of men, and as I watched them work, I saw that they were trawling on a commercial scale. After lunch, Ahmad sent me to an outreach office close to the city center for further education. Once there, I peeked into a conference room where young men were poring over maps of Benin, the West African nation best known as the birthplace of voodoo, in preparation for a mission there. The missionaries reminded me of Mormons, not only in their cheery excitement, but also in their linguistic aptitude. One older man caught me browsing a German translation of the Koran, then introduced himself in fluent, idiomatic German. He claimed he had never been to a German-speaking country but had studied so he could talk to people on the Web.

Not all these people were Salafi, and by no means could I be sure they were all jihadi. I suspect many were not. Some talked of Hell and Paradise, and others of justice and love. But they shared an evangelicism that made at least one portion of their conversation predictable. At the end of every exchange, they invited me to embrace Islam, as Hesham had in our first meeting, with a profession of faith, the *shahadah*: *I witness that there is no God but God, and Muhammad is His Messenger.* I always declined, and they rarely badgered me.

I soon returned to Cairo, and to the tailor shop of the most tenacious angler of them all. Hesham asked, with increasing insistence, for me to say the *shahadah*—to speak the words, no matter what I felt within. According to orthodox theology, a necessary element of conversion is intent. You can't accidentally say the words, or say them when you're drunk or lying, and have the conversion count. But he treated the phrase as talismanic, something that could, by its utterance, switch me irreversibly from one category of being to another. *La ilaha ilallahu, wa Muhammad ar-Rasulillah.* Say it. Blammo, now you're a Muslim.

"Just say it," he said. "Repeat after me."

"I can't," I said.

"Why not?"

"Because I don't believe it's true."

"Doesn't matter," he replied. "Allah likes it when his slaves say this. Just say it." *Slaves!* I thought. But he was speaking in a way that came naturally—what shame could there be in servitude to the all-powerful creator of the universe?

"Wouldn't I be lying?" I asked. "And isn't lying worse than saying nothing at all?"

Intent, however, was not Hesham's priority. "You have your part to do, and Allah has his part," he told me. "Your part is to say the words. And if Allah loves you, he will put the belief in your heart. But you have to do your part with the tongue, and then he helps you with the heart." I asked him if I would, upon saying the words, even without belief, be a Muslim.

"Yes," he said, moving onto shakier ground. He told me that there was a division of labor, and that my job at this stage was to speak the words, to eschew pork, to learn to pray. One day this would lead to a beautiful moment when action, speech, intent, and understanding would unite. He saw the world as filled with potential Salafis who could, with just a little coaxing, be converted and cleansed. The main thing was getting them in the front door. New Muslims could be minted by the truckload each day, as long as they could be brought into Hesham's presence, taught a little theology, and induced to mouth a few Arabic words.

I treated our meetings as a combination of journalism, ethnography, and intellectual sport. Eventually, he must have decided that our conversations were either too rich, or possibly too boring, to have only in private, so he arranged audiences. Hesham had become a minor celebrity on Al Hafez, a Saudi-backed Islamist cable TV channel that sprang up as one of the flowers of the Arab Spring. (Mubarak's government would have banned any show hosted by a supporter of the Blind Sheikh.) He invited me onto his show (*The Court of the Scholars*) as part of a panel featuring himself and Gamal ʿAbd al Sattar, a professor of Islamic creed and philosophy at Al Azhar University. I demurred at first, out of embarrassment at my ignorance, and out of fear that I would accidentally say something that would get me mobbed and murdered outside the studio. But he persisted and offered me wide leeway: "You can even ask whether the Prophet Muhammad, peace be upon him, was a child molester."

So I went on camera. The professor wore a suit and tie. Because of the short notice, I was stuck wearing a wrinkled pinstriped linen shirt. I spoke English, and Hesham translated for the home audience. I pressed both Hesham and ʿAbd al Sattar on how they reconciled the sadism of eternal punishment with a loving God, and they replied in the usual ways: God punishes us because he loves us, like a parent; we are his servants, so anything he does to us is his choice and prerogative. These answers satisfied believers but not me. I asked whether they thought that punishment for nonbelievers, especially apostates, could be considered a form of compulsion, which (famously) is Koranically forbidden in matters of religion.[32] In the end, this farce succeeded in making me look and sound shabby, which was partly the point. No souls were saved, but we had a good time, and judging by the viewer response ("Has the foreigner converted yet?" asked caller after caller to the show's switchboard), it made good television.

But the most interesting audiences were smaller. Twice in his shop, Hesham had discussed my conversion while accompanied by understudies, as if he were an attending physician in a Salafi teaching hospital. They were female—each dressed in a full, black, figure-covering cloak with a *niqab*—and he did not explain their presence (or why they were there without a *mahram* or male relative), other than to say they were learning from him. It felt impolite to meet their gaze, and they never spoke, although they sometimes nodded vigorously when he scored points against me.

One day early in 2012, there was another young woman in his workshop. She wore no *niqab,* just a veil wrapped tightly around her oval face. She remained silent and gazed at the floor, and as usual I tried not to look. But about twenty minutes into the sparring session, she looked up, and we locked eyes. Hers surprised me: they had the epicanthic folds of an Asian woman. I assumed she was Malay or Indonesian. But how did she get here? I wanted to keep looking, but I looked away again, hoping I might soon steal another glance.

Hesham excused himself to fix us tea. As soon as he disappeared into the kitchen, the woman signaled me discreetly. "Do you have a phone number?" she whispered in English. "For emergency." I could now see that her veil sat lopsided, as if she had just started wearing it. From her voice and accent I deduced two things: that she was Japanese, and that she was terrified of Hesham.

After begging for my phone number, she asked me if I ever had "trouble" in Egypt and how I got out of it. I mumbled something about making sure I had friends to help me out. Then I tried to be a friend. I asked her where she was from, and she explained that she was from Yokohama and until recently had been teaching Japanese in Vladivostok.

"Do you speak Russian?" I asked in Russian, hoping she could speak more freely in a language Hesham didn't understand. At this, her lungs filled with oxygen, and she let forth a long, scared, and unnervingly loud explanation of her predicament.

Her name was Hoshi, and she had graduated from a Japanese university with a degree in Russian. Disowned by her parents, she moved to Vladivostok, then fell in love with a Siberian shooting instructor. The romance fizzled, and she sought refuge from loneliness by going online. Two Egyptian men lured her to Cairo with the promise of friendship and a job. On arrival, at the insistence of these two—now her best and perhaps only friends—she converted to Islam.

"Were they Salafis?" I asked.

"What is Salafi?" she said.

After she converted, everything went badly: The job didn't work out. Her landlord robbed her, and her two friends dropped her off, nearly broke, at Hesham's doorstep before cutting off contact. She told me he ran "the Organization"—when I asked Hesham, he called it "the Charity for New Muslims"—that worked systematically to snag converts and teach them pure Islam. It sounded as if a primary tactic was to isolate them.

The fishers of men had caught an unusual fish. I thought of the German speaker I had met in Alexandria and speculated about whether Hoshi's former friends had approached her with practiced Russian or Japanese. The invitation to Cairo sounded suspiciously like a trap—a ruse to get her alone, at the mercy of strangers, and easy to pressure. Whether she had been lured as part of a scheme, Hoshi declined to guess. (She still felt fondly toward the two men who encouraged her to come to Egypt.) But now she was getting the Salafi hard sell, and she wanted out.

The Salafis of the Organization were not letting her escape into disbelief without a fight. Hesham had installed her in an apartment where she could be monitored. She didn't feel safe there. If she left, Hesham might assume she had left Islam. I didn't even want to ask him how he would punish someone who committed apostasy under his care. Given the stakes, violence seemed possible, and rage certain. I didn't encourage her to leave Islam. Nothing Hoshi said made me think she wanted to—only that she wanted to leave Hesham.

Her concerns were more immediate than apostasy. She feared that if she were to stay, she would be cut off from the world. "That tailor guy let me talk to an American woman who converted," Hoshi said. "She said they would not even let her leave the apartment." They had already been hinting that she should hand over her phone and computer. Hoshi had been offered a job at a health spa, and Hesham had called up her boss to inform him that she quit. Her wallet was nearly empty. She worried her passport would be taken away next.

Hesham returned with the tea, suspicious when he heard us gabbling in a language he didn't understand. I told him that she explained that she needed a place to stay and that I had offered a spare room in the apartment my wife and I were renting. "Don't worry!" he said. "I have a very nice place for her in Mohandiseen." Mohandiseen was the part of town where the American woman said she was confined.

Hoshi looked stricken. "If you need a place, we're happy to help you for a few days," I told her in English. "And if you need help," I added in Russian, "call me."

Within hours the texts started coming. "I want to leave the Organization," said one. "Please can you meet me today as soon as possible," said another. Since she said her phone was being monitored, for a little extra security, I asked her to write in Russian, which she did. A friend who spoke Russian helped me write back. The friend was reluctant. "I have to live in this city," she said crossly, not wanting to get on the wrong side of jihadis.

The next day, Hoshi slipped out of her apartment when no one was looking and, at my direction, took a taxi to the Zamalek Marriott. A five-star resort with a lush garden, an Irish bar, and a casino named for the wine-swilling poet Omar Khayyam, it had once served as a royal palace, and its golden colonnades retained a royal splendor. In comparison to Hesham's blank-walled shop, it felt like the palace of Caligula. I sat in the garden and waited.

When Hoshi walked past the columns, I recognized her only by the roundness of her face. With no one to fear, it lit up and transited the garden like a moon along the horizon. Her veil had slipped to her shoulders.

I told her that if she felt endangered, I would help her. I passed her my mobile phone, which had the Japanese consul waiting on the other end, and for about fifteen minutes they discussed options. Satisfied that she was comfortable with her plan, I pressed cab fare into her hand and sent her away.

A few days later, she called again, saying that she had extracted herself from the Organization. I had referred her to a couple of cheap, Japanese-friendly hotels, and I think she stayed at one for a night or two. "Be careful of that tailor guy," she said at the end of our chat. "He says I should not talk to you. He thinks you are spy."

Soon after, her phone line was dead, and I stopped hearing from her.

Months later, Hoshi emailed: she was still in Cairo and would meet me for dinner. I took her to a French restaurant, and she described how she had left the Organization, fending off persistent entreaties from Salafis who had found her new phone number. The calls eventually stopped, and now her main struggles were with the rapists who prowled the hallways of her downtown flophouse.

She got a job at the spa, where she raised tiny carnivorous fish that nibbled the dead skin off the legs of wealthy Egyptians for cosmetic purposes. Was she happy? No. "It is so disgusting," she said. "The fish keep dying." But neither was she asking for help. She was saving cash for a trip home, and someday she'd make it.

But what kept her in Cairo, she said, was not religious or financial but personal. She felt she owed the Egyptian friends who had invited her here, and whose families she believed had ostracized them for associating with her. "Most of all," she added, "I don't want Egypt to be a bad experience."

When I heard that, I wanted to cry. To me, dodging sex criminals and babysitting tanks of fish sounded only marginally better than being Hesham's prisoner. Ironically, her rootlessness and low expectations, which imperiled her in the first place, may have saved her from that worse fate: many others who join cultish jihadi groups crave membership in a grand cosmic narrative that leads somewhere darker. She just wanted friends. Hoshi's willingness to be satisfied with "not having a bad experience" meant her ambitions were modest, and she could resist the potentially fatal appeal of a truly megalomaniacal group like the Islamic State. Sadness and loneliness drove her to Egypt, and more sadness and more loneliness might have eventually driven her all the way to Syria.

But she was still a sad case, immune to help. If she considered her Cairo experience salvageable, she was incorrigible after all, and I was delusional in thinking I could save her. Her delusion had created my own. "You are not in a Murakami novel," my Russian-speaking friend warned me, referring to the Japanese writer whose heroines tend to vanish or get caught in tough situations.

Mostly I despaired for her. Her broken home life had been just a start. Then came romantic rejection in Siberia and now another devastating experience in the land she hoped would provide a new life, religion, and maybe love. To return to Tokyo would mean going back to one of the most expensive civilizations on earth, and also one of the loneliest.

Soon after Hoshi left me at the Marriott, and before I knew she had extricated herself, I stopped by Hesham's shop. I asked about her, and he told me that I shouldn't worry, that he had "taken care of" Hoshi. He probably intended those words to sound paternal. But after I had watched him blur the line between compulsion and invitation, they now had a Mafia-like ring to them. His friendly face shone with the cruel smile of a jailer.

"Do you think I'm a spy?" I asked.

It didn't matter if I was a spy or not, Hesham said. He was telling me about Islam. And the message didn't vary according to who heard it, just as Islam hadn't changed between the seventh century and the twenty-first.

I told him that it might not matter to him whether I was a spy. But

I didn't want him to think I had come to him falsely. I had arrived presenting myself as a skeptical journalist and would soon be leaving as one. He shouldn't think the hours we spent burning our fingers on tea were a CIA plot.

He repeated: God didn't care whether I was a spy or not. The only thing that mattered was whether I spoke the words, and whether when I met my maker, I would respond to his questions as a Muslim. Would today be the day I took *shahadah*? he asked.

I said no to Hesham many times, but that time was the easiest.

MADNESS AND METHODOLOGY

Our task is not to reach closure. Indeed, at present this is factually impossible, for we lack the majority of the necessary data. We know the pornography of Jonestown; we do not know its mythology, its ideology, its soteriology, its sociology—we do not know almost everything we would need to know in order to venture a secure argument.

—Jonathan Z. Smith, "The Devil in Mr. Jones"[1]

Every jihadist generation gets its own precocious intellectuals. The 1970s and 1980s had the Blind Sheikh (born 1938), and the 1990s had Abu Muhammad al Maqdisi (born 1959), a Jordanian cleric who became the intellectual architect of Al Qaida. Thinking of reasons to kill people is a young man's game, so every decade or so produces new minds to incarnate its worst ideas.

In 2013, Cole Bunzel, a Princeton Ph.D. candidate who studies the Islamic State, began to notice a cleric preaching and writing under many pseudonyms—Abu Humam al Athari, Abu Sufyan al Sulami, Abu Hazm al Salafi—and rapidly rising to prominence. In these and other guises, this man stridently defended ISIS and its leader, Abu Bakr al Baghdadi, against Al Qaida. Baghdadi had moved to dissolve and absorb the latter's Syrian affiliate, Jabhat al Nusra, and the cleric murmured hopefully about Baghdadi's victory and eventual rise to the office of caliph. By early 2014, Bunzel reported, the man had arrived in Syria and unveiled himself as Turki al Bin'ali, "the Caliphate's scholar-in-arms."[2] A Bahraini national, he is about thirty-three, roughly the age of Bunzel himself.

Bin'ali hails from a well-known Bahraini family and grew up in Busaiteen, near the kingdom's airport. The area is a warren of dusty streets and comfortable villas, heavily populated with air force officers from the country's ruling Sunni minority. According to the biographies of Bin'ali posted online by his students, he has lived and studied in Dubai, Jordan, and Saudi Arabia, and has been imprisoned in Gulf states for preaching jihad. Several of his relatives have since been arrested or charged with supporting the Islamic State, and Bahrain stripped Bin'ali himself of his citizenship in January 2015.[3] As the Islamic State's mufti—analogous to a chief justice and attorney general wrapped into one—Bin'ali is responsible for the weightiest matters of religious policy—who is a Muslim, who is an apostate, who is eligible to be enslaved, and who must be killed. As a doctrinal enforcer, he has kept the movement pure and leads the efforts to educate—and when necessary, punish—deviants within the Islamic State.[4]

After Bunzel first watched an online video of a Bin'ali lecture, he shared it with Bernard Haykel, his adviser at Princeton. They agreed that the young sheikh was "a genius—fucked up, but a genius." In Bin'ali's rulings and recorded sermons, one can see a fearsome, lawyerly brilliance, a glee in dismantling the logic of his opponents, and an adolescent confidence in the rightness of his judgments.

Most impressive, Haykel and Bunzel later told me, is Bin'ali's machinelike recall. His sermons are a rhetorical spectacle, focusing on recitation of hadith—that is, the reports of the sayings of Muhammad—and the details of the millennium-long game of telephone that attaches to each, starting from the first person who heard the saying from the Prophet's lips, and then proceeding through all those who have conveyed that memory up to the present day. "When he speaks, he puts on a world-class oratorical performance," Haykel says. "He is a master of his métier, a performer of the same category as a Laurence Olivier or a John Gielgud."[5]

Whether Bin'ali's sermons and writings inspire awe or nausea depends on perspective. He quotes liberally from Ibn Taymiyyah and Ibn 'Abd al Wahhab, and like those men, he shows little deference for scholarly or legal precedent. Bin'ali sets a match to centuries of non-Salafi Muslim theology and law. He disregards all but the earliest precedents, favoring scripture, as filtered through Ibn Taymiyyah. Scholars' arguments have traditionally had great influence on the practice of Islam, but in the end, they are just opinions—this is religion, with no right answers to be determined conclusively in this life—and Bin'ali rejects most of them. Only the authority of the Koran and Sunna of the Prophet matter; precedent and prior interpretation count for little. An analogy to U.S. law will unavoidably fail in its particulars but may be useful as illustration: imagine if a bright man happened upon the U.S. Constitution as it existed in 1791 and tried to construct a legal system on that basis, without a jot of consideration for any of the Supreme Court opinions and pieces of legislation that followed in the two subsequent centuries. Bin'ali has undertaken a task of comparable boldness for Islam.

Every Muslim scholar to whom I have shown Bin'ali's sermons has ended up exasperated—by his brashness, his violence, his rhetorical style. "*Mutakallaf,*" said one. (In plain English: "What a poseur.") Some react with pained expressions, as if unexpectedly in the presence of loud bagpipe music, or a malodorous fellow passenger on public transit. How does an Islamic scholar argue with someone who denies that the last millennium of Islamic scholarship ever happened? At the same time, though, some will acknowledge his creativity and nerve. Bin'ali is citing scripture in a learned and brilliant way—just without obeisance to previous scholars.

It helps, too, that his Arabic is, like the caliph Baghdadi's, impeccable. The average educated Arab cannot speak classical, fully voweled Arabic. It is as different from modern spoken dialects as Spanish is from Latin. To speak without notes or prepared text is therefore a staggering parlor trick—and Bin ʿali does so for nearly an hour at a stretch, while discussing complicated theological topics, intermittently using a form of unmetered Arabic verse called *saj ʿ*.[6] When a new jihadist statement comes out, Bunzel compares the written text with the text as delivered, marking grammatical errors in red, as if it were an undergraduate paper. "Usually there are lots of mistakes," Bunzel told me. "Baghdadi and Bin ʿali are perfect."[7]

What does Bin ʿali believe? His office of fellow scholars in the Islamic State has become a veritable factory of fatwas, signed and unsigned. Bunzel has catalogued many of these, and other researchers (such as the Iraqi-Welsh polymath Aymenn Jawad Al-Tamimi and the American Aaron Y. Zelin) have done the same. Collectively, Bin ʿali's writings show an indifference to the worldly lives of both Muslims and infidels, a hatred of idolatry, and an intellectual stubbornness so pronounced that Bin ʿali surely counts it as a virtue. By far the most salient influence on his thinking is Ibn ʿAbd al Wahhab, the eighteenth-century Arabian cleric and follower of Ibn Taymiyyah. Bunzel cites Bin ʿali as the likely author of one of the clearest statements of the Islamic State's ideology, an indoctrination pamphlet titled *This Is Our Creed, This Is Our Methodology*. Its main message is that Islamic State followers should heed and avoid the "nullifiers of Islam," a standard Wahhabi list of beliefs and actions that invalidate one's claim to be Muslim.[8]

For a man his age, Bin ʿali has a long record of misbehavior. He was a bright student, but his views—including endorsement of violence against the state—made him unemployable as a government scholar in his home country and ineligible to study in the most prestigious institutions in Saudi Arabia or Egypt.[9] But in Amman, the capital of

Jordan, he found an ideal patron: Abu Muhammad al Maqdisi, the Al Qaida grandee from the 1990s. A Jordanian of Palestinian descent, Maqdisi has a fair claim to being the most important jihadist unknown to the average American newspaper reader. He remains aligned with Al Qaida, siding with the group against the Islamic State—and now, against his former student.

Born in the West Bank in 1959, Maqdisi studied widely in the Arab world, and for a few weeks in Yugoslavia (where he found the Serbo-Croatian language bewildering and the women's skirts too short). He embraced jihadi-Salafism, and Arab dictators were the first targets of his excommunication. In the 1990s, he pronounced the kings of Jordan and Saudi Arabia infidels, and the Jordanians threw him in prison. Once there he found many eager students, including Abu Mus'ab al Zarqawi, who would go on to found the Iraqi Al Qaida affiliate that would become ISIS and, ultimately, the Islamic State.[10]

After his release, Maqdisi taught Bin'ali by phone and online, from his Amman madrassah. By then, Maqdisi's former student Zarqawi had gone to war in Iraq, and the divisions between the eventual Islamic State and Al Qaida were widening. At issue, starting in 2004, was Zarqawi's penchant for bloody spectacle and his hatred of other Muslims. Zarqawi reveled in gore, particularly the gore of Shia and other apostates, and he pioneered the practice of on-camera beheadings and bombings calibrated and placed to maximize Muslim casualties. Maqdisi wrote to his former pupil and warned that he needed to exercise caution and "not issue sweeping proclamations of *takfir*" or "proclaim people to be apostates because of their sins."[11]

The distinction between apostate and sinner may appear subtle, but it is a key point of contention between Al Qaida and the Islamic State. Both groups say denying the holiness of the Koran or the prophecies of Muhammad is straightforward apostasy. But Zarqawi and the state he spawned have taken the position that apostasy is also revealed by many other acts. These include, in certain cases, selling alcohol or drugs, wearing Western clothes or shaving one's beard, voting in an election—even for a Muslim candidate—and being reluctant to call other people apostates. By themselves, none of these would normally rise to the level of capital offense. But if practiced persistently, they could be interpreted as denial of their own inherent sinfulness, which amounts to denial of God's law. Maqdisi chastised Zarqawi further. His *takfiri* followers are possessed of "hollow zeal," he wrote. "For these [people, a proclamation of] *takfir* does not require proof; it becomes a sort of [instinctive] vengeful reaction that does not spare anyone except those who completely share their path and beliefs."[12] He lodged one sharp criticism he would come to regret. In addition to their zeal, he said, these "youngsters" were neglecting their duty of planning for the long term. Violence for its own sake was all well and good, he said. But proper jihad aims not just to hurt the enemy but ultimately to establish an Islamic state.[13]

Bin'ali fully assimilated that objection. He traveled to ISIS territory no later than the beginning of 2014, around the time when Jabhat al Nusra, the Al Qaida faction with which Maqdisi was aligned, formally went to war with ISIS. Bin'ali has since written several philippics against the Islamic State's detractors, Maqdisi among them, and he has repeatedly stressed that Maqdisi is complaining about the Islamic State's having done only what Maqdisi himself told them to do. In an essay about the acts of "revival" performed by the Islamic State, Bin'ali lists accomplishments that make the scattered terrorist attacks of Al Qaida look unambitious by comparison. Chief among the achievements is the establishment of precisely the state Maqdisi had called for:

> The Islamic State has revived the core of Islam. People now clearly differentiate between belief and disbelief, loyalty [toward believers] and disavowal [of infidels]. Even children now learn what most adults did not know before.
>
> The Islamic State has even revived what had vanished

from jurisprudence of jihad and transferred what is written in the books to practical application on the ground.

Islamic State has revived the Islamic model of domestic and foreign policy, the guidelines and rules of foreign relations, formerly unknown even to scholars, let alone laymen. The Islamic State has revived matters related to leadership and allegiance. These matters are in the hands of the public today, [but] previously were only accessible to the elites.

To this parade of victories he added the revival of laws about finance, shedding blood, and modesty; the institution of morality police or *hisbah;* and *jizya,* the tax on Jews and Christians permanently residing in Muslim lands, which until recently "was a fantasy in the minds of many Muslims." Finally, he added, "the most significant revival is defeating tribalism and [splitting into] groups" such as the Muslim Brotherhood, Salafis, or indeed Jabhat al Nusra. The Islamic State aimed to bring unity to the Muslims.

Maqdisi and his followers responded venomously. By what right did Bin ʿali and Baghdadi declare themselves able to speak for all Muslims? Was it not the duty of the whole Muslim *ummah* [community] to appoint its caliph, and hadn't the split between ISIS and Jabhat al Nusra demonstrated that the *ummah* was in no position to unite on this or any other issue? Abu Muhammad al Jawlani, Nusra's leader, called on Baghdadi to not "force your ignorant thoughts on the *ummah.* O people of the Islamic State, wake up and return to the *ummah!*"

Bin ʿali retorted that Nusra's fetishization of the *ummah* amounted to veiled or unwitting endorsement of democracy. God never intended for the whole *ummah*—which contained both good Muslims and bad—to make these decisions. Indeed, "the Prophet Muhammad told us that the majority of the *ummah* are in delusion," and that it would split into seventy-three sects, only one of which would be right. "Do they want us to follow the seventy-two Hell-bound sects and be governed by them and let them decide for us?" The true leaders should be the ones who follow the model of the Prophet.

Bin ʿaliʾs insubordination is all the more astonishing because Maqdisi had once given him his highest endorsement. In the mid-2000s, having been jailed repeatedly by the Jordanian government, Maqdisi anointed Bin ʿali as one of a small number of deputies who would run Maqdisiʾs school in case of his incapacitation.[14] Bin ʿali became known to some as "little Maqdisi."[15] Gradually, Maqdisiʾs esteem for his pupil slackened. Joas Wagemakers, a professor at the University of Utrecht who wrote an intellectual biography of Maqdisi, says that in the 2000s, Maqdisi would refer to the Islamic State's forebears not as "scholars," the term one might apply to a peer, but as "seekers of knowledge" [tullab ʿilm], a less reverent term that acknowledges their scholarly intention without acknowledging attainment.[16] Now Maqdisi might wish to take back even that.

Overall, though, Bin ʿali followed Maqdisiʾs path more closely than the latter would like to admit. Bin ʿali is executing in reality a plan that Maqdisi had endorsed in theory. Maqdisi opened the gates to excommunication of Arab leaders with his pronouncements against the Jordanian and Saudi royals. He just never did anything about it—and now he can only stew enviously. As the Arkansas politician Jim Johnson said of Orval Faubus: "The sonofabitch hit the jackpot on my nickel."

Bin ʿaliʾs intellectual exertions exposed the mind of the Islamic State. The world would soon see its face.

ISIS, as it was then called, expanded in 2013 and 2014, while most of the world was luxuriating in its first year in a long time seemingly without important news from Iraq and Syria. The Syrian civil war looked frozen, or frozen enough to ignore for the time being. Iraqis and Syrians, of course, cared a great deal about the events in their Sunni-dominated desert borderlands, and Muslim communities in

Europe and Arabia worried as young men and women began slipping away to join a mysterious group growing in the Levant.

Those who were paying attention, however, noticed the coming of something serious. At the end of 2013, *The Independent*'s Patrick Cockburn wrote that Abu Bakr al Baghdadi deserved the title "Middle East leader of the year."

> There is one leader in the Middle East who can look back on the achievements of the past year with unmitigated satisfaction. He leads an organization that was supposedly on its way to extinction or irrelevance three years ago, but today it is an ever more powerful force in the vast triangle of territory in Iraq and Syria between Mosul, Baghdad and the Mediterranean coast. One of the most extraordinary developments in the Middle East is that 12 years after 9/11 and six years after "the Surge" in Iraq was supposed to have crushed al-Qa'ida in Iraq, it is back in business.[17]

The Islamic State in Iraq had begun that year as the older Iraqi sibling of Jabhat al Nusra, a Syrian jihadist group. In April 2013, the Iraqi side informed its Syrian counterpart that the two groups would unite under Baghdadi and become ISIS. The Syrian group, led by Abu Muhammad al Jawlani, did not take the news of its absorption well and fell out with Baghdadi, with Jawlani's Jabhat al Nusra dominating in Syria's west and Baghdadi's ISIS straddling the Iraq-Syria border in the east.[18]

At that point, few outside Baghdadi's inner circle knew what he looked like, how he walked, whether he could inspire a crowd or was devoid of charisma. He was, we now know, born in 1971 to a pious lower-middle-class family in Samarra, Iraq. He earned a doctorate in Koranic recitation from a university in Baghdad, and in the 2000s, he ascended through the ranks of Al Qaida and became a trusted courier for the group.[19] Unlike some of his predecessors as leader of Al

Qaida in Iraq, he avoided photographs and cultivated his own personal security from an early stage. Baghdadi had appeared previously only in grainy prison mug shots taken by American military police during detentions for insurgent activity in Iraq in the mid-2000s. They showed a man with the tanned face of a day laborer but the wire-rimmed spectacles of a scholar. And records are so unreliable that the man in the photo might not have been him. Some speculated that Baghdadi might be a composite of multiple leaders, their identities hidden behind a decoy.

On June 10, 2014, ISIS fighters sacked Mosul, and for the next few weeks, its leaders plotted a major event, the Islamist equivalent of a debutante ball, where the world would finally meet Baghdadi. In Iraq, the United States had labored mightily to ensure that chiefs of Al Qaida died in quick succession, but in Syria, Baghdadi enjoyed safety from American drones and special operators. When it became clear that his organization had seized—and would keep—Iraqi territory, the United States began looking for signs of his movements.

Knowledge of the rhymes of history might have helped them predict where, if not when, he would reveal himself. Zarqawi, Baghdadi's forerunner, died in a drone strike outside Baʿquba, Iraq, in June 2006—eight years too early to see the conquest of Mosul. His associates remembered him as a Moses-like figure, granted a chance to see his promised land but not to set foot in it. They knew, too, that he idolized Nur al Din al Zengi (1118–1174), a warrior against the Crusaders. The decision to orchestrate Baghdadi's debut at the Grand Mosque of al Nuri, the site of Nur al Din's inauguration as leader, may have been a tribute to Zarqawi.[20]

On July 6, 2014, at the beginning of Ramadan, Baghdadi stepped from shadows into light, and this formerly spectral figure became vivid and real. In footage from the event, Baghdadi moves slowly, with the authority of a man obliged to move for no one at all. His beard is streaked with gray, and his clothes are all black, the regnal color of the Abbasid caliphs, the last to rule from Baghdad and Raqqah. The worshippers in the mosque look unprepared. Some are wearing dirty T-shirts, others sweaty tunics. This occasion of possible world-historical importance caught them by surprise.

Baghdadi first greets the congregation, then sits down for the call to prayer. During the call, he stares ahead and picks his teeth with a *miswak,* the Salafi-mandated gingery dental twig. Finally, he pauses for several seconds before rising and ascending the pulpit. His delivery is even and precise. He moves his body almost not at all, save for his right hand, which rests on a brass banister and periodically rises, with the index finger up, to stress a point.

He emphasizes the obligatory nature of jihad, and the great blessings of the holy month of Ramadan. During this month, he says, virtuous acts are worth a thousand times more than in other months. "This is the month in which the Prophet commanded armies to fight against the enemies of God, the month in which he would wage jihad against the polytheists," he says. "And God likes us to kill his enemies and make jihad for his sake."

Then, turning to the matter of the office of caliph, he chides Muslims for having gone without a caliph for so long.

> As for your mujahideen brothers, God has bestowed upon them the grace of victory and conquest, and enabled them, after many years of jihad, patience, and fighting the enemies of God, granted them success and empowered them to achieve their goal. Therefore, they hastened to declare the Caliphate and place an imam. This is a duty upon the Muslims—a duty that has been lost for centuries and absent from the reality of the world and so many Muslims were ignorant of it. The Muslims sin by losing it, and they must always seek to establish it, and they have done so, and all praise is due to God.

He accepts the job of caliph under duress:

> I have been plagued with this great matter, plagued with this
> responsibility, and it is a heavy responsibility. I was placed as
> your caretaker, and I am not better than you. So if you found
> me to be right then help me, and if you found me to be wrong
> then advise me and make me right and obey me in what I
> obey God through you. If I disobey Him then there is no
> obedience to me from you.

Then he recites Koran and leads prayers. The first row of worshippers behind him have AK-47s with them in the mosque, and their
faces are blurred. The whole exercise, prayers included, takes about
twenty minutes.

Cole Bunzel watched a video of Baghdadi's debut after learning of
it through online jihadi chatter.[21] "It was one of the more amazing
things I have ever seen," he told me. At first the chatter merely indi-
cated that something exciting was in the works. Then, when the official video emerged, the group's supporters became ecstatic.

Any Muslim with an elementary knowledge of the history of his
religion would hear Baghdadi's caliphate declaration and recognize
its implication: that to support him was compulsory, and that Baghdadi would fight anyone who did not obey him. Baghdadi's speech
echoed—almost to the point of plagiarism—the speech given by his
namesake, Abu Bakr al Siddiq (570–634), the immediate successor to
Muhammad as leader of the Muslims. After the Prophet's death in
632, Abu Bakr al Siddiq spoke to his supporters:

> O people, I have been appointed over you, though I am not
> the best among you. If I do well, then help me; and if I act
> wrongly, then correct me [. . .] Obey me so long as I obey
> God and His Messenger. And if I disobey God and His Mes-
> senger, then I have no right to your obedience.

The similarities between Baghdadi and Abu Bakr al Siddiq tran-scend rhetoric.[22] The original Abu Bakr kicked off his caliphate (which lasted only two years) with a campaign of consolidation. Some early Muslim factions declared that their allegiance was to God and his Prophet, not to Abu Bakr, and they refused to pay taxes [zakat] now considered a cornerstone of Islam. Abu Bakr responded by fighting and subjugating them, in what are known as the Wars of Apostasy (or the Ridda wars).[23] Baghdadi's decision to emphasize the Abu Bakr connection implied that he, too, would begin his rule by attacking and subduing (former) Muslims: Kurds, Shia, and others loyal to other governments or ideologies.

Baghdadi had been a key figure in Iraqi Al Qaida circles for years already, so in a way his ascent continued the trajectory of jihad in Iraq—another leader, another high-value target with a short life ex-pectancy. By declaring himself caliph, though, he could issue binding orders and, in effect, create law. Islam, which most Muslims had re-garded as a religion, once again became a religion and a state.

Most of the world's Muslims heard this call and dismissed it.[24] The Islamic State's supporters expected this indifference. They had long been told that most Muslims were apostates. The Islamic State's minority status only increased the prestige of following Baghdadi: there would be more room in Camp Faith for the believers, and a greater share of the riches in Paradise. When I heard the call myself, my mind went straight to Hesham. An early piece of Islamic State propaganda cited a famous Koranic passage: "It was we [God] who created man, and we know what dark suggestions his soul makes to him: for we are nearer to him than his own jugular vein."[25] Hesham had quoted me that same vivid verse, and I read it again in the Is-lamic State's propaganda with a shock of recognition. The verse en-courages mindfulness—a good thing in itself, but dangerous when combined with violent self-loathing. The Islamic State and Hesham preyed on a constant feeling of self-incrimination, a reminder that no life is sinless and every soul has its own enemy within. They then weaponized that fanatical sense of shame by declaring their jihad the only absolution. The guiltier the conscience the better, since there is more sin to expunge. The recruit's fear grows more intense, and the need for absolution more urgent, with each thump of the jugular. All those discussions of hellfire with Hesham had an effect, however mild, even on me. The effect on others might be strong enough to send them to Mosul, in hopes of praying behind the caliph.

After I last saw Hesham, I spent most of the year in the United States, and we spoke rarely, by phone. In July 2013, the Muslim Brotherhood's Muhammad Morsi—who had been elected president in the fairest election Egypt had ever held—was toppled by a military coup after only a year in office. The general who replaced him, ʿAbd al Fattah al Sisi, reinstated the Mubarak-era policies and even looked a bit like a younger Mubarak.

Hesham began protesting Sisi's government. On August 14, 2013, the military moved against the protesters in Rabaʿa Square, killing as many as a thousand of them. Days later, Hesham called me to say he had survived only because God diverted the bullets around him, like a stream around a boulder. He said many of the other Salafis I had met through him—the Alexandria group, my debate opponent on his show—had already left Egypt for Turkey, Qatar, and Africa.

In 2014, I returned to Egypt to see what Hesham himself was doing. The Islamic State had established itself, but not everyone from the older generation of jihadis had pledged to the caliph. Older jihadists grumbled that the Islamic State was a bunch of upstarts, disrespectful of its jihadist elders. The Blind Sheikh and many others had spent decades in prison for jihadist activities and sympathies. And now Baghdadi *commanded* obedience, with hardly a grateful nod to the generations that preceded him.

Hesham's loyalties therefore remained in doubt. He had never stated membership in a terrorist group or explicitly supported any specific acts of violence. But all his discussions with me seemed to foreshadow what had since become the program of the Islamic State, and I wanted to know more about his reaction to its emergence.

On an August afternoon, after more than a year without contact, I dropped by his workshop. Walking up the stifling, dark stairwell, past a doorman sleeping through the afternoon heat, I wondered if Hesham might have gone to Syria already. Everything he had said to me was consistent with support for the Islamic State—but also with support for competing jihadi groups, such as Al Qaida. The only question was whether he had the courage to shorten his life for the convictions that he had spent the last two decades urging on others, including me.

I was relieved to find him sitting alone, wearing dirty cotton pajamas moist with sweat. He had a full teacup in front of him, and it must have been sitting there for some time, because it had equilibrated to the temperature of the shop and wasn't giving off any steam. I wondered if his time in prison had taught him to sit still. In the ten seconds I spent watching him from the doorway, he didn't move at all. I thought he was asleep, perhaps dreaming of caliphates, until I tiptoed closer and saw his eyes, glazed but open.

They came alive when I said a *salam,* and he stood up and shook my hand hatelessly, saying he was pleased to see me. He looked around, embarrassed, and I felt bad for not giving him a chance to tidy up. Then again, there was nothing to clean up: a dress-form dummy stood next to him, but his shop was bare, the bolts of cloth and works in progress noticeably absent. Business was not good.

He said he was well—"Not arrested yet!"—and called an apprentice to get me a cold orange soda. The Egyptian economy had shriveled under Sisi, he told me, and he didn't have work. "I have a family," he told me, "and times are really, really tough."

About Morsi he remained contemptuous. "Morsi prayed, he memorized the Koran, he fasted during Ramadan," Hesham said. This made him a fine Muslim. But he was undone by ambition. "When he became president, he became different from anyone else: he became responsible for ruling by Islam." Hesham said he would have forgiven Morsi for bringing Islamic law along slowly, committing to stoning adulterers at a later date. But Morsi gave no reason at all for his rejection of Shariah and intimated no plans to stone anyone ever. He could at least have shut down the casinos and belly-dancing shows— but instead he extended their licenses. These were actions of disbelief, even if undertaken by a self-described Islamist. They nullified his faith. Thus Morsi, once a good Muslim, became no Muslim at all.

But like the Blind Sheikh and Ahmad ibn Hanbal before him, Hesham refused to excommunicate Morsi by name, saying only that Morsi had committed *kufr* and must be held accountable. "The imam, the president, the leader, and the king are not like ordinary people," Hesham told me. They are judged more harshly, and they leave themselves open to charges of *kufr* because they are required to consider issues—such as whether to ban gambling—that ordinary people never face. This was the "heavy responsibility" of the imam, mentioned by Baghdadi in his Mosul sermon. His own deference to scholars (including the Blind Sheikh) grew out of humility and fear of error. His now-canceled cable show had been called *The Court of the Scholars,* but he hastened to add that he wasn't one. For a layman, errors in matters of faith could be catastrophic. For a president or caliph, the opportunities of soul-imperiling error were more abundant.

To avoid missteps, Hesham said, a sovereign had no choice but to obey the scholars. He told me a story that illustrated the dangers of leadership. When Sulayman the Magnificent (1494–1566), the Ottoman caliph, died, he asked to be buried with a small box. Many wondered whether Sulayman expected to take a little treasure of gold along to the afterlife. His grand mufti, Abu al Su'ud, opened it up. "Inside they found all the *fatawa* [religious decisions], all the advice he ever got from the scholars," Hesham said, "just in case Allah asked him why he did what he did." (Abu al Su'ud was, according to this apocryphal tale, displeased to discover the extent to which his caliph had established a paper trail that could inculpate him before the Almighty.[26])

"Why would anyone want to be a ruler?" I asked. "Or a scholar, for that matter?"

"Very good," Hesham said, his favorite words of praise when I anticipated the next step in a lecture. "The people who know this responsibility—*they run away from it.*" Again, he turned to the greatest hits of Sunni governance. ʿUmar ibn ʿAbd al ʿAziz (682–720), the eighth Umayyad caliph, so feared God's punishment that he declared nearly all sources of state revenue off-limits, removing his own ability to claim them for discretionary use.[27] When he found his government had a surplus—it had cared for the poor, paid the debts of the indebted, and given money to the young to start families—he ordered that bread be baked and left out on the mountaintops for birds. He didn't want to risk the chance that God would hold the fall of a sparrow against him.

Centuries later, the job of caliph still sounded like the worst on earth. An incompetent tailor might end up broke and bored. An incompetent caliph will burn for eternity. Hesham agreed that the job would be unattractive. But he added an important caveat. "If there is no one to take it but you," he said, "then you have an *obligation* to take it." In the history of Islam, he said, the greatest rulers found themselves compelled to serve because no one else could.

"And that's what happened with Abu Bakr al Baghdadi," he said, broaching the topic I thought he would avoid. Baghdadi had spoken of the office of caliph as onerous, a "heavy responsibility" that "plagued" him. The rhetoric struck the right note. Hesham said the questions that determined whether Baghdadi was required to take office were simple. "Who's doing Islam right now?" he asked, growing more animated. "Who's practicing *khilafah* [caliphate]? Nobody!"

The mention of Baghdadi sent adrenaline through his veins, and I rocked on my heels for a second, taken aback by the restorative power of the caliph's name. Hesham had wanted to impose harsh punishments on thieves and apostates before, but he had lacked an Islamic government to administer them. Now he had it. He had disapproved of Mubarak or Morsi before, but had no choice other than seething acquiescence. Now he had a caliph, and he could direct his feet to an Islamic State.

I decided to be blunt. "What do you think of the Islamic State," I asked, "and why aren't you there?"

"I'm too old for that," he said. "Too old for traveling." He continued with a few noncommittal words about the Islamic State itself. "I don't attack them, and I don't defend them," he said, his hands raised again defensively, in the stick-up position. "I don't attack someone I don't know."

It beggared belief that he didn't know enough about the Islamic State, since the media had been talking about little else for months now. And even if Hesham knew just a little, he would at least be aware that Baghdadi had *ordered* him to submit, using a familiar language of religious obligation. The Islamic State described the oath of allegiance as *bay'a*—a term from early Islam for the contract between the Prophet (or his successor) and a subject. The analogy suggested that a tepid response to the invitation would be a serious sin.

As for being too old—the Islamic State had published videos of men older than Hesham living within its borders in a state of spiritual bliss and physical comfort. These were men old enough to draw full pensions from their home governments in Europe, but who threw in their lot with the caliphate instead.

"Why don't you at least give your allegiance to Baghdadi?" I asked.

Hesham's legal mind spun into motion. "Even if I am convinced one hundred percent that Abu Bakr al Baghdadi is *khalifah,* I can't give *bay'a* to him," Hesham explained. "That would mean I am under his command, and he is responsible for my protection and safety. If I don't have money, he'll give it to me, if I don't have food, he'll feed me." The physical distance made a relationship of *bay'a* impossible—

conveniently, for someone who did not seem to have the will to emigrate to a war zone. "He can't command me now, because the way is
cut between us."

Again, he alternated excuses and romantic speculation. "I've seen
pictures," he said wistfully. He meant the Islamic State propaganda.
"They have enough food, enough everything. If you live under their
protection, it's beautiful." Seeds that once yielded a single stalk of
wheat now, under the Islamic State's care, gave three or four. Miracles
were happening.

"The *Dawlah Islamiyyah* [Islamic State] came to save people from
terror and find protection and freedom," he continued. They were
Sunni saviors. He considered them the possible fulfillment of prophecy: a caliphate that would arise out of nowhere, as Muhammad foretold, and clear away the rule of Muslims by tyrants. "You can't fight
ʿaqida [creed]," Hesham said. "What's wrong in what they're doing?

"Who is with them, who is supporting them? Nobody. And yet the
whole world cannot stop them. How are they so strong? It's not because they have the best weapons. It is because they are being *supported by Allah*. And when Allah is with you, who is going to beat
you?"

I decided I wouldn't get anything more from him. Hesham had
enough Ibn Hanbal in him to avoid making an outright declaration
of fealty to Baghdadi, or of excommunication against Morsi. But
here, in this city of punctured dreams and bitter compromise, his
dream remained intact—and closer to fulfillment than ever. I pitied
his family, for whom he cared and was responsible, just as a caliph in
receipt of valid *bayʿa* would be responsible for him.

When I stood to leave, I thought of Hesham in his New York days,
measuring the *Color of Money*–era Paul Newman for an elegant wool
three-piece. My wife had been urging me to buy a suit. At the door,
as a parting entreaty, Hesham told me Newman would pay five grand

and up, but since he was desperate, he'd charge me less than a thousand. I told him I'd think about it.

I got into a taxi and headed home. Slaloming past cars and pedestrians, I texted my wife to find out what she thought of his proposal. *You are not,* she wrote back, *under any circumstances to give money to a supporter of ISIS.* She has been a source of sound advice for a while now.

In midsummer 2014, around the time Baghdadi revealed himself, the Islamic State published the first issue of its English-language magazine, *Dabiq.* It is named for a Syrian town that figures in the apocalyptic cycles in Islamic prophecy. Distributed online as a 68-megabyte PDF, the issue was polished and well edited. The cover featured a map of the Middle East as a single borderless caliphate. I was in Connecticut at the time and was able to download the first issue in just over a minute. If Hesham downloaded it in Cairo, it probably took much longer.

Students of the art of propaganda will someday read *Dabiq* alongside issues of *Der Stürmer* under Streicher or *Pravda* under Bukharin. Even in this company, the competence of *Dabiq*'s messaging stands out. Purely from the perspective of journalistic tradecraft, it deserves full marks—hip sans-serif fonts of varying size keep the design vibrant; full-bleed photos are tidily chosen and cropped; the text itself reads smoothly, with professional copyediting, and a variety of genres of writing, from features to pull quotes to charts. It is entirely in English, with heavy doses of transliterated (but untranslated) Arabic. Content aside, it looks like a scrappy new men's magazine.

The issue aimed to reach at least two distinct audiences, with rhetoric custom-tailored for each. The first was non-Muslims, and the main function was to scare the bejesus out of them. A page-three photograph of wounded U.S. soldiers, wreathed with photoshopped flames, served that purpose, as did a martial tone and a steady flow of images of battle-hardened jihadists. The editors were making a promise: If you are not on our side, we will kill you.

The second and more important audience was a Muslim one—and not just any Muslim audience, but one literate in the language of the faith. The cover's banner headline—"The Return of Khilafah"—was accompanied by a date from the Islamic calendar—month of Ramadan, year 1435—and, in smaller letters, three other headlines. The first, "Reporting on Iraq and Sham," rounded up news stories from the region; the second, "Imamah [leadership] is from the Millah [people] of Ibrahim," concerned the renewal of monotheism from followers of Abraham (a prophet in Judaism and Christianity as well as Islam); and the third, "From Hijrah to Khilafah," explained the strategy that had begun with an influx of fighters into Syria, and had since led to the reestablishment of the caliphate.

As these headlines make clear, the magazine will baffle anyone completely ignorant of Islam and its history. It is the work of someone at home with the aesthetics of Western popular culture, philosophy, and religion, and also with the official doctrine of the Islamic State. The density of untranslated Arabic phrases and references to specific figures from early Islam render large sections incomprehensible to the uninitiated.[28] Context reveals the meaning of some words, but for the average reader, the experience of reading an early issue of *Dabiq* is not so different from encountering the Cockney-Russian pidgin of *A Clockwork Orange* for the first time. If you know only some of the lingo, by the end of the issue *Dabiq* will either have repulsed you enough to force you to put it down—or it will have initiated you into new concepts and new Arabic words, and brought you closer to the mentality that its editors are trying to promote. It is a lesson in a foreign language, smuggled in under the subterfuge of being a magazine about politics and religion. The effect is one of brainwashing.

Obscure though the Arabic may be to most non-Muslims, to anyone primed to believe that Islamic civilization began degenerating after the death of the last Companions of the Prophet, not a word would have seemed out of place. The first issue quotes the semi-official Islamic State slogan that it is establishing itself on *al minhaj al nubuwah* [the Prophetic methodology], that is to say, the political and religious recipe dictated by the Prophet. The phrase alludes to a prophecy by Muhammad—quoted in the article "From Hijrah to Khilafah"—which promised the rise of a caliphate on the Prophetic methodology, then a period of "harsh kingship" (supposedly referring to modern-day Middle Eastern despots) followed by the restoration of the caliphate. The phrase "Prophetic methodology" is ubiquitous in the Islamic State, not only in propaganda, but also on letterhead, street signs, and bumper stickers.

Other Prophetic pretensions are more subtle. "From Hijrah to Khilafah" also referenced one of the key words in early Islamic history, *hijrah*, which usually refers to Muhammad's emigration from Mecca to Medina. Muhammad had been preaching Islam for years in Mecca when the city's rulers rejected him and drummed him out of town. His journey to Medina (known then as Yathrib, 210 miles north of Mecca) in the year 622 marks Year Zero of the Islamic calendar. The Islamic State fighters' own *hijrah*-like flight from their disbelieving home countries to the hinterlands of Syria and Iraq implicitly promises a similar historical reboot.

Muhammad's supporters who joined him for the dangerous journey to Medina were known as *muhajirun* [emigrants, or *hijrah* makers]. *Dabiq* and other official outlets use the same name to refer to the foreign fighters for the Islamic State. Early Muslims consisted of two factions—the *Muhajirun* from Mecca and the *Ansar* [helpers] indigenous to Medina, who welcomed the *Muhajirun* on arrival. The Islamic State calls the local people of Syria Ansar. Righteousness, like fashion, comes in cycles—and for the creators of *Dabiq* all the great concepts and key words from Islam's past are relevant once more, and the seventh century is back in style.

Muhammad's armies strengthened enough to return to Mecca

eight years later, conquer it, and convert the holdouts from the Prophet's tribe of Quraysh who had sent him packing in 622. Among the most famous acts of the Muslims upon arrival in Mecca was to destroy the pagan idols that had been worshipped there for generations. True to form, an article in *Dabiq* quotes Baghdadi promising to destroy the figurative pagan idols of the lands from which the latter-day *Muhajirun* have emigrated. The Islamic State will, he says, "trample the idol of nationalism [and] destroy the idol of democracy."

The initial war against Muhammad's Meccan adversaries prompted the first classical uses of the word "jihad," and the Islamic State follows suit—implying that anyone who doesn't recognize its activities as holy war would not recognize Muhammad's either.[29] *Dabiq* calls frontline fighting duty "making *ribat*" or "doing *ribat*," after the classical and medieval word for a frontier outpost on the edges of the Islamic world. One recruiting poster shows a man behind a machine gun, on watch in the cold dawn hours. "This Muslim is doing *ribat*," it says. "What have you done for Islam today?"

Dabiq also speaks of *bay'a*, the binding loyalty pledge between believer and caliph that Hesham was reluctant to make. The word can be used in a secular sense—Saddam Hussein demanded *bay'a*—but in the *Dabiq* article "Halab Tribal Assemblies," the pledge is packed with religious allusion. During the Prophet's consolidation of power, and its preservation by Abu Bakr and the other early caliphs, tribes convened to offer their allegiance in formal ceremonies. The seventh-century pledges of *bay'a* involved a physical act, a laying of hands called *safqah* or *musafahah*. Historical reenactments of these allegiance ceremonies are depicted in *Dabiq*, as if a camera crew were present at the Prophet's own meetings. The photo spread of the meeting ends with a shot of a dozen men leaning in to put their hands together, like a football team breaking a huddle.[30]

Finally, the magazine blasts Muhammad Morsi and Ismail Haniya (Hamas's elected prime minister of the Palestinian Authority) as *tawaghit* [tyrants]—in the same category as Mubarak and Sisi—with a "deviant methodology," i.e., democracy. These men's followers, the article said, compromised their jihadism. They instead "became embarrassed of acknowledging [sic] [Shariah] fundamentals, such as takfir of the clear tawaghit and murtaddin [apostates]." The worst offenders were the Iraqi Sunnis who allied with the United States and others in the Sunni "Awakening" (a term, the author said, "used to beautify their apostasy and treachery") to drive the Islamic State's predecessors into exile or retreat. Naturally, that exile is likened to the persecution of Muhammad by the Quraysh, before the *hijrah*. "This was a test decreed by Allah," it said, "so he would see the patient mujahedin and expel the weak-hearted from their ranks, and thereby solidify the newborn Islamic State and prepare it for greater responsibilities." That these topics had been banished from public discussion by Middle Eastern governments for so long ensured a frisson of subversion for jihadists who read about them.

If *Dabiq* worked its sorcery through savvy packaging of historical precedents, the Islamic State's rapidly proliferating propaganda videos derived power from their sheer brutality. On June 12, 2014, soon after the fall of Mosul, the Islamic State seized an Iraqi Air Force training camp near Tikrit, at a base named for Scott Speicher, the fighter pilot who was the first U.S. serviceman killed in the 1991 Gulf War. As the Islamic State approached, the Iraqi cadets—most of them Shia—left the camp in buses. Islamic State fighters stopped and apprehended about 1,500 of them.

In the video ISIS released, the young cadets cower in the backs of trucks, their faces haunted with fear, worry, and incredulity. They walk in single file, heads bowed and level with the buttocks of the man ahead: this is the pose of subjugation that the Islamic State forces upon its prisoners before execution. The cadets lie down, and masked men shoot them. At first the cadets appear dead, but on closer inspection many are still alive. They lie facedown, hoping to be overlooked. One by one they are not. A body jerks here, a head explodes in a fine pink mist there. The submissiveness, hunched march, and cowed silence drain all dignity from their deaths. Did the cadets give up hope and obey their captors, just to live a few more minutes? Did they not believe their ears and eyes, as the bullets kicked skull and brain into the air around them? If anyone tried to run, his act of defiance did not make the final cut.

I found the video posted in full on the Web. Like many others, I at first did not understand what I saw. Peter Bouckaert, the emergencies director at Human Rights Watch, warned the perpetrators:

> The photos and satellite images from Tikrit provide strong evidence of a horrible war crime that needs further investigation. They and other abusive forces should know that the eyes of Iraqis and the world are watching.[31]

In hindsight the statement is touching in its belief in the capacity of ISIS to feel shame, and to worry about the opinion of the world's moral authorities. Worse atrocities have happened in other wars, but most perpetrators of mass murder hide or deny their crimes. The Islamic State wanted the largest audience possible.

In the second half of 2014, more videos—of executions, amputations, and battles—emerged, and the Internet made them as easy to see as they were hard to forget. It took little effort to figure out the search terms that would elicit the rawest footage from Syria and Iraq. "Islamic State" yielded too many results, but *dawlah islamiyyah* combined with *khilafah, muwahhid* [monotheist—a synonym for "Islamic State fighter"], *rawafidh* [derogatory for Shia], *sahwa* [for Iraqi Sunni enemies of the Islamic State], and *jahannam* [Hell, to which the foregoing were being sent by soldiers of the *khilafah*] brought a steady stream of horrors.[32] Islamic State supporters posted many of them to YouTube, and for hours or days before the service deleted the videos, the world could watch forlorn men kneeling in the desert, or by the side of a river, getting shot in the head and tumbling over, blood spurting from their wounds.

Some videos were snuff: claustrophobic and lo-fi records of the taking of a life. But many transcended that genre. They were not furtive. They were highly contextualized, filled with meaning and importance, both political and religious. The production values were high. Several videos showed battlefield footage that resembled nothing modern journalism has ever captured—or at least, has ever shown to its audiences. In the western deserts of Iraq, at what looks like high noon, cameras roll while Islamic State fighters ambush Iraqi Army convoys. They keep rolling as the mujahedin close distance on foot and inspect wrecked army vehicles and bodies of dead enemy soldiers. There is no shelter in sight, just small hills and desert with vegetation barely higher than one's knee.

The cameraman slows his pace. It's not clear where he's going. Eventually he stops, flanked by three fighters, at a point where a culvert runs under the road and connects two sides of a shallow wadi. The camera tilts down to show a squad of unarmed soldiers squirming in the ditch, trying to hide in a drainage pipe that could scarcely fit a five-year-old child, let alone several grown men. The soldiers of the caliphate kill them all with tidy little sprays of bullets to their clustered heads, nary a round wasted. It would have been more challenging to kill squirrels.

The same images that filled me with loathing soothed the hearts of their target audience. The comment sections of the YouTube videos— the moral cloacae of the Internet at the best of times—featured many cheers, some from people posting under their real names. Many admired the style and derring-do of the fighters. The fighters themselves realized that image was everything, presumably having had a generational affinity for selfies even before going jihadi. Islam Yaken, twenty-one at the time of the caliphate's announcement, became the most famous Egyptian recruit, due to his prolific social media activity. In mid-2014, he posted pictures on Twitter of himself riding a horse and brandishing a Chinese-made cutlass. He encouraged his mother and others to join him, and he promised them safety, spiritual reward, and an environment of piety. His previous selfies, taken just a year before, showed a gym rat with his shorts pulled down to the pube line, for maximum ab exposure.

It was tempting, in the aftermath of the atrocities—and especially once the selfies of the fighters began showing up online—to dismiss the Islamic State as an army of psychopaths and self-dramatizing losers (with a detectable level of repressed homoeroticism). The Islamic State's forces had its share of each, and horrified observers could be forgiven for not wanting to look at the kill shots and glam shots for any deeper significance. Sane people naturally wanted to avoid the emotional and spiritual cost that came with watching the videos. What could it profit a person to flip through the photo albums of wanton murderers? These were madmen too bloodthirsty to create a coherent philosophy at all, let alone be serious adherents of Islam or any other system of thought or belief.

But these prejudices did not survive scrutiny. In instances of what at first looked like nihilism or idiocy, hints of a deeper meaning could be found by those willing to look. Consider two recruits from Birmingham, England—Yusuf Sarwar and Mohammed Nahin Ahmed, both twenty-two—who ordered *Islam for Dummies* and *The Koran for Dummies* from Amazon.co.uk before traveling to Syria in 2013.[33] Their case became a cliché of foreign-fighter coverage, a permanent exhibit of the fatuity of the jihad. But the coverage was all too glib. That Sarwar and Ahmed are in some sense fools there can be no doubt. But questions remained. Were these purchases intended for themselves, or for novitiates whom they expected to see in Syria? Do these books not reveal that they were, in fact, eager to educate themselves about Islam, and that doing so was among their highest priorities? (If they had also ordered *Middlemarch, Jonathan Livingston*

Seagull, and *Pork Mastery: 24 Delicious Pork Recipes,* I might admit that their priorities lay elsewhere.) Books about Islam, even primers with embarrassing titles, are normal reading material for sincere recent converts to a militant path.

But the ridicule persisted. The subtext of these gloating non sequiturs was a desire to imagine the Islamic State's fighters as barbarians, incapable of the high-minded savagery that Westerners perfected in, say, the intellectualized totalitarian environments of Nazi Germany or the Soviet Union under Stalin. Many observers, both Muslim and infidel, wittingly or unwittingly harbor preconceptions of Muslims as brutes and barbarians. The brainless-jihadi cliché fit that mental model well. But the cliché breaks down in many, many particular cases. Islam Yaken, the six-pack jihadi, is one. The early tabloid stories concentrated on his vainglorious monstrosity and the inconsistency between his pious jihadism and horny adolescence. He had joked with his friends about the women he had bedded, and now he believed himself a modern-day *muhajir.* The contradiction glared.

Within months, though, a fuller picture emerged. Mona El-Naggar of *The New York Times* interviewed his friends and father, who described a path of discovery:

> In his quest for answers, Mr. Yaken found Sheikh Muhammad Hussein Yacoub, a popular Salafist preacher with tens of thousands of followers. Sheikh Yacoub appeared regularly on at least two television channels, calling for Egypt to enshrine Shariah law in its new Constitution [. . .]
>
> Just as Mr. Yaken's religiosity began to peak, Egypt's army removed President Mohamed Morsi of the Muslim Brotherhood by force, reversing the gains of the broader Islamist movement. When the army moved to consolidate its power, silencing all opposition, Mr. Yaken's faith in the political process faltered.

The last time Mr. Yaken went to pray at his neighborhood mosque, in August 2013, he looked noticeably different.

"He had shaved his head and beard," Sheikh Ramadan Fadl, an imam at the mosque, recalled. "When I asked him why, he said he was going to jihad."[34]

He worshipped at the bench press until he began worshipping God. In December 2014, Yaken posted his own account of his moral failings and the temptations of secular success. He relates his discovery of Islam, reaches out to other Muslims and calls them to piety, and finally insists on the necessity of jihad. He was lured by a friend who went to fight, then called home, urging him to join. Yaken marvels at his friend's conviction, how he set off to fight without hesitation or consultation:

> After the call, I sat down, did *wudu* [ablutions], and prayed *istikharah* [a prayer for divine guidance in a time of personal indecision], and went to memorize Koran. I was surprised to find that the portion that day was from Sura al Imran [about those who fled the Battle of Uhud]:
>
> *[Remember] when you [fled and] climbed [the mountain] without looking aside at anyone while the Messenger was calling you from behind. So God repaid you with distress upon distress so you would not grieve for that which had escaped you [of victory and spoils of war] or [for] that which had befallen you [of injury and death]. And God is [fully] acquainted with what you do.* (Koran 3:153)

Yaken concluded that he should not turn his back on jihad. He read on:

> *And never think of those who have been killed in the cause of God as dead. Rather, they are alive with their Lord, receiving*

provision, rejoicing in what God has bestowed upon them of
His bounty, and they receive good tidings about those [to be
martyred] after them who have not yet joined them—that
there will be no fear concerning them, nor will they grieve.
(Koran 3:169–170)

Now he was galvanized for martyrdom. "The next day," Yaken
writes, "I went to recite Koran to my sheikh, and afterward told him
I wanted to go for jihad to Syria."[35]

Naturally, Yaken flatters himself by claiming inspiration from
God. But all reports suggest that his conversion was sincere—and his
narrative follows a perverse logic. His concerns, if not his methods
and conclusions, engage the same moral issues in the Koran and
mainstream Muslim thought: What is the nature of good and evil?
What pleases God, and how does He want us to live? What should we
understand from the example of His Prophet, and how does that example fit in the modern world? For inspiration he consults holy
scripture and clergy, using orthodox practices like *istikharah* and
reading of the shared texts of all Muslims.

One of the photos Yaken posted on social media after he made it
to Syria showed a bucket filled with severed heads, hashtagged
"#headmeat."[36] Irrespective of whether his adventure to the land of
the caliphate was spiritually fulfilling, the imagery it produced was a
kind of pornography. And like all pornography, it aroused strong reactions, ranging from titillation to revulsion, and sometimes both at
once. These reactions share an intellectually disarming effect. As in
the case of porn, they resist detached analysis. The scholar of religion
Jonathan Z. Smith noted a similar tendency in the failure to understand the mass suicide at Jonestown in 1978. The problem, he said,
was an unwillingness to undertake the difficult task of "looking,
rather than staring or looking away."[37]

That unwillingness has left many of those most qualified to opine on the Islamic State mute or unhelpful when the public has solicited their analysis. The Islamic State's self-presentation is suffused with religious language, tropes, and pomp—but when I asked experts on religion for their opinion on the group's religious foundations, they typically denied any meaningful link and instead changed the subject to American foreign policy, neo-Baathist power-politics, abnormal psychology, or secular grievance. The rise of the Islamic State is indeed incomprehensible without examining these factors. And yet none precludes the role of religious belief, and none absolves scholars of religion of their responsibility to use the tools of their discipline to help the public understand a phenomenon with religious dimensions. The notion that religious belief is a minor factor in the rise of the Islamic State is belied by a crushing weight of evidence that religion matters deeply to the vast majority of those who have traveled to fight. The scholars' training in Islamic studies rendered them uniquely capable—linguistically, culturally, pedagogically—of explaining the Islamic State's religious claims. And yet in the months after the declaration of the caliphate, I could find hardly a single tenured professor whose writings about the Islamic State revealed acquaintance with the group beyond having read about it in *The New York Times*. Almost no one could quote the group's scholars, let alone engage their arguments, even though the Islamic State's propagandists had strewn those arguments all over the Internet.

Instead, prominent scholars declared, reductively, that "much of what [ISIS does] violates Islamic law" (as if Islamic law admitted just one correct interpretation, let alone one determined by Western secular scholars, or even a group of Muslim religious ones), that its understanding of Islam is "warped or distorted," or that its adherents "have little actual knowledge of Islam." The last claim, usually adduced with no evidence or context, is true of foot soldiers of the Islamic State, but it is also true of the religious knowledge of every army in history. (Deep knowledge of ideology is always a specialized skill. Few Christian laypeople have sophisticated knowledge of academic or theological debates about Christianity, and other than a few JAGs, U.S. soldiers typically do not have, or claim to have, nuanced understanding of the U.S. Constitution. Yet no one would say that lay Christians are unmotivated by their faith, or that American wars have nothing to do with the ideals or founding documents of America.) Major figures in Islamic studies—precisely the people to whom journalists and policymakers looked—gave whole talks on the beliefs of the Islamic State without citing any of its fatwas and other scholarly output.[38]

Even worse were those who knew little to nothing of the Islamic religious context and who opined confidently anyway. Some made up evidence entirely. In September 2014, the sociologist Kevin McDonald informed readers of *The Guardian* that "ISIS jihadis aren't medieval—they are shaped by modern Western philosophy." He wrote that Baghdadi, at his inaugural speech in Mosul, "quoted at length from the Indian/Pakistani thinker Abul A'la Maududi, the founder of the Jamaat-e-Islami party in 1941 and originator of the contemporary term Islamic state."[39] Since Maududi had drawn his conception of statehood from the French Revolution, McDonald concludes that Western European secular phenomena are ultimately to blame for the group's savagery. It is true that in constructing a totalizing state power, the Islamic State has learned from fascist and authoritarian styles incubated in the West—as Saddam Hussein did in Iraq. But Baghdadi has *never* quoted Maududi, nor has any other Islamic State ideologue. And to stress his occult debts to "ideas at the heart of the 17th-century scientific revolution," as McDonald does, ignores the much greater influence of Islamic discussion from late antiquity and the medieval period. The only lengthy quote in Baghdadi's inaugural address—other than from the Koran or hadith—was from Abu Bakr al Siddiq, the direct successor to the Prophet Muhammad.[40] The importance to the Islamic State of early modern European concepts of citizenship is dwarfed by the concern it places on issues fashionable in fourteenth-century Damascus—issues like the permissibility of revolt, the law of apostasy, and how to live an Islamic life in non-Muslim lands. Moreover, the Islamic State explicitly rejects the brand of Islamism that Maududi espoused and hereticizes him for engaging in party politics and democratic processes rather than demanding a caliphate on the Prophetic model.

One of the most common means of fleeing analysis of the Islamic State's religious claims involved fixating on ex-Baathists within the Islamic State and accusing them of puppet-mastering the whole enterprise and tricking the rank and file into true belief. Liz Sly of *The Washington Post* contributed a fascinating and well-reported story on these ex-Baathists—one of whom, according to her sources, was "a masked Iraqi man who sat silently through [Islamic State meetings], listening and taking notes."[41] The head of the Islamic State's Iraqi wing, Abu Muslim al Turkmani, was a Baathist army colonel with no record of Islamism before the fall of Saddam. Tariq Ramadan, a professor of Islamic studies at Oxford and prolific writer on contemporary politics in the Muslim world, also noted the presence of ex-Baathists among its leadership.[42] He told Al Jazeera that the Islamic State was not religious, but merely "playing with politics referring to religious sources"—as if politics and religion were separable, and a history of Baathism among some high-ranking officials negated the sincerity of all theological claims and canceled the thousands upon thousands of documented acts of piety by Islamic State followers and leaders alike.[43] In some quarters, the relief at discovering the group's covert secularism is palpable.

But the relief is sadly premature. First, it ignores the fact that the Islamic State's founding fathers, a number of whom survived to see the caliphate, were not Baathist at all. Most were not Iraqi, but instead, like Zarqawi, Jordanians and Syrians united by jihadist service in Afghanistan. Those who were Iraqi and joined the group early were, like Abu Bakr al Baghdadi, men with long-standing jihadist belief—or they were Saddam loyalists who, among all insurgent groups fighting the United States, chose the most aggressively religious. The simplest explanation is that they were extreme Islamists. But in any case, the Islamism came first and the influx of Baathists second, while Zarqawi was firmly in charge.[44] Even if hypocritical Baathists—nonbelievers who preach jihad in public but sip scotch and smoke cigars in private—secretly run the Islamic State, why do they invoke religious justification not only in public but among themselves, in internal communiqués, which are littered with religious language and quotation, in documents as minor as rent-control edicts and childhood vaccination cards?[45] Why do these crypto-Baathists take such pains to craft a cynical religious message, spread over thousands of pages and hours of propaganda, unless that religious message is convincing to the rank and file? The foot soldiers view their mission in religious terms and spend great energy on piety and devotion. "I [find] no support for the claim you sometimes hear about jihadists' being hypocritical opportunists who don't really care about religion," says Thomas Hegghammer, a Norwegian government researcher who is one of the most respected analysts of jihad. "Some of them may have been unobservant before they join, but once they're in, they seem very meticulous about observance."[46]

In my conversations with scholars of Islam, few of the people who dismissed the Islamic State as a product of false Islamism—Jacobinism with an Islamic veneer—were able to name a single cleric or scholar associated with the Islamic State, or a fatwa or other statement by that scholar. The level of ignorance is as appalling as if a scholar of Marxism declared the Soviet Union "not Marxist" and turned out to be unfamiliar with the name Trotsky or Lenin, or the title of anything either of them wrote. Since 2012, tens of thousands of men, women, and children have migrated to a theocratic state, under the belief that migration is a sacred obligation and that the state's leader is the worldly successor of the last and greatest of prophets. If religious scholars see no role for religion in a mass movement like this, then they see no role for religion in the world.

Happily, that initial dereliction of duty has subsided, and reputable scholars have begun interrogating the group's beliefs and writings. But relative to public interest in the subject, there are still vanishingly few professors who work in the field of jihadism. The reasons are sometimes political. "Middle Eastern studies is entrenched in political activism," says Hegghammer. "In top [religious studies] departments, you'd be hard pressed to find anyone who specialized in jihadi studies. These people just don't exist, or don't get tenured."[47] One specialist in jihadism, Joas Wagemakers, also attributed his lack of colleagues to a sense of proportionality within Islamic studies. Although jihadism holds contemporary interest, it is hardly the most important or interesting aspect of Islam. Consider the great intellectuals of Islam—Ghazali, Ibn Khaldun, Avicenna—and then compare them to an inventive modern crank such as Maqdisi, the subject of Wagemakers's own scholarship. "They're like Bach," Wagemakers says. "[Bach's] contribution to music is unimaginably brilliant, and if you wrote a five-hundred-page book on Bach it would hardly be the first word about his music. Studying Maqdisi is like studying Beyoncé—a great singer, but her contribution to music as a whole is nil compared to Bach's." There are no conservatories with chairs in Beyoncé studies, and there are few jobs for Islamicists who study jihad.[48]

If there is an exception to this distaste for jihadi studies, at least within the American academy, it is in Princeton, New Jersey. A disproportionate number of jihad analysts have spent time at Princeton University or at the nearby Institute for Advanced Study. Hegghammer has twice served as a visiting member at the institute. Will McCants, a historian of jihadism and author of a book about the Islamic State,[49] now works at the Brookings Institution but earned his Ph.D. at Princeton, as did Jacob Olidort, a Salafism expert at the Washington Institute for Near East Policy. Jacob Shapiro teaches politics at Princeton and is probably the foremost young social scientist who studies terrorism. Cole Bunzel, the Bin'ali watcher, is a graduate student there.

The key figure in Princeton's history in Jihadi studies is Bernard Lewis (born 1916), the most famous living historian of the Middle East and an affiliate of the Near Eastern Studies department since 1974. Lewis, who is now as famous for his right-wing politics as for his academic research, became a court scholar of neoconservative Washington in the 1970s, through his friendship with Richard Perle.[50] But even early in his career, Lewis argued that religion mattered more to politics than was commonly supposed. In 1953, he suggested that modern secular scholars were guilty of projecting their secularism on others:

> The medieval European, who shared the fundamental assumptions of his Muslim contemporary, would have agreed with him in ascribing religious movements to religious causes, and would have sought no further for an explanation. But when Europeans ceased to accord first place to religion in their thoughts, sentiments, interests, and loyalties, they also ceased to admit that other men, in other times and places, could have done so. To a rationalistic and materialistic generation, it was inconceivable that such great debates and mighty conflicts could have involved no more than "merely" religious issues.

The result, he claimed, was a wild-goose chase for hidden nonreligious causes:

> Historians, once they had passed the stage of amused contempt, devised a series of explanations, setting forth what they described as the "real" or "ultimate" significance "underlying" religious movements and differences. The clashes and squabbles of the early churches, the great Schism, the Reformation, all were reinterpreted in terms of motives and interests reasonable by the standards of the day—and for the

religious movements of Islam too explanations were found
that tallied with the outlook and interests of the finders.[51]

Lewis's intellectual heirs in his department (who have not always
been in political sympathy with him: they range from neocons to
Bernie Sanders supporters) have made Princeton unusually congenial for study of the Islamic State. Until her death in 2015, Lewis's
former doctoral student Patricia Crone occupied the chair in history
at the Institute for Advanced Study; her students refer to her, in
hushed tones, as a "goddess" for her command of sources in early
Islamic history. Michael Cook, another Lewis student, occupied
Lewis's former chair at Princeton from 1986 to 2007.

Neither shied from emphasizing the effects of religion. Cook's recent work brings religion back into the scholarly analysis of politics.
His newest book, *Ancient Religions, Modern Politics* (2014), argues
that Islam's scriptures and history are obstacles to Muslims' peace-
able living in non-Muslim states. Islam's claim on the lives of Muslims disposes them, more so than Christians or Hindus, say, to seek
reflection of their faith in the authority of the state. In particular, the
insistence—expressed repeatedly in scripture—on "a divine monopoly in the domain of law" inclines devout Muslims to seek sovereign
status for religion above other considerations.[52] Religion, he argues,
"provides its modern adherents with a set of options that do not determine their choices, but do constrain them"—like "a menu dis-
pensed by a waiter anxious to sell the house specials."[53] Cook denies
that these scriptural guides doom Muslims to any particular politics—
certainly not to allegiance to Abu Bakr al Baghdadi—but he does say
that the scriptural resources make secularism or non-Muslim rule
enduringly unpalatable.[54]

Representing the youngest generation in scholarly descent from
Lewis is Cole Bunzel, the thirty-one-year-old Princeton Ph.D. candi-

date who tracked Bin'ali's rise within the Islamic State. For many academics, spending hours on Facebook, Twitter, and online forums is a distraction. For Bunzel it is work. Through subterfuge and persistence, Bunzel secured invitations to elite and open-admission online forums for jihadis, long before Baghdadi's name became well known. Within these forums, Bunzel watched the evolution of jihad in real time. The history of the Islamic State can be read in his reports and blog posts, written for a community of fellow jihadologists.[55]

In April 2013, Bunzel noted a portentous development. Abu Bakr al Baghdadi, then still the unseen leader of the Islamic State in Iraq (ISI), announced that his group had moved into Syria and absorbed its Syrian counterpart, Jabhat al Nusra. A post by Bunzel on the jihadi studies website Jihadica.com was the first to observe the shift, which marked the end of ISI's existence as an independent group.[56] In October of that year, Bunzel reported early statements from Abu Muhammad al 'Adnani, the Islamic State's official spokesman. These statements left no doubt about the group's long-term aims. 'Adnani laid out the plan:

> Our objective is the formation of an Islamic state on the prophetic model that acknowledges no boundaries, distinguishes not between Arab and non-Arab, easterner and westerner, but on the basis of piety. Its loyalty is exclusively to God: it relies on only Him and fears Him alone.[57]

Rarely are terrorist leaders so transparent and concise: this was the plan, and three years later, it was reality. The subsequent statements attributed to Baghdadi and 'Adnani shared that one's audacity and candor, and in time a much larger community of scholars read them all as soon as they were released. The statements have become the subject of Kremlinological scrutiny: like wolves over a carcass, the jihadologists tear the messages apart for fresh signs of what the group might be planning and who, exactly, is doing the planning.

Bunzel's main research area is the early history of Saudi Arabia. Once ISIS began churning out videos and publishing statements, Bunzel says, the group's debt to Saudi scholars—both past and present—became evident. The voices of the foreigners in the propaganda have been suggestive all by themselves, Bunzel says. He hears "Saudi accents—lots of them." The Islamic State is officially at war with Saudi Arabia. But their mutual hatred is a case of Freud's "narcissism of small differences," driven as much by similarity as by disagreement.

The two sides each claim to be the rightful heirs of the clerics who attended the birth of premodern Saudi Arabia. In 1744, Ibn ʿAbd al Wahhab, a cleric influenced by Ibn Taymiyyah, struck a deal with the central Arabian warlord Muhammad Al Saʿud. Saʿud and his family would rule as kings and control earthly affairs. In exchange for their protection, Ibn ʿAbd al Wahhab would not question the Saʿuds' legitimacy and could preach a hard *takfiri* line against the Shia, Sufis, and other innovators. Ibn ʿAbd al Wahhab's theology surpasses Ibn Taymiyyah's in intolerance. He viewed a wide range of beliefs as prima facie apostasy, without need for the "first we show you the dagger" safeguards. But he let his king rule unmolested. That arrangement, inherited by subsequent kings and Wahhabi clergy, has remained in place formally ever since.

It lasted, more or less, through the nineteenth century. But the first three decades of the twentieth century tested it, possibly beyond its breaking point. Starting in 1902, Muhammad Al Saʿud's great-great-grandson ʿAbd al ʿAziz began consolidating power in the Arabian Peninsula, and as his territory grew, he was increasingly forced to administer it not as a desert tribal society but as a modern territorial state with fixed borders and international relations. The British sped that process of border delineation along by promising to bomb ʿAbd al ʿAziz if he ventured too far north. The imperatives of running a modern state trumped the religious imperatives of the deal with Ibn

'Abd al Wahhab, and Saudi Arabia slowly began to resemble just another modern country.

By 1933, the consolidation of power was complete, and in 1938, prospectors struck oil. That accelerated the development of relations with the outside world, and with them social change in the kingdom. Supercharged by cash, Wahhabism's austere brand of Islam—up until then an obscure religious idiosyncrasy from the boondocks—became a familiar presence in communities where a more tolerant Islam had flourished. To take full advantage of their oil wealth, 'Abd al 'Aziz and his successors compromised on aspects of Wahhabism that had previously gone unchallenged. The Arabian Peninsula had officially been a Muslims-only zone. Non-Muslims could visit and work for short periods, but they could not stay permanently, since the Prophet was said to have forbidden the coexistence of religions in the Arabian Peninsula. Before the discovery of oil, this stricture hardly needed enforcement, since few non-Muslims had any reason to stay in Arabia. After the discovery of oil, the Saudis needed skilled guest workers to extract and refine it, and would eventually need unskilled ones to work as domestics and do the cheap labor that Saudi royals no longer deigned to do for themselves.

Bunzel identifies Sulayman ibn Sihman (1850–1930) as the intellectual founder of the faction that would oppose the liberalization of Saudi Arabia. Ibn Sihman, the top Saudi cleric of his generation, opposed not only the admission of non-Muslims to the kingdom but also permission for Muslims to travel *out* of the kingdom to non-Muslim lands. On this and several other points, he is the champion of the hard-liners who regret the direction Saudi Arabia has taken over the last century. The Islamic State quotes him approvingly, and it has associated him with an implied alternative history of Saudi Arabia in which the Sa'uds kept their vow to Ibn 'Abd al Wahhab. The most committed Sihmanists claim that Saudi Arabia has relinquished its Islam and that its royal family are *munafiqun* [hypocrites] who preach the truth but have apostatized in their hearts. The Saudi government has abolished slavery and allowed permanent embassies, staffed by infidel diplomats. Foreigners drink alcohol and indulge in other impure behaviors. In 1990, during Operation Desert Shield, Saudi Arabia's chief mufti ʿAbd al ʿAziz bin Baz declared that tens of thousands of infidel soldiers could reside in the Kingdom indefinitely to protect it from Saddam Hussein.[58] The hardscrabble tribal society of the eighteenth century is gone.

The Islamic State suggests backtracking to the fork in the path of history and taking the other route. It aspires to be a more religiously muscular Saudi Arabia, under less merciful management.

Few things threaten that dream more directly, then, than the possibility of being outdone in piety. The Islamic State enjoys nothing more than to see its enemies' heresies and hypocrisies paraded before the world, to prove that all products on the jihadist market save its own have been contaminated—some in the 1930s, some five years ago, some more recently still. It believes it has already made its case against the rulers of Saudi Arabia, who had permitted debauchery, punished jihadism, and conspired with infidel Americans for decades. The next enemy to undermine was Al Qaida.

The leaders in Raqqah chose their most difficult enemy first: Abu Muhammad al Maqdisi, Binʿali's former teacher turned critic of the Islamic State. He was a jihadist of unimpeachable credentials. By late 2014, Maqdisi and Binʿali had traded nasty public letters, with Maqdisi accusing Binʿali of barbarity and arrogance, and Binʿali calling Maqdisi a lily-livered fair-weather jihadist. In October 2014, when the Islamic State held several Western hostages and dangled before their families the possibility of their release, Maqdisi called for the Islamic State to extend mercy to Alan Henning, a British cabbie who had entered Syria in 2013 to deliver aid to children. No mercy was forthcoming. At the time, Bunzel read Maqdisi's call and thought it would hasten the captives' deaths. "If I were held captive by the Islamic State and Maqdisi said I shouldn't be killed," he told me, "I'd kiss my ass goodbye."

The U.S. government saw an opportunity. It tried to heal the two men's rift and win the hostages' freedom. In December 2014, representatives of the United States asked Maqdisi to intercede with the Islamic State on behalf of Peter Abdul Rahman Kassig, a former U.S. Army Ranger who had come to Syria as an aid worker. With money supplied by the FBI, Maqdisi bought a phone and was allowed to correspond with his former student. They discussed an exchange of Kassig for an Al Qaida operative in a U.S. penitentiary. This trade would have been, in the words of Stanley Cohen, the American lawyer who facilitated negotiations, "a present of sorts from Turki al Bin'ali to Muhammad al Maqdisi."[59] The Americans declined that proposal, and soon the Jordanian government stopped the chats and used them as a pretext to jail Maqdisi again. Kassig's severed head appeared in a video a few days later, in the town of Dabiq—namesake of the propaganda magazine. Kassig's death was a tragedy, but the plan's success would have been a bigger one. Reconciliation between Maqdisi and Bin'ali would have begun to heal the main rift between the world's two largest jihadist organizations. Cohen says the negotiations were "sandbagged" by the Jordanians, who were eager not to be revealed as less effective in advancing American interests than Maqdisi. Moreover, he says, Maqdisi's people showed "NO interest" in "merging with or working with ISIS." Instead, they evinced "ridicule and disdain for ISIS" and thought the Islamic State "provided a convenient pretext and cover for additional U.S./Western militarism."[60]

It would be hard to overstate the pleasure the Islamic State took in watching its enemies fight, squabble, and debase themselves. The United States ended its jihadi matchmaking program after Kassig's murder, but Jordan had its own turn trying to rekindle the Bin'ali-Maqdisi romance. On December 24, 2014, the Islamic State took prisoner a Royal Jordanian Air Force pilot named Mu'dh al Kasasbeh after he ejected from his F-16 over Syria. The Islamic State toyed with the Jordanian monarchy as it sought his return. *Dabiq* featured an interview with Kasasbeh days after his capture. The magazine refers to him as "MURTADD" ["APOSTATE"]:

DĀBIQ: Have you seen videos produced by the Islamic State?

MURTADD: No, I haven't.

DĀBIQ: We will make sure the jailers provide you with the opportunity to see "Although the Disbelievers Dislike It" [featuring the simultaneous beheading of about two dozen Syrian airmen]. Do you know what the Islamic State will do with you?

MURTADD: Yes . . . They will kill me . . . [61]

Maqdisi thought he could still bring Bin'ali around. In February 2015, with the blessing of the Jordanians, Maqdisi proposed a trade: Kasasbeh for Sajida al Rishawi, an Iraqi woman who had intended to blow up a wedding party at Amman's Radisson Hotel in 2005 but botched the job and was caught. It's unlikely that Maqdisi cared about Kasasbeh—who, as a serving officer in the Royal Jordanian Air Force, probably qualified as an apostate in Maqdisi's eyes—but to save the life of a holy warrior like Sajida would be a blessed act.

But by then the Islamic State had already burned Kasasbeh alive. They just wanted Maqdisi to grovel. When Maqdisi demanded proof of life, his correspondent in the Islamic State "eventually claimed to have the video showing [Kasasbeh] was still alive, [but] he subsequently stated he couldn't play it for Maqdisi because the Internet connection was too slow."[62]

Days later, the whole world received proof of death, and Maqdisi emerged looking foolish, having negotiated for a pile of ashes. (Within hours, the Jordanians executed Rishawi in retaliation.) Maqdisi went on a Jordanian talk show, sounding sane and moderate, and rebuked the Islamic State for negotiating in bad faith and for violating Islamic laws of war by burning a captive. Bin'ali responded witheringly. In a signed statement, he pointed out the distinguished history of the Prophet's Companions' use of execution by immolation. Subsequent jurists, too, approved of burning. Shafi'i and Hanafi clerics allowed it, and all Sunni schools of jurisprudence have invoked the doctrine of *qisas*—eye-for-an-eye punishment—to justify burning those who had killed with fire, as Kasasbeh had (allegedly) done in airstrikes. He also alluded to the justification for the immolation that was included in the immolation video itself, in a pull quote from Ibn Taymiyyah. The quote claimed that if a public display of punishment would cause enemies of Islam to cease fighting or give up, then punishments such as these were defensible. *Dabiq* echoed his rebuttal in a subsequent article.[63]

Bin'ali excoriated Maqdisi for giving his television interview at all, and for not objecting to the show's title, "The Martyr Pilot Mu'dh Kasasbeh." Whether one thinks Bin'ali bested Maqdisi in the argument over burning, Bin'ali succeeded in making Maqdisi look priggish and servile. He had appeared on what looked like a Jordanian clone of *Charlie Rose* and become a tool of the Jordanian monarchy and the United States. No one who kept allies like these could claim to be the world's foremost jihadi ideologue. The younger cleric effectively declared his teacher an infidel.

Bunzel and others chronicled the public duel in a series of blog posts. The feud gave the impression, Bunzel says, of a rift widening and of a changing of the international jihadi guard.

Among the others who recognized the significance of the split were Maqdisi's peers in the Al Qaida brain trust. Bunzel quotes Hani al Siba'i, a senior Al Qaida–linked figure living as a refugee in the United Kingdom, ruefully denigrating Bin'ali as a once-promising protégé, now lost to extremism. For years, Siba'i has justified Al Qaida's killing and maiming of non-Muslims. From his West London home, he has also opposed the Islamic State, charging its leaders with extremism, failure to consult their fellow Muslims, and splitting the jihadist community, among other sins. To this welter of abuse, Bin'ali has answered with icy calm. Compared to Maqdisi and Siba'i, Bin'ali is a shadow or a ghost, or, as Bunzel calls him, "the Silent Mufti." Bunzel quotes Siba'i again before adding his own comment:

> "This community [the Islamic State] is the graveyard of ex-tremists . . . and only the truth shall prevail . . . You will know, succeeding generations in the future will know, that what I am saying is right." Yet in all likelihood it is Siba'i and his ilk who are headed for the graveyard first. Perhaps sym-bolically, Siba'i's once-acclaimed website was permanently deleted within days of his comments. Impressively, the Silent Mufti seems to be quietly winning.[64]

My next task was to find a mufti who was not so silent.

MUSA CERANTONIO

"A cafe called 'The French Baguette,'" Musa emailed me, setting a place for our first meeting, in December 2014. "If you are driving, there is ample parking across the road from it, and if coming by public transport, it's very close to Footscray station." We had traded fewer than half a dozen emails at that point, and my first reaction was to look the place up on Yelp to see if it might be fancy enough to require nice attire, or at least closed-toe shoes.

When I arrived and saw Musa, I chuckled at my concern. This was not a man who goes to restaurants that require neckties. He was large, with a sturdy physique that will probably turn to jelly if he lives to see his late thirties. He wore sneakers and dungarees (cuffs rolled up) and a long beard that he sometimes stroked, as if it were a Bond villain's cat. Indeed, his facial hair made him look more like a fan of *The Lord of the Rings* at Comic Con than a recruiter for the Islamic State.

The more he described his vision of the Islamic State, however, the more he seemed to be living out a drama worthy of a medieval fantasy novel, only with real blood.

That Musa was free to meet me was surprising in itself. As perhaps the most famous jihadist in Australia (Junaid Thorne, a twenty-seven-year-old part-Aboriginal preacher from Perth is a close second), Musa has regularly been labeled a "terrorist," "ISIS supporter," and worse by the tabloids. On July 11, 2014, a Philippine SWAT team broke into Musa's apartment in Lapu-Lapu, which he may have intended to be a waypoint en route to Syria and the Islamic State. Musa was deported to Melbourne and his passport was confiscated. Yet there he was five months later—a free man—drinking coffee in the window of what turned out to be a Vietnamese, not French, bakery. In our conversation—the first of many—he outlined the non-negotiable articles of creed that the Islamic State was uniquely poised to champion. "I would go so far as to say," he told me, "that Islam has been reestablished."

The name "Musa Cerantonio" is one of those lovely translinguistic hybrids: "Musa" is the Arabic equivalent of "Moses," and "Cerantonio" is Italian. Musa was born Robert Cerantonio, and he is Italian enough to talk to his *nonna* in her native tongue—a dialect of Calabria. ("Roberto," she asks him, still not sure what to make of his conversion from Catholicism, "perché sei diventato turco?" *Why have you turned Turkish?*) One of Musa's aliases, "Al Qillawri," is Siculo-Arabic—the extinct dialect of Muslim Sicily—for "the Calabrian."[1] The archaism is deliberate: the last time anyone used "Qillawriyya" to describe Calabria was the ninth century, when the Moors conquered Sicily for Islam, using Calabria as a beachhead.

Islam doesn't require converts to take an Arabic name, and Musa says he didn't plan to at first. But his new Muslim brothers kept asking when he would choose a new name, so he went with Musa. His blended name also confers a special status, because it marks him as a convert—a Muslim who didn't luck into Islam by birth, but instead came to it by will. The first jihadist I ever met was a Pakistani follower of Osama bin Laden living near Peshawar in early 2001. "If you convert to Islam," he promised me, "you will be better than all of us."

I first noticed Musa on jihadi social media in the summer of 2014, soon after Baghdadi's caliphate declaration. His name came up in a number of tweets, Facebook posts, and videos circulated by Islamic State supporters for propaganda purposes, and it struck me as noteworthy that an apparent convert had achieved literal cult status for his preaching. That Musa's star was rising was soon confirmed by the United Kingdom's center of scholarship on the Islamic State, the International Centre for the Study of Radicalisation (ICSR) at King's College London. The center issued a report in April 2014 tracking the social media accounts that were most active in supporting foreign fighters in Syria. These accounts ensured that potential recruits received a stream of doctrine and news along the way to full radicalization. The leading disseminator, known as @ShamiWitness, pumped out updates and exhortations at a furious pace for his seventeen thousand Twitter followers. Among clerics, most popular and influential were a Palestinian-American named Ahmad Musa Jibril[2] and Musa Cerantonio, who had twelve thousand Facebook fans when the site shut down his page in May 2014.[3]

These three men had something else in common: none of them had visited or emigrated to the Islamic State, even as they encouraged others to do so. I corresponded briefly with @ShamiWitness and tried to interview him in November 2014. At the time, many analysts thought he was Egyptian. Just weeks after our correspondence, however, he was outed as Mehdi Masroor Biswas, a pizza-loving computer programmer living in Bangalore, India. Jibril, who has since silenced his Twitter account, is on parole in Detroit for bank and mail fraud, failure to pay income tax, and money laundering. These men may not have had the fortitude to make the journey, but many of the tens of thousands who did make the trip looked to them for facts and motivation. The primary role of the disseminators is to perform mass outreach [*da ʿwa*] for the Islamic State, as Hesham the tailor did for Salafism on a bespoke basis. And to do that, what matters is the message and its effect, not the integrity of the messenger.[4]

A great deal has been made about the Islamic State's ability to recruit online—as if the recruitment begins with a normal person innocently Googling "Syria" and ends days later with the same person beheading an Alawite on Instagram. ICSR's director, Peter R. Neumann, told me that recruitment rarely, if ever, happens primarily online. "I don't believe we've seen a single case of a fighter who traveled to Syria without knowing someone [in real life] who went there first," he told me in late 2014.[5] The contagion spreads in person. To see epidemiological proof, put a pin in a map for the home city of every European foreign fighter now in Syria. If online chatter alone were sufficient to convince people to emigrate, you would see an even distribution of pins, closely correlating to population centers. Instead, the pins cluster. In some major cities, one sees few pins. But in other cities of modest size, the pins stick out like porcupine quills. The German town of Dinslaken, in the Rhineland, has sent more than twenty fighters to Syria, out of a population of seventy-two thousand. Nothing about Dinslaken would give the impression of a hothouse of jihadism. (When I visited, the only outward sign was a set of stickers, placed in bus shelters, promoting the freeing of "Muslim prisoners." The prisoners were all jihadists.) Horst Dickhäuser, the city spokesman, says defensively that Dinslaken doesn't have a disproportionate problem with jihadism. But if its per capita rate of jihadism applied to the rest of Germany, then Germany would have contributed twenty thousand people to the Islamic State, not the mere thousand or so that it has. In truth, Dickhäuser said, Dinslaken had the misfortune of being home to a single persuasive individual, the son of a local businessman, who convinced others to emigrate, then skipped town. "The head of the group has vanished from Dinslaken," Dickhäuser told me, clearly wishing I would do the same.[6]

Similar stories abound, with a Patient Zero spreading the Islamic State germ from person to person in other places: Portsmouth; Molenbeek; Cardiff; the small town of Lunel, France.[7] The function of social-media propaganda, Neumann suggested, is to provide a growth medium for the germ once it has been contracted. Then, on their own time and through easily accessible sermons, articles, and videos, individuals can nurture and feed it, and finally dedicate whatever remains of their lives to the Islamic State's expansion.

Neumann and his colleagues called Musa a "new spiritual authority." Musa translated statements and speeches by Islamic State leaders into English, and *muhajirs* followed him online and looked to him as a source of orthodoxy and interpretation, a teacher of the doctrines of the *khilafah*. I got to know him well, and in a way, he became my teacher too. From the French Baguette we walked to a Sudanese place for lunch. The short trip took us through the back streets of Footscray—a multicultural suburb of Melbourne that is the original home of Lonely Planet, the travel-guide publisher. We passed African restaurants, Vietnamese shops, and young Arabs walking around in the unofficial Salafi uniform of scraggly beard, long shirt, and trousers rolled up to midcalf. In this crowd, I would have felt at least as comfortable in a jihadi-chic beard, or a dashiki, as I did in my chinos and button-down shirt. Musa wanted to talk about Islam, and so did I: if Islamic State supporters looked to him, then he could show me what and how they think.

Musa was born in Melbourne and grew up Catholic in Footscray. His mother works at an assisted-living facility, and his father left when Musa was a child. In mid-2014, when he was deported from the Philippines, Musa moved back with his mom in a middle-class residential area of Footscray. All the neighborhood streets are named for British colonial projects or battles. He lives on Khartoum Street.

As a young student, he showed no particular inclination toward jihad, though his mom later told me he was a physically aggressive player of Australian rules football and prone to fighting on the pitch. He visited Rome as a teenager and came away appalled by the "idolatry" of the Catholic Church's art and spectacle. In 2002, at seventeen, he converted to Islam and soon fell in with Tablighi Jamaat, a global outreach organization that calls Muslims to piety. (Some of the Alexandrians Hesham sent me to meet were Tablighis, although Tablighis are not primarily Salafi.) Musa was drawn to the religion, he says, in part because it combined logic—no tortuous explanations of the Trinity, say—with reverence for Jesus, the Muslim prophet whose return to earth and coming role in the Islamic State Musa now spends a great deal of time contemplating.

Musa studied, online and in person, with sheikhs in Australia and the Middle East and mastered enough Arabic and Koran to be sought as a speaker and teacher. He has a talent for languages, and has spoken to me in comprehensible Italian, Arabic, and Spanish. Additionally he claims survival levels of Portuguese, French, Bosnian—"mostly bad words"—Chinese, Tagalog, and Chavacano (a Spanish-based creole spoken in the southern Philippines). He delivered sermons around Australia and abroad, and he came to know Muslim intellectuals of international prominence—some of whom he now considers infidels.

On YouTube, one can find enough Cerantonio speeches to observe not only a religious progression, from extreme to very extreme, but also a physical one, from boyish convert to experienced teacher. In 2011, a Saudi-backed television station called Iqraa ("Recite!," the first word of the Koran revealed to Muhammad) asked him to go pro, and he moved to Cairo to work as a televangelist. On his show, called *Ask the Sheikh,* he tested the boundaries of religious speech as he

grew increasingly political. Eventually he began calling for the establishment of a caliphate controlled by a single absolute leader and run
strictly according to Shariah.

I found Musa's account of his attraction to this version of Islamism
psychologically incomplete. He says that Islam requires an imamate
along caliphal lines, and that a proper reading of texts brought him to
that inevitable conclusion. But the conclusion is obviously not inevitable, since most Muslims reject or ignore the call for a caliphate. I
asked several times about the source of his good fortune in discerning Islam's political obligations, and he never volunteered an explanation beyond the rectitude of his reading.

Any attempt to speculate about Musa's psychology is just that—
speculation—but there is a species of convert psychology that might
be relevant. In his Iqraa TV appearances, he acquits himself well, and
he shows a level of scriptural knowledge impressive not just for an
adult convert but for any Muslim of his age. He may or may not have
been able to stump the sheikhs of Al Azhar, but Musa was grappling
with the texts seriously. Converts—though feted and congratulated
for their conversion—by definition bloom late, and native-born religious people unintentionally denigrate them by implying that their
late start is a permanent handicap. *You may be zealous, but if you
come to Islam seventeen years late, how can you catch up?* Some converts tire of the pats on the head they receive from less knowledge-
able and less pious lifers. And yet they profit from the attention they
get, which (patronizing or not) is disproportionate to their achievement. After all, not many twenty-something native-born Muslims
get their own television shows. Still, Musa's viewers may have tuned
in out of amusement that a newcomer was presuming to lecture people who had grown up in the faith. The applause he received might
have been offered in the same spirit as Samuel Johnson's famous
snicker about preaching by female Quakers: "[It] is like a dog's walking on his hinder legs. It is not done well; but you are surprised to
find it done at all."[8]

One response to belittling skepticism is retrenchment. In some cases, that means adopting the most extreme views and dipping as far back as possible into philosophy and history, so that no one could possibly question the authenticity of one's position. Consider the Catholic convert who seeks out a pre–Vatican II priest for confession, or the Jewish convert who nags his secular Jewish in-laws about how they should keep a kosher kitchen. Musa may have felt a similar impulse to outdo his peers—and nothing could be more irreproachable than to dress in the Salafi style and preach the revival of an ancient institution despite the disapproval of the authorities around him. Neither the leader of Egypt at the time, Muhammad Morsi, nor the Saudis funding the station desired the resurrection of a caliphate in any way, so Musa was told to drop the subject and preach less politically. His refusal to do so got him fired and, as a sort of severance package, beaten by members of the station's staff. He left Egypt in 2012 and hasn't returned.

But the dream of a caliphate was lodged in Musa's mind, and he started scanning the globe for a suitable place to establish one. The caliphate, Musa told me, is not just a political entity or a Muslim dictatorship but also a vehicle for salvation. He quoted a Prophetic saying that to die without pledging allegiance is to die ignorant [*jahil*] and therefore die a "death of disbelief."[9] Consider how Muslims (or, for that matter, Christians) believe that God deals with those who die without hearing about the one true religion. Their souls are neither obviously saved nor definitively condemned. Similarly, Musa said, the Muslim who acknowledges one omnipotent God and prays, but who dies without pledging himself to a caliph, has placed himself in a middle space between Islam and disbelief. He has failed to live a fully Islamic life and dies in a state of sin.

Historically, the caliphate has been the best-known template for Muslim government, and some Muslims consider it the sole divinely approved form of rule. At its center is the caliph (*khalifah*), whose title literally means "successor" (and who, as Hesham pointed out, must bear the burden of implementing God's law).[10] According to Sunni tradition, the government works roughly like this: A caliph—chosen by a select group of elites—requires obedience from his subjects in exchange for his competent implementation of Islamic law and institutions. Recall the inaugural speech of the first caliph, Abu Bakr al Siddiq, later cribbed by Morsi and by Baghdadi: The caliph should seek his subjects' advice and govern justly. If he stops ruling by God's law—for example by ignoring prohibitions on alcohol and fornication, or by not punishing wrongdoers as prescribed in scripture—his subjects are obliged to depose and kill him.

By Musa's reading of Sunni law, few are eligible to assume the role of caliph. That explains, in part, he says, why it took so long for Baghdadi to come along and declare himself. To understand how exclusive the club of potential caliphs is, imagine if the world's 1.6 billion Muslims were to stand together, and then take their seats as we named criteria that excluded them from eligibility. To begin with, the caliph must be a free Muslim adult man; that excludes slaves—even Muslim ones—and all women and children. He must exhibit probity and mental integrity; that excludes half-wits, cowards, and flagrant sinners. (Gulf princes known for boozing and carousing may take their seats, along with anyone unwilling to lead men into battle.)

The upstanding free Muslim male warrior-scholars (already it's a small group still on their feet) must also be *physically* intact. They cannot be missing a limb or a digit or an eye. That would exclude nearly all senior Taliban, who almost to a man have tripped over land mines in combat and lost eyes or feet or hands. (Mullah 'Umar, the leader of the Taliban until his death in 2013, claimed the quasi-caliphal title *amir al mu'minin* [prince of the faithful]—but he was missing an eye.)

Finally, the caliph must be from Muhammad's tribe, the Quraysh.[11] According to hadith, Muhammad said, "The caliphate is reserved for

Quraysh." The caliph need not descend directly from Muhammad, Musa says, but he must absolutely be a member of his tribe. This constraint gets rid of nearly everyone else. The Saʿud clan—the rulers of Saudi Arabia—are not Qurayshi. Nor was Osama bin Laden. Bin Laden came from a prominent family of Yemeni Hadrami extraction, and so would have fooled no one if he claimed patrilineal descent from the Quraysh. ("The Bin Ladens are like the Kennedys," one Middle Eastern specialist told me. "Everyone knows their genealogy.")

Qurayshi descent isn't rare. Saddam Hussein claimed to be Qurayshi. More credibly, King Muhammad VI of Morocco claims Qurayshi descent, as does Abdullah II of the Hashemite Kingdom of Jordan. Since both kings are military officers, they could plausibly have claimed caliphal status, Cerantonio says—if they had not already disqualified themselves by violating earlier criteria. "[Abdullah II] is clearly not a Muslim," Cerantonio says. If he were Muslim, he would be ruling according to Shariah, and would have declared himself caliph long before. The same complaint applies to the Moroccan king, who is rumored to be gay—a probable additional disqualifier.

If, by the end of this winnowing process, there is even one person who fulfills all the relevant criteria, that person *must* assume the position of caliph. Musa is clear: he would follow such a person, even if the caliph were in theological error. "If a Qurayshi man came along and offered to rule by Islam, we would have followed him as *khalifah* [caliph] even if he were a Sufi," he says.

Cast out of Egypt, Musa became more determined to establish a caliphate. Any little place would suffice. There is a tradition, he told me, that said that even a single street or stretch of road could be a caliphate, as long as all the conditions of validity were met.

He headed to the Philippines, where one of his brothers had lived and worked, and began looking for a physically intact Qurayshi man. If a caliphate-seeking group succeeded in taking territory on or near the southern Philippine island of Mindanao, this man could become its caliph. Such a task may sound preposterous, but Musa says the Muslim areas of the southern Philippines are rich with support for a Qurayshi caliphate. He soon married a Filipina convert to Islam, Joan Navarro Montayre, three years his senior. (They have no children, but Musa has two young kids from a previous marriage to an Australian of Lebanese descent.)

Musa's Mindanao dreams were preempted by ISIS. By 2013, ISIS supporters had begun talking online about the possibility of a caliphate. This chatter spurred Cerantonio to accelerate his ministry. In one sermon, recorded in Melbourne after his first Philippine sojourn, he mocked Muslims who approached the caliphate as gradualists. He called for jihad:

> The Prophet told us that the return of the *khilafah* is going to be a time of great warfare and tribulation. The answer to Palestine is not by holding hands with the *kuffar* [infidels]. It is not by begging the UN to accept us as a nation. The answer is, as the Prophet told us, to fight the *kuffar* until the religion belongs to Allah.
>
> For the first time, the *ummah* is waking up. . . . We're not going to slowly return ourselves to strength. We are going to return to the Islamic state.

That the wake-up call was coming from Syria, he says, piqued his interest. "*Sham* [the Levant] has a very special and strategic place for the *ummah*," he told me, citing both Koran and well-known hadith. "The best of men will come from *bilad al Sham* [the nation of the Levant], and Allah has blessed it, out of all nations." The Koran and hadith mention *Sham* multiple times (and Mindanao not once), including in portions devoted to apocalyptic battles and the coming of a Muslim messiah.[12] Geography and prophecy were aligning.

In June 2014, he watched the news as ISIS seized Mosul. When

ISIS leaders gave speeches and published official statements, he trans-lated them into English. (Many of the English translations floating around the Web still bear his name.) "[The translation] took longer than I expected, especially 'Adnani's speeches, because his language is very hard, especially the poetry," Cerantonio says. "I did it and [ISIS supporters] loved it. The next speech came out and they're like, 'Are you gonna do the translation?'" About half a dozen speeches later, a formal production cycle was created, with Musa contributing transla-tions and others creating supporting graphics, videos, and more. A representative of ISIS asked him to be "the official translator for the *Dawlah,*" he says. "I was just speechless. This shows how easy it is to move up in the ranks in the *Dawlah,* I guess."[13]

"They said there was a sister from Sudan who was my go-to person if I didn't understand something." He says he declined any official role but promised to keep translating independently. "That was a very wise decision, to say the least," he says, considering the legal consequences of formalizing a working agreement with a terrorist group.

Among the very few left standing in the casting call for caliph was Abu Bakr al Baghdadi. He fulfilled every criterion—piety, physical integrity, Qurayshi descent—and therefore had no choice but to re-vive the caliphate. When Baghdadi made the announcement, Musa was ecstatic—and frustrated. "I was in a hotel [in the Philippines], and I saw the declaration on television," he told me. "And I was just amazed, and I'm like, *Why am I stuck here in this bloody room?*" The Muslims had their legitimate caliph, and at that point there was only one option. "If he's legitimate, you must give him the *bay'a* [alle-giance]," Cerantonio says. "This is why people are hastening to give the *bay'a,* rather than saying, 'Well, let me meet [Baghdadi] person-ally!'" to examine his bona fides. "No, no, no. Does he fulfill the few conditions? Yes. And really he's the only person in the world who fulfills them. Do we have a single ruler in all of the world who is a Muslim, who is from Quraysh, and rules by Islam? Only one."

I assumed Musa gave *bay'a* immediately, but he corrected me: "I didn't say that I'd pledged allegiance." Under Australian law, he reminded me, giving *bay'a* to the Islamic State was illegal. I realized he had never actually affirmed his support for the group, in so many words. "But I agree that [Baghdadi] fulfills the requirements," he continued. "I'm just going to wink at you, and you take that to mean whatever you want." Then he winked.

Musa's failure to reach Syria has been a source of consternation for him and of comedy for his opponents. Here was a purported believer in caliphates and in the divine selection of Baghdadi—but instead of making haste to the battlefield, he was stuck, living with ovine docility, under the government of the female atheist Julia Gillard.

Musa had moved to the Philippines by 2013, and he told me he and his wife had planned to travel in June 2014, after Baghdadi's declaration. He was cagey about the destination ("It's illegal to go to Syria") but led me to believe he aspired to emigrate ("make *hijrah*") to Sham. Things did not go as planned. A group of Kashmiris intercepted money that had been sent from Yemen to the Philippines for his travel, he says. Local authorities wanted to arrest and deport him, so he stayed offline and off the phone, except in crowded public areas where the police wouldn't be able to geolocate him. In early July 2014, his Twitter account displayed a message claiming to followers that he had nearly arrived in Syria: *Insha'Allah I will be arriving in Ash-Sham very shortly, keep us in your du'a [prayers], getting ready to travel. May Allah bless and protect our Imam, our Amir, our Khalifah, Abu Bakr al-Baghdadi.* A Facebook post followed, indicating that he had arrived.

In fact he was still in the Philippines. He says his lies were meant to trick the police (if they thought he was already in Syria they might call off the hounds). He later told the reporter John Safran that he hadn't, strictly speaking, lied. He says he gave his Facebook credentials to a friend in Syria, and the friend posted under his name. "From an Islamic point of view," he says, "I'm not actually lying, because he's the one saying 'I'm in Syria' on my account."[14] His wife then slipped up and made a phone call that was intercepted by the government. Musa was arrested and deported to Australia for overstaying his visa. Joan remained in the Philippines.

When Musa and I first met in December 2014, the Islamic State had existed in name for five months. Its relentless slaughter had made that time pass slowly for me, as happens when every day brings something new and terrible. Musa wasn't the first supporter of the Islamic State I had met, but he was the first ready to speak in what was all but officially the group's English-language voice, with appreciation for its master plan. Many of the online fanboys hid their faces. Musa hid nothing, and to have him munching Sudanese lamb in front of me was like having one of the blood-soaked slaughterers on Twitter step through the screen, *Purple Rose of Cairo*–style, to meet me halfway between his world and mine. Musa did not claim (and indeed denied) membership in the Islamic State. But it was clear that he thought the group was a marvel, a thing of beauty, and a confirmation of prophecy.

Far from being intolerant, he eagerly debated with me and offered thoughtful corrections. My writing about the Islamic State had not always been generous: I had, in an article for *The New Republic*, alleged that the Islamic State was modeling itself after the *salaf* and was painstakingly reviving the practices of late antiquity; I called them "the most monstrous squad of historical reenactors of all time."[15] Musa took issue not with "monstrous" (gentlemen could disagree over that) but with my suggestion that the Islamic State was backward-looking.

"You understand that there are Islamic State fighters wearing Nike Air Jordans?" he asked me. "They're not using swords"—Musa hadn't seen Islam Yaken's cutlass—"they're using RPGs."

"And Twitter," I added. "But they're also trying to revive laws that existed only in the century after the life of the Prophet. They might be using modern technology, but they're trying to bring back old law."

Musa shook his head. "They're not saying that they're doing [these things] *because* they were done this way 1,400 years ago. No. They are doing it because it was commanded by Allah. It's something meant for all times," he said. "So they're not looking back. They're looking up. They're not medieval. They're forward thinkers."

On the topic of slavery, too, he conceded the facts—the Islamic State practices slavery, and slavery (including sex slavery) has a scriptural and historical basis in Islam—without conceding the interpretation. What the Islamic State was doing, he said, is slavery. "It's getting someone who was free and forcing him to not be free."

But Musa viewed this as a mercy. He used an argument (associated in U.S. jurisprudence with Oliver Wendell Holmes)[16] that "the greater includes the lesser"—that is, if it's permissible to do something, then it's permissible to do lesser versions of the same thing. To the Islamic State, killing infidels is patently permissible. So what's wrong with keeping them alive to do chores around the house? "If we've got no problem actually fighting *kuffar* [infidels], I don't see why we'd have a problem with enslaving them," he says. "There is that sort of guilt associated with it because of the slave trade in the USA, and even among some Muslims, the slave trade with Africa—but this is a person who has declared war against Allah and his Messenger, and this person could be killed."

I likened this reasoning to that of George W. Bush's Office of Legal Counsel, whose attorneys famously authorized torture, since if the government could kill a terrorist then surely it could waterboard one.

"It's a strange logical deduction," Musa allowed. He stopped—not because he had been caught in a contradiction or error but because he had been caught in an irony. Irony was something he could appreciate, while error, a binary phenomenon, was something to avoid. ("You're a Muslim or you are not," he told me. "Islam is one hundred percent. You take away one part, and it's no longer Islam.") In the presence of something not wrong but merely peculiar—such as being the methodological bedfellow of former deputy assistant attorney general John C. Yoo, author of the Bush "Torture Memos"—Musa went quiet and was briefly bemused. So much about his view of the world looked bizarre to me, and it was a relief to discover that it could look bizarre to him too.

Musa paid for our meal. We then spent a couple hours walking around Footscray before returning to the French Baguette for Vietnamese coffee. Each cup of *cà phê đá* comes with about a quarter inch of condensed milk. We drained our cups, enjoying threads of sugary glue on our tongues. These were crude pleasures, not so different from eating straight from the sugar bowl, and they felt childish and mundane. Musa's confidence in his interpretation of Islam felt similarly indulgent: just as Hesham luxuriated in his certainty, Musa spoiled himself with self-confidence. Listening to him was at times like watching one of those competitions in which people eat enormous piles of hot dogs in a matter of minutes. He had shed normal inhibitions. The object of his gluttony was purity, vindication, the bliss accompanying banishment of uncertainty and participation in righteous struggle. Others might detect overindulgence in self-confidence and pause to examine themselves for hubris. Musa had no such safeguard. His appetite was an intellectual and spiritual one, but it was no less saturnalian than the hot-dog eaters'. I was disgusted but also entertained.

When he wasn't advocating slavery or violence against infidels, Musa's inversion of the conventional categories of good and evil gave him an impish glee. He loved to find alternative interpretations of events and to test out shocking moral theories to see where they led. One day, at his mother's house, I noticed some *Wizard of Oz* knickknacks sitting by the wall. When I asked about them, Musa grew giddy and explained that his mother loved *Oz,* and he had crafted a sermon devoted to an alternate reading of the film, comparing it to the killing of Osama bin Laden by the United States.

In his analogy, Glinda the (supposedly) Good Witch is George W. Bush, and Bin Laden is the (again, supposedly) Wicked Witch of the West. But the world and the moviegoers have, in both cases, been misled. Recall that the Wicked Witch of the West is the sister of the Wicked Witch of the East, whom Dorothy crushed with her tornado-borne Kansas farmhouse. Dorothy steals the ruby slippers off the feet of the Wicked Witch of the East. "The Wicked Witch of the West is completely justified in wanting her sister's shoes. She's the next of kin!" Musa says. "Those shoes belong to her. She doesn't even want blood money [*diyah*]!" Glinda the Good Witch, he says, "is the most evil character in the movie. She puts the shoes on Dorothy, knowing that they're going to lead her on a mission to kill the [real] good witch" and eliminate her rival witch as well as the Wizard. "She uses Dorothy as a patsy."[17]

Here came the inversion. "Osama is the Wicked Witch of the West of our times," Musa explained. "He's passed off as being this evil man, whereas George Bush is passed off as being good and appealing. Glinda's dressed in pink; she's white; she has fair features. The Wicked Witch of the West is darker, the Other." Dorothy—the world's infidel population—is tricked into undertaking a long murderous quest, in the guise of fighting against terror. But the only victims are the blameless Wicked Witch, and Glinda's rival, the Wizard himself.

It occurred to me that Musa was an advocate of religious genocide but also a huge dork.

For a few months after he was forced to return to Australia, Musa behaved himself. He stayed offline, or at least stopped writing under his own name, and if he vowed allegiance to Baghdadi, he did so privately. The authorities, he told me, had been "pretty honest" about their intention to monitor and prosecute him, whether for "racial vilification" (a catch-all crime on the Australian books that could be interpreted to outlaw hate speech against non-Muslims), for recklessly or accidentally encouraging someone to join a terrorist group, or for supporting the Islamic State. But nothing that Musa had provably done or said was then illegal in Australia, and the police let him go. However, the government amended its laws late in 2014 to abridge speech freedoms, and lawmakers may well have had Musa in mind when they made the changes. As of December 2014, it was a crime to attempt to travel to Syria. The law would now presume that any *muhajir* was emigrating for terrorist purposes. The pro–Islamic State statements Musa had made in 2014 might get him jailed if he repeated them in 2015.

Meanwhile, the Islamic State was hard at work, several time zones to the west. It formally annexed Boko Haram, in Nigeria, and in western Iraq it captured Ramadi, the capital of Anbar province. Following these victories, the Islamic State broadcast footage of Iraqi soldiers' executions, with the Speicher Base massacre as its template. Most chilling to me were the shaky, raw videos of Anbari towns minutes after they had fallen. The corpses of Iraqi soldiers lay on the ground in front of houses and government buildings, the blood soaking their uniforms. In places like Mosul, Islamic State forces had eased themselves into power and become comfortable, with the local Sunni population cowed into accepting their rule. The Islamic State was holding territory, and looking more and more like an enduring government.

Musa had begun studying history at a local university. With a few of his buddies, he fared well in local quiz bowls devoted to Islamic topics and trivia. His team's name was Al Ghuraba' [the Strangers], after a hadith he quoted to me more than once. "Islam began as something strange," it said, "and it will return to being strange, as it was in the beginning. So blessed be the strangers." I could see how the theme of strangeness, foreignness, and inversion attracted him. It reminded him that when other people said his religion was weird, he could take their insult as a compliment. Who could doubt that the Companions were strangers, too, and had faced ridicule for their monotheism and devotion to their Prophet? The *muhajirs* were also strange, odd as well as foreign, forced into alien lands having been ejected from their own. Ibn Qayyim (1292–1350), an acolyte of Ibn Taymiyyah, had told Muslims to thank God for their strangeness at moments when they were blessed to feel it:

> Those who are strange are the true people of God. This strangeness does not make the stranger lonely. In fact, when he abandons the deviant people, he is most happy and sociable, and when he socializes with them he is most lonely. So, his allies are God, His Messenger, and the believers, even if the majority of the people oppose him and push him aside.[18]

Fewer Islamic State supporters mentioned him in their online exchanges, except to urge each other to "make *duʿa* [pray]" for his safety and *hijrah*. The moment of *hijrah* never came. I met several Islamists, online and in person, who sneered at him privately for being a loudmouth and a hypocrite. ("If he really wants to go to ISIS, he can stuff himself in a box and ship himself to Syria," one scoffed. "Or he can get in a boat and sail.")

In the fall of 2015, I asked Musa if I could join him and his followers for Friday prayers. He consented, on the condition that I not photograph anyone. "On *Jumuʿah* [Friday]," he wrote to me, "we usually have the *khutbah* [sermon] at 12:30 and then play indoor soccer for an hour. You're welcome to join in if you like."

We met at RecWest, a YMCA branch in Footscray that he and his friends had been using as a mosque. The rain was spitting down.

When I came in, knocking the wetness from my sneakers, I asked a middle-aged woman with large earrings at the front desk where I could find the radical Muslims. Chewing gum, she paused to think, then remembered that Musa's crew had reserved a room at the other end of the building.

Musa and his flock were already there. He greeted me warmly and introduced me to more than a dozen others—Lebanese, Turks, some Australian converts. The oldest, a man in his sixties, wore a windbreaker with the word *tawhid* [unity, monotheism] emblazoned on the back. The youngest, that man's grandson, toddled around during the sermon. Most of the others were in their twenties, and one—twenty-four-year-old Hamza Granata, a Sicilian-descended convert, born Antonio Granata—had his whole torso tattooed with Gothic letters and symbols. Tattoos are generally forbidden in Islam, and I wondered whether he now considered them a mark of shame from his former life, and a permanent exhortation to piety in his new one.

The room was carpeted and intimate, and it contained no obvious religious signs. It could just as easily have been used for a book club or a tai chi class. "We used to pray at other mosques," Musa explained. "But after a while we just didn't feel comfortable praying behind the imams." (The imam leads prayers, with the congregation behind him as they all face Mecca.) As the world grew enraged over the conduct of the Islamic State, imams across Australia denounced Baghdadi and began to promote patriotism and democracy. This, Musa said, was too much. His former imam, whom Musa had known since his conversion, had swapped out his non-political sermons about "charity, goodness, whatever" for ones that Musa actively despised, about loyalty to Australia. "I asked him about this after the *khutbah* [sermon]. And I wish I didn't ask him, because it only got worse." The imam recognized the validity of courthouse weddings and declared Islamic marriage invalid. "I know he was ignorant to some degree, but that takes the cake."

They stopped going to mosques altogether. "For a few months,"

Musa told me, "about forty of us prayed in a local park." Their op-position to the major mosques became so vehement that Musa and his men began to regard them as valid targets for destruction. They invoked the case of *masjid al dhirar* [the mosque of opposition] from early Islamic history. After Muhammad's flight to Medina from Mecca, a group of the Ansar built a mosque in support of the Prophet, and with his blessing. Later, though, those Ansar turned against him, and the Prophet ordered the mosque razed, despite its prior consecration.[19] The story confirms that the hypocrisy [*nifaq*] of an imam can nullify a mosque's holy status, and can require believ-ers to seek its destruction. Normally a mosque is inviolate. Musa's men considered just about every mosque in Melbourne a *masjid al dhirar*.

The men wore shoes during prayer, in contravention of the eti-quette of most mosques. "It's Sunna," Musa said with a shrug, mean-ing that Muhammad prayed in shoes. "When I went to the Grand Mosque in Mecca, I wore shoes." After small talk and introductions, Musa assumed a position at the front of the room, and rested his hand, with affectation, on a wooden stick and began his sermon. Whatever sense of welcome I had felt vanished as he began to speak, then yell, about the recent victories of the Islamic State:

> This is the time that every single Muslim has been waiting
> for, when we see these cities of disbelief handed back to the
> *Ahl-al Sunna* [Sunnis]. . . . How could one not find happiness
> in this time? O Muslim, look inside of your heart and ask
> yourself, is it that I love something other than the religion of
> Allah? Is it that I prefer rule, other than by the Shariah of
> Allah? Is it that I feel kindness for disbelievers?
>
> This is something that gives us joy: justice; the liberation
> of a land; bringing it under the rule of Allah; seeing the hap-
> piness of its people taken out of oppression. As our *khalifah*
> [caliph] (may Allah protect him) said, "There is no honor, no

protection, nothing for you of safety except under the shade of the *khilafah* [caliphate]."

We may not agree on every matter. But Allah has commanded us to hold fast and follow the imam who rules among you justly, rules by Islam and commits no acts of *kufr* [disbelief]. We ask Allah the Almighty to continue to expand his victory, so that we may find that the lands which were the lands of Islam returned to the lands of Islam. . . . Liberate the Najd [central Saudi Arabia], the lands of Baghdad, all the lands of this *ummah* [Muslim community], so that we may be of those who earned your pleasure and mercy, and so we may enter into *jannah* [Paradise]. . . . We hear and we obey.

The men lined up to pray, shoulder-to-shoulder, even though the room could accommodate at least three times their number. Hanging on the wall in front of them as they bowed in prayer toward Mecca were wooden plaques commemorating various community leaders in Footscray, most of them dead Australian Catholics of Italian descent.

After prayer, the group broke up, and we departed for locker rooms and toilets to prepare for indoor soccer. Hamza Granata, the tattooed one, turned out to be especially skilled, and he gave the impression of playing at roughly half capacity, to keep things sporting (the jihadist way of soccer being more forgiving than the jihadist way of war).[20] None of the men treated me with anything but acceptance, even when I scored a hat trick (Hamza scored ten goals) and once drilled a wild shot right into the busted knee of the grandpa, who was watching in the bleachers and later tossed me an energy drink.

The bond between Musa and his friends was tight, and I struggled at first to understand it. After watching their little fraternity for a few hours, I didn't fear that they were, say, plotting a terrorist attack on Melbourne. Few criminal conspiracies rent out space at the Y. Instead, I detected a monastic vibe. They were striving for self-improvement. They met to study Arabic, to critique the legal opinions of other Muslims, to discuss politics and life. Even the way they played soccer felt abnormal for young men. Hamza, the best player, did not celebrate goals gratuitously, and the competition did not feel like a displacement of a fighting instinct, a way of burning off excess rage. It was, Musa told me, "something the brothers do to stay physically fit." Some viewed their commitment to the religion as an atonement for whatever miscreant behavior they may have previously engaged in.

Afterward, Musa and I walked to his home, a few minutes away. It was a comfortable, one-story house. As I entered, I saw samplers on the wall and women's shoes, and I remembered that he still lived with his mom, Paula, and I had no idea what she would think about a stranger inquiring about her jihadist son. I readied my most ingratiating smile. "This is Graeme," Musa told her. "He's showering here."

"Nice to meet you," I said.

"Want a cup of tea?" she responded, handing me a towel.

I said yes, and she sat down on a sofa in the next room to read a stack of gossip magazines. When I emerged from the shower, Musa gave me the Wi-Fi password and motioned to a breakfast nook next to the window, where I sat reading the newest issue of *Dabiq* on my phone as he showered. Outside the window was an unkempt yard and a small shed. One of Musa's three brothers, Nick, also bushy-bearded but not Muslim, wandered through the room a few times, but he spoke only when Musa asked him to turn down the television. Neither his mom nor his brother seemed fazed by Musa's esotericism.

Once Musa finished showering and my tea was served, we began talking about crime and punishment, slavery and terrorism. His mother was about ten feet away during the first part of the conversation, but once she lost interest in her magazines she walked off to another part of the house. Musa, meanwhile, was discussing the permissibility of immolation as a method of execution.

The main duty of the caliph, he had told me, is the implementation of God's law. The Koran says: "Whoever does not judge by what God has revealed—they are infidels."[21] That verse and others like it formed the basis for many prior acts of excommunication against secular Muslim leaders. The body of law in the Koran itself is small: unlike Leviticus in the Bible, it contains no litany of prohibitions and punishments, and its criminal code can be summarized on the front and back of an index card. Muslims must therefore rely on the record of elaboration by the Prophet, in word or deed, to know what acts are divinely forbidden and how they are to be punished. Collectively those crimes are called *hadd* [limit] crimes, because they are beyond the boundary of what God has permitted. Islam considers the crimes to be perpetrated against God. The Islamic State's Aleppo province circulated a concise table with its list of these crimes:[22]

CRIME	PUNISHMENT
Blasphemy against God	Death
Blasphemy against the Messenger	Death even if he repents [Blasphemy against Muhammad is deemed unforgivable because the victim of the offense is dead, and therefore not available to accept repentance and apology.]
Blasphemy against the religion	Death
Fornication	• For those who are *muhsan*: stoning • For the non-*muhsan*: 100 lashes and banishment for a year [A person who is *muhsan* is one who is free (i.e., not enslaved) and Muslim, and has had intercourse with a spouse at least once during marriage. Once *muhsan*, always *muhsan*—even after divorce. Fornication by *muhsan* people is therefore nearly synonymous with the English "adultery," although under Islamic law, divorced people can be punished for adultery even if they have sex (not necessarily with each other) after their divorce.]
Homosexuality	Death for penetrator and receiver[23] [The method of execution for sodomy in the Islamic State is to push the accused off a tall building.]
Theft	Cutting off the hand
Drinking wine	80 lashes

CRIME	PUNISHMENT
Calumny	80 lashes
Spying for infidels	Death
Apostasy	Death
Highway criminality [*qat' al tariq*][24] [This category encompasses highway robbery (brigandage; besetting travelers, or anyone out of reach of civilization) but also home invasion, i.e., breaking into a house while armed and taking property.]	• Killing and taking wealth: death and crucifixion • Killing: death • Taking wealth: Cut off the right hand and left foot ["cross amputation"] • Terrorizing the people: banishment from the land

One of the distinguishing characteristics of these punishments, as the Islamic State sees them, is the absence of judicial discretion in their delivery. There is little room for mercy. In the case of fornication, the Koran says, "Let not compassion move you, in a matter prescribed by God"—hence the rule that the caliph must implement these punishments without exception.[25] In a document posted online, the Islamic State quoted a hadith about an incident in which a Qurayshi woman was found guilty of theft, and her tribesmen asked a friend of Muhammad to intercede with him and beg on her behalf for mercy. Muhammad replied indignantly:

> The nations before you went astray because if a noble person committed theft, they used to [let him go unpunished]. But if a weak person among them committed theft, they used to inflict the legal punishment on him. By God, if Fatima, the daughter of Muhammad, committed theft, Muhammad will cut off her hand![26]

The caliph (and the victims, in some cases) can exercise discretion over the punishment of non-*hadd* crimes, including battery and murder, and indeed it is considered honorable for the victim's family to accept blood money [*diyah*] in lieu of the life of the murderer. But because *hadd* crimes are violations of commands from God, they must always be punished as prescribed. (The Koran and hadith do not state a clear logic for why minor crimes like drinking wine are etched into Islamic criminal law for eternity, while larger ones like murder are not.) Nor is it coincidental that the Islamic State carries out the sentences publicly. (Koran: "Let a party of the Believers witness their punishment.")[27] By the time of our soccer match, the Islamic State's followers were circulating photo and video exhibits of public *hadd* punishments on a daily basis. Nearly always the spectacle followed the same protocol: parading of the criminal; public announcement of the crime, usually through a loudspeaker; and finally carrying out the sentence.

I found it heartening that Musa blanched when I asked him about the *hadd* punishments. "You see some [Islamic State supporters] who love to watch videos of beheadings," he said. "I'm quite the opposite. I mean, some of them *love* it." For him, the *hadd* punishments were obligatory. "But they aren't there to make us feel better. To take control, and to implement the *khilafah,* this is compulsory. There will be blood, and that's just one of the realities."

I asked: shouldn't the Islamic State's judges and executioners worry that their judgments could be faulty? "Amputation is irreversible. That's a lot on your conscience."

"You don't want to play with something as serious as human life," he admitted. But the *hadd* punishments are non-negotiable. Errors in application would be rectified. "As a Muslim, I'd say that Allah will compensate you for your suffering," if you are wrongfully punished. "Someone who doesn't believe in the afterlife would struggle to understand that. As Allah says, 'To kill one innocent person you've killed all of mankind.' That's how serious it is. But the *hadd* goes on," he said, unexpectedly channeling Sonny Bono.

These punishments require a recalibration of intuitions, and Musa was there to help me adjust my expectations, as he did with the Land of Oz. I had been picked up by a moral twister and deposited somewhere other than Kansas—in the mental world of the caliphate. The punishments, he agreed, may seem savage—but aspects of the process leading to them are merciful. Some punishments may never be meant to be implemented at all. Shariah court judges are encouraged to dissuade the accused from confessing. Moreover, through a doctrine called *satr* [concealment], even *witnesses* should recant or refuse to produce their true, incriminating testimony. Muhammad is said to have said: "Whoever keeps hidden what would disgrace a believer, it is as though he had restored a buried baby girl to life from her tomb."[28] The threat of punishment matters more than the punishment itself.

Musa said the punishments purge criminals of their sin and allow them to meet God with a clean record. "You may have seen images from the *Dawlah*," he said, "of people who looked happy to be receiving their punishment." What he said was true: some victims are smiling. In what strikes many outsiders as the sickest of scenes from the Islamic State, condemned sodomites are hugged and congratulated by their executioners as they are led to their deaths. Blindfolded, the victims are marched up to the roof of a tall building and pushed off the edge. They, Musa would say, are truly blessed: they spare themselves worse punishment in the afterlife, having paid the price for their crime in this one. And they go to God as Muslims, with the last words on their lips praise for their creator.

"A woman committed *zina* [fornication] while she was married," Musa told me. She came to the Prophet and said, "*Ya Rasulullah* [O Messenger of God], I've committed *zina*: torture me, purify me." The Prophet turned her away, pointing out that she need not confess, and that he would never know if she didn't. But she continued to beg for punishment, as the child of her sin grew inside her. The Prophet told her not to come back to him until she had weaned her baby. "The day that the child could feed himself, she came to him, and the child had a piece of bread in his hand, to show that he could feed himself. She said: 'Purify me.'"

With the Prophet looking on, she was stoned. One of the killers grunted vehemently—"Take that, you fornicator!"—as he winged a fastball into her cranium. The Prophet admonished him: "She made repentance so great that if all of the people of Medina were to make repentance, hers would even be greater than theirs. Indeed, she is in *jannah* [Paradise]."

"Shall we get lunch?" Musa asked.

We drove from Footscray into central Melbourne, to a Chinese restaurant run by Uighurs—Musa's accent turned the Central Asian ethnic group's name into "WEE-gah"—who specialized in spicy plates of meat and noodles. Along the way, he obeyed every stoplight, drove only slightly over the speed limit, and paid for parking in full. Why, I pondered, did this ideologue who recognized no law but God's and no leader but the caliph behave so meekly? Friends had asked whether I feared meeting with him, since he presumably viewed me, like all who resist the Islamic State, as a legitimate target for murder. It had not occurred to me to worry. Musa's home Wi-Fi network was named after a Monty Python sketch, and he professed appreciation for the gay British polymath Stephen Fry. He sent me interesting emails about Semitic philology. I never feared our conversations at all, nor could I see him strapping on a suicide bomb.

But the Islamic State itself was a much tougher customer, and I was foolish to take for granted that Musa's winsome dorky nature would remain dominant over the jihadi within. In an infamous September 2014 video (repeated on loops in many subsequent videos, especially after the Paris attacks in November 2015), the Islamic State's spokesman 'Adnani gave me fair warning. He told his followers:

If you can kill a disbelieving American or European—especially the spiteful and filthy French—or an Australian, or a Canadian, or any other disbeliever from the disbelievers waging war, [then] kill him in any manner or way however it may be. Smash his head with a rock, or slaughter him with a knife, or run him over with your car, or throw him down from a high place, or choke him, or poison him. If you are unable to do so, then burn his home, car, or business. Or destroy his crops. If you are unable to do so, then spit in his face.[29]

I asked Musa to reconcile his peaceful behavior with the Islamic State's command to violence. He told me, first, that most graduates of Melbourne's Islamic schools either openly or secretly supported the Islamic State. But he said nothing required them to obey 'Adnani blindly. "Do we have problems with the Australian government and military? Yes," he said. "Do we think that it would be beneficial for Muslims to have global attacks? No." He claimed that a consensus has been reached among local Islamic State supporters that emigration to the caliphate is obligatory though illegal ("I myself have no plans to go") and that attacks at home would be "unwise" though permissible.

"Let's just say every Muslim in Australia right now went out and killed a random person. Does that bring Shariah to the land? No. It will bring absolute chaos," he said, noting that the chaos would hurt Muslims and likely make immigration harder. "So let's just say that instead we got half of the Muslims here, shipped them off overseas, trained them, and began to expand the *Dawlah* until it gets to Australia. Is this more likely? Of course. Have some sense!"

"Don't you still owe obedience to the caliph?" I asked. "He says to attack. Why don't you attack?"

According to Musa, Baghdadi and 'Adnani were working with bad information. "The [Islamic State] leaders don't understand Australia, so we respectfully disagree with them," Musa said. He wished he could convey his opinions to them so they would understand why such attacks would be counterproductive. "We want to open up dialogue [with them]. At the moment we think that there's no wisdom in [attacks on Australia]. We would want to say [to 'Adnani and Baghdadi] that 'Look, we haven't been consulted.'" But for the moment, that consultation is impossible. "What do we do? Go to the Australian Federal Police and say, 'Is it okay if we, you know, give Baghdadi a call? It's in your interests!'"

In the months after that conversation, the Islamic State increased its attacks on foreign targets—both attacks directed from its headquarters in Syria and attacks it inspired but did not necessarily control. Australia, which had contributed a disproportionate number of its citizens to the ranks of the Islamic State, remained mostly untouched.[30]

Not for the first time, Musa's arguments conveniently excused his remaining in Melbourne, slurping noodles and sweating his way through plates of lamb. He must have sensed my skepticism, because after he came back from praying in a back corner of the restaurant, he was ready to defend himself.

The belief that attacks on Australia and other Western targets could bring Islam to the whole world, he said, was a relic from the old days of Al Qaida. That group, he said, attacked the West because it acted as a vanguard military movement. It existed for no purpose but to attack—and it deserved praise for its bravery. But it could not build a state. Al Qaida's approach was at once too patient and too hasty. In its haste, it focused on spectacular, immediate attacks, putting no trust in the morrow. Then it waited passively for the rise of the caliphate. The Al Qaida model reached its apotheosis on September 11, 2001—and, Musa asked, what did it get for its troubles? (This intra-jihadi criticism of Al Qaida is, as Thomas Hegghammer notes dryly, "something that we've heard since roughly September 12.") The American response sent Al Qaida's leadership scurrying over the Hindu Kush and into hiding in Pakistan. Since then, its victories have been few and small.

The Islamic State, he said, was correcting Al Qaida's errors. When confronted with one of the core obligations of Islam—the appointment of a caliph—Al Qaida delayed and delayed. "[Some] believe if you shout out '*khilafah!*' enough it will magically appear," Musa said. "You could almost say that Osama had this view: just attack the West enough and things will fall into place." The Islamic State has focused on building a state, while farming out attacks on the West to autonomous agents overseas. Only when it began suffering terrific defeats in Syria and Iraq—largely because of U.S. air support for Kurds and Iraqis—did it pivot completely toward encouraging attacks, large and small, and undertaking big operations like the November 2015 Paris massacre. The first unambiguous statement from the Islamic State encouraging attacks in lieu of immigration did not come until May 2016.[31]

Musa sometimes calls Osama bin Laden "Sheikh Osama"—a term of respect—but he clearly regards him as a bit of a Kumbayah figure among jihadis. "Osama addressed the Islamic State in Iraq [2006–2013], saying, 'You are the dream that the *ummah*'s been waiting for.'" He was a unifier. "Osama was like, 'Guys, I love you! Keep it up! This is what we want—but at the same time, don't ruin it [by building a state too soon].'"

Documents seized in the raid on Abbottabad that killed Bin Laden in 2011 confirm this impression. The leader of Al Qaida in the Arabian Peninsula, Nasir al Wuhayshi (aka Abu Basir, 1976–2015), wrote to Bin Laden to suggest the establishment of an Islamic state in Yemen. Bin Laden replied:

> Yemen is the Arab country most suited to the establishment of an Islamic state, but this does not mean that the

necessary fundamental elements for success for such a project have yet been realized. . . . Being deliberate in this matter is a good thing, and to explain further, establishing the state before the elements necessary for success are put in place most often will lead to aborting the effort wherever it takes place, because establishing a state and then toppling the state represents a burden that exceeds the energy of the people.[32]

"Al Qaida was a [flawed] theory of how to get somewhere," Musa says, "and the *Dawlah* is that realization of that theory."

For Al Qaida's current chief, Ayman al Zawahiri, Musa's derision is intense. The Islamic State has made one of its core missions the theological purification of jihadist ranks. Zawahiri, like Bin Laden, encouraged ecumenicism. On July 9, 2005, he wrote to Zarqawi—then up to his elbows in Muslim and infidel blood—and encouraged him to get along with Sunnis of all types. He pointed out that Mullah ʿUmar of the Taliban was a Maturidi (and therefore out of line with Salafi or Hanbali theology) but a great guy nonetheless. Zarqawi had taken up the mass killing of Shia civilians in Iraq, and Zawahiri asked him to stop. "Why kill ordinary Shia, considering that they are forgiven [for apostasy] because of their ignorance?" he asked. He warned that ordinary Muslims would never understand or forgive his wanton violence against the Shia.[33]

Musa defended Zarqawi. "Zawahiri was telling the Islamic State in Iraq off, saying, 'You guys are just going overboard [with killing Shia]. Too much bloodletting, too much!' And of course, you know, Zarqawi just shrugged and said, 'Up to you. We'll continue with our stuff. We have to establish our state.'" Zarqawi kept on killing as many Shia as he could. To deny that the Shia deserve death is to deny that their deviancies (veneration of false imams, modification of the *shahadah* to include allegiance to ʿAli) are deviant—clear cases of *shirk*, for which ignorance is no excuse. "Certain factions of Al Qaida were very, very soft on the Shia," Musa says, both in anger and sorrow. "It's something I don't like to talk about too much. But I would say [Zawahiri's side] held [anti-genocidal] views that could even lead to [their own] apostasy."

Now Zawahiri appears in Islamic State propaganda as a target of ridicule. Islamic State supporters mock him for having given allegiance to Mullah ʿUmar of the Taliban, who in addition to several other flaws—missing an eye, not Qurayshi, not Salafi—had been dead for several years. *Dabiq* publishes unflattering photographs of Zawahiri, which make him look decrepit, as if waiting for a bowl of Jell-O at a jihadist retirement home.

Over the next few days, Musa and I wandered the city, drinking coffee and hot chocolate. Jihadists can make good tour guides. Musa knew restaurants everywhere that served halal food: a Thai Muslim place near Footscray, an Ottoman restaurant further out of town. Many of the conventional sites held no interest for Musa, so I never saw Melbourne's art museums or nightlife. But some sites gained special significance under his tutelage. At the Royal Arcade—a posh Victorian shopping mall in the central business district—we looked at two hideous statues that ring in every hour by striking bells on either side of a clock. They represent Gog and Magog, the Biblically (and Koranically) foretold creatures that will ravage the earth at the end of time. Musa talked me through the ways in which those statues did and did not conform to prophecy. The statues are wearing Mongol attire, and they fit the Christian view of Gog and Magog as bogeymen from the Far East. He stressed that according to Islamic revelation, they should be depicted as peoples, not individuals, and that their rapacity would make the Mongols look no more aggressive than Black Friday shoppers.

He was having a good time, I could see, teaching me all the things he thought I should know, and thereby ensuring that I (and by extension you, dear reader) could be held accountable when the Day of Judgment comes. By now he had spent so much time binding me to Islam that I probably looked like a giant ball of twine, with my infidel head and hands barely sticking out. That I would burst into flames in Hell, then spend eternity being tortured by demons (one source says they will floss unbelievers' gastrointestinal tracts, from lips to anus, with a rusty chain), didn't bother him.

Every once in a while, the pre-jihadist Musa, with relatable human sympathies, would emerge. One morning, when he picked me up from the apartment I was renting, he told me that his aunt, who was not a Muslim, had just died. We had spoken the day before about the Day of Judgment. He had informed me that before Paradise or damnation, most mortals would face the Punishment of the Graves [ʿadhab al qabr], a palate cleanser for the coming eternity of either pleasure or pain. Even Muslims and righteous people—with the exception of martyrs and prophets, who go straight to Paradise—will have their ribs squeezed until they touch each other and crack. His aunt would have been experiencing this process now. According to scripture, her howls of pain could be heard by animals and genies but not by humans.

We had spoken of little besides death for days. Musa was subdued and pensive, and before we drove off, he said of his aunt, "She was not a Muslim, and all things are now between her and Allah." I sensed sadness and a hint of regret—although I'm sure he would deny it— that he was obliged to believe in, and celebrate, his aunt's torture.

Everywhere in Melbourne he faced memories of a previous life. One afternoon we drove past an ice rink. "I think that will be the sign that the Islamic State is truly enduring," I told him: "Once it has its own indoor ice rink."

Musa said he used to skate at that rink. He told me, sheepishly, about a time in his youth when a girl, "drunk out of her brains,"

showed up in disco attire and skidded around the ice until she stumbled into his arms. "Something was wrong with her," he tutted, adding that others, and not he, helped her up. His prudishness reminded
me that I was talking to a married man, with two kids in the western
suburbs of Melbourne and a wife in the Philippines, and that among
the downsides to his life in Australia was indefinite physical separa-
tion from Joan. He mentioned that the Philippine authorities had
tortured her after the raid that led to his deportation.

"It must be frustrating to have your wife so far away," I said.

Musa replied that it was—but it was also his preference. The Australian government wanted her to come to Footscray to domesticate
him, to urge him to get a job, make money, fill his mind with something other than jihad. To me that sounded like a shrewd strategy.
Married life takes time, and it demands compromise and empathy,
the precise virtues his jihadism rejected. I think he understood that.
He said he preferred that she stay in the Philippines while he looked
for ways to leave Australia. When his brother considered getting
married in Thailand, Musa encouraged the idea, in case the Australian government could be persuaded to grant him a passport to attend.

On my last morning in Melbourne, we picked up his daughters
from his ex-wife's house before going to the airport. They were cute,
boisterous kids. The older one was entering grade school. After a few
attempts to teach them new Arabic words, Musa sang the *Speed Racer*
song with them, before returning to our discussion of the pain of
living outside the caliphate. The kids sat in the back, quietly and politely.

"The Prophet said not to live among the *kuffar* [infidels]," he said,
shrugging. The Koran commands Muslims to move to Muslim territory at 8:72 ("But those who believed and did not emigrate [make
hijrah]—for you there is no guardianship of them until they emigrate") and 4:89 ("do not take from among them allies until they emigrate").[34] Living among infidels, some traditions have pointed out,

forces Muslims to abide by unholy laws and customs, and tempts them to ignore their own. If you are the only Muslim around, who will disapprove when you neglect prayer, sneak a beer, or refuse to give alms? Who will pray with you, and where will you find a butcher to sell you meat slaughtered as God intended? The point of an Islamic state is to command good and forbid wrong, to make a halal life easy. Although Muslim scholars have disagreed about whether living among infidels is inherently sinful or merely undesirable, the plain meaning of the command that Muslims should live among Muslims is something Musa violated every day. The rows of one-story houses we passed as we drove looked like one of the most boring suburban subdivisions imaginable—perhaps on par with a down-market area of Phoenix. "[Muhammad] said, 'You shouldn't be able to see the fires where they cook, or their houses at a distance. Stay away from them, live amongst the Muslims.' This is an obligation, Islamic State or not," Musa said.

I reminded him of an opinion, infamous in jihadist and non-jihadist circles alike, issued by Nasir al Din al Albani, who was considered the most important Salafi scholar of the last century when he died in 1999. In response to the partition of Palestine, Albani advised the Palestinians to simply leave. "It is obligatory for them to leave," he wrote, and to go to "a land in which they are able to observe Islam." Get out, move to Muslim lands, heal your wounds and live the kinds of lives available only under rule by Islam. Return to destroy Israel, in the fullness of time.[35]

"I know a lot of people read what [Albani] said and say it sounds like treachery," Musa reflected. It sounds like giving up on the Palestinian cause and conceding Jerusalem, the third holiest city in Islam, to infidels. "But I have to be fair and say I understand him. He's not saying to give up. He's just saying to go live among Muslims, then come back and reclaim your land. History has shown many examples of this happening. The Prophet left Mecca [for Medina], and he came back victorious."

When we said goodbye at the airport, Musa gave me a large, special-edition Cadbury's chocolate bar flavored with Vegemite, the tarry, salty Australian spread made from dead yeast. Few non-Australians like Vegemite, and many who taste it gag and suspect it is an elaborate prank, an instance of the same odd Aussie sense of humor that produced Yahoo Serious and Prime Minister Tony Abbott. The chocolate bar was the perfect parting gift from Musa—something revolting, encased in sweetness.

As I removed my luggage from the back of his car, I watched his face in the rearview mirror, detecting no wistful glances at the departures board and its menu of forbidden destinations. I wondered whether he really envied my passport, or whether his imprisonment on the continent of Australia was a price worth paying for the chance to live here in comfort, and sing with his kids on weekends. So much of his identity was bound up with his refusal to compromise. But he looked willing to compromise plenty—to act like a normal person with emotions and beliefs that had nothing to do with savage violence. At the Qantas counter, the check-in agent asked if anyone unknown to me gave me anything to take on board. I felt the hefty brick of chocolate in my coat-pocket and said no.

A year later, Musa sent me a chat message with a picture of more kebabs. I had floated the possibility of another visit, and the images of fatty meat, dusted with cumin and chili powder, were an invitation. "It will be good to see you," he wrote. "I should be free. Just let me know when you'll be here exactly." I wrote that I was considering May 12 to 16, 2016.

That meeting never happened. In early May, Musa and five other Australians—including Hamza Granata (the tattooed, messianic Messi) and the brother of the Perth-based firebrand preacher Junaid Thorne—acquired a twenty-one-foot-long Fraser motorboat and towed it sixty-one hours from Melbourne to the far northeastern tip of the Australian mainland. On the evening of May 10, all five were arrested near Cape York, Queensland. According to Australian media, Musa had told a Sydney psychologist, Hanan Dover, that he planned to flee Australia.[36] I heard about his detention in time to save me the trip to Footscray.

None of the men had seafaring experience. If they were planning to cross from Cape York to New Guinea, they would have had to traverse over a hundred miles, the distance from Cuba to the Florida Keys. Had they made it, they would still only have reached the croc- and shark-infested waters of southern New Guinea. To continue onward to Syria, or even Mindanao, would have been ambitious. Wags on Twitter suggested that Musa and his friends be allowed to try their luck, and be given provisions for half of their journey, just to make things interesting.

I tried to envision the improbable scene of five hairy mujahedin desperate not to look suspicious while hauling a deep-sea fishing boat across the Outback. Did they want to get caught? After all, they can now say they did what they could to reach the caliphate. And they will probably never have to leave Australia.

In 2013, Musa wrote a short essay about the Muslim victims of the 2004 tsunami in Banda Aceh, Indonesia. He quoted a hadith about martyrdom. Muhammad told his followers that martyrdom can take multiple forms:

> One who is slain in the way of God is a martyr; one who dies in the way of God is a martyr; one who dies of plague is a martyr; one who dies of cholera is a martyr; one who is drowned is a martyr.[37]

Musa may have been a hypocrite. But if he was sincere, a rough crossing would have been a no-lose proposition.

. . .

In our earliest conversations, Musa had mentioned a conspirator—a "teacher," he said—with greater love of *khilafah* than his own. I made a note of Musa's teacher's name, Yahya Abu Hassan, and committed to investigating him later. They both identified as Muslim, but their Islam had peculiarities that Musa was eager to explain. They were not, he said, Salafi. Musa said he and his teacher—also a convert—were revivers of a small school of Sunni jurisprudence known as Dhahirism. (The sound *dh* is alien to English—a buzz pronounced with the tongue near the back of the front teeth, more like an English *z* than a *d*.) Musa first encountered the school in a book by the Salafi-oriented writer Bilal Philips, who rejected the Dhahiris but portrayed them in a way Musa found appealing.

Islam is irreducible to law, and there are aspects to the Muslim tradition—literary, mystical, cultural—that are remote from juristic discussion. But law has been central to Muslim intellectual life since the earliest days of the religion, and Musa's insistence on his affiliation with the Dhahiri school [*madhhab*] suggested a further dimension of his attraction to the Islamic State. To identify as Dhahiri is eccentric, even pretentious. Nearly all Sunni Muslims adhere to one of four schools: Hanbali, Hanafi, Maliki, or Shafiʿi. They have coexisted for more than a millennium, and with an understanding that their differences—while significant—should not be a source of acrimony.

The differences among the schools are complex, but chief among them is disagreement about the sources of ultimate authority in legal argument. All agree that the Koran trumps all else, along with the things we know Muhammad commanded or did. All four schools believe the opinions of individual Companions of the Prophet (*sahabah*) deserve deference. So if Abu Bakr al Siddiq did or said something, but what he did or thought isn't confirmed in the Koran or hadith, Abu Bakr's word nonetheless carries some weight. The schools admit further sources of authority. If, for example, the leaders of Medina after Muhammad's death agreed on a practice or legal ruling,

Malikis consider themselves bound by it. Hanafis and Malikis both accept that 'urf—the customs and conventions that prevailed at the time of the Prophet—can be a source of guidance, if the Prophet and the Koran are not known to have opposed those practices.

Musa's legal school, the Dhahiris, are a minority so small that many Muslims believe they are extinct. There are no Dhahiri congregations of significant size. The sect was founded in the ninth century by the Iraqi Dawud al Dhahiri and reached its zenith in eleventh-century Andalusia.[38] By far its greatest exponent was Ibn Hazm (994–1064), the wealthy son of a vizier to the Amirid state in Córdoba. Ibn Hazm grew up in poor health, but he came to see his comfortable upbringing, and the lazy intellectual attitudes it fostered, as a greater handicap than physical illness. As a young man, he realized with shame he didn't know how to pray properly, and he renounced political office to become a religious scholar and writer. "In a way," the Ibn Hazm scholar Maribel Fierro told me, "he was a convert."[39] Intellectually, he was omnivorous and produced texts of astronomy, theology, literature, and poetry, as well as works that straddle or confound those genres. He was also known, according to his biographers, as a skilled impromptu poet—the best street-corner rapper in eleventh-century Córdoba.[40]

In a bustling metropolis several weeks' journey from other hubs of Islamic legal scholarship such as Baghdad and Medina, Ibn Hazm developed an idiosyncratic legal school that was as much his as Dawud al Dhahiri's. His methodology anticipates aspects of the legal originalism of, say, Antonin Scalia or Clarence Thomas. It enjoins Muslims to read texts narrowly, preferring their "apparent" [dhahir] meaning and avoiding "hidden" [batin] meaning.[41] The Koran and Sunna of the Prophet contain a complete guide to life, Ibn Hazm said, so Muslims should trust them. "We have neglected nothing in the [Koran]," God says. "We revealed the Book as an explanation for everything."[42] If God wanted to guide Muslims, why would he conceal his true meaning?

Like all Muslims, Ibn Hazm accepted the sayings and reports of the Prophet as a source of authority. If the Prophet commanded something, Muslims must do it, even if the Koran is silent on the matter. Most schools of Islamic law have agreed that it would be better to rely at times on the opinions of scholars, rather than rely on poorly attested, "weak" hadith. Ibn Hazm suspected that reliance on opinion over hadith was a gateway to error, and he argued for the strictest adherence to revealed sources.[43] To Dhahiris, nothing counts but the Koran, the Sunna of the Prophet, and the *consensus*—not the individual opinions—of the Companions. That means '*urf* is worthless, and the word of Abu Bakr al Siddiq counts for nothing unless all the other *sahabah* agreed. God commanded believers to follow His law and the example of His Prophet—not to follow the Prophet's followers.

Reading this way makes it difficult to derive new rulings from those sources. All four of the major schools accept analogical reasoning [*qiyas*] as a way to derive law. *Qiyas* is straightforward: find a legal ruling on one issue, and see if it might apply to a similar one. If the Prophet said that children shouldn't use a particular curse word (in the hadith, it's "oof!") when speaking to their parents, then surely he meant to prohibit other curses. The Koran says not to drink date wine. By analogy, surely this means Muslims should abjure bourbon and beer as well—to say nothing of crystal meth. Dhahiris are unique in rejecting *qiyas* altogether[44]: they say that meth is forbidden not because it is analogous to wine, but because it is an intoxicant, and intoxicants are forbidden. To forbid PCP on grounds of analogy is unnecessary.

Musa gave me another example of Dhahiri reasoning. He quoted hadith: "If a dog drinks from your bowl, then you must wash it seven times."[45] From this guidance, many Muslims have understood dogs to be unclean. Touching unclean creatures invalidates prayer, and you have to bathe before you can pray again. Many Muslims will shun dogs on this basis alone. When Pervez Musharraf, then president of Pakistan, publicly cuddled his Pekingeses, Pakistani Islamists seized on his affection for dogs as a sign that he was not a believing Muslim.

But Dhahiris reject this reasoning. The hadith says only that *you must wash your bowl seven times*—not that dogs are unclean. Pigs are unclean [*najis*], and touching them would require bathing before prayer. On what basis do we add dogs to the category? Dhahiris say there is none. "If the Prophet meant 'The dog is an unclean animal,' by Allah we know he would have said, 'The dog is an unclean animal,'" Musa said. "How dare they come along and say, 'I know what Allah meant!' You've gone from washing your plate to not touching dogs at all—all based not on text but on your own reasoning. I see a dog, I'll pat the dog. No problem." He paused. "Really, cleaning your bowl thoroughly after a dog licks it just seems like good hygiene."

To Dhahiris, the impulse to look for legal authority beyond the established sources bespeaks a weakness of faith. It also resembles a juridical power grab, an attempt to elevate man, through his interpretive power, to the status of God. Dhahirism sliced authority so finely that it suggested that God was silent on many things that busybody clerics desperately wanted to control. Since only a few things are expressly forbidden, then all else is permitted. Dhahirism is, in this sense, the most libertarian of Islamic legal schools.

Dhahirism can lead to peculiar conclusions. Ibn Hazm, for example, endorsed the practice of adult breastfeeding as a way to allow unrelated women and men to socialize or work together without sin. When a person feeds from a woman's breast, he becomes her kin, and therefore she no longer needs to wear a veil around him. The Prophet suggested this practice (as a joke, some say), but most Muslims would agree that modern customs make the solution unworkable.[46]

To continue, pruriently: I was told by one non-Dhahiri Islamist that Dhahiris have unusual views of non-penetrative intercourse. The obligation to fast during Ramadan daylight hours is agreed upon by all Muslims, including Dhahiris. They also agree that sex is forbidden during daylight in Ramadan. But Dhahiris point out that "sex" refers to vaginal intercourse. So for these Dhahiris, the Ramadan menu of daytime sexual pastimes still includes oral sex, frottage, manual stimulation, and anything else that isn't vaginal sex. If God wanted to forbid hand jobs, he would have said so.

No one, including Musa, claims that Dhahirism is the official legal school of the Islamic State. The Islamic State has not officially endorsed any legal school, and its relationship with the very concept of splitting Islam into distinct legal schools is complicated and antagonistic. But its legal rulings include tantalizing quotes from Ibn Hazm (along with quotes from other, non-Dhahiri scholars, such as Ibn Taymiyyah, a Hanbali). Bin ʿali quotes Ibn Taymiyyah far more often than Ibn Hazm, and since Ibn Hazm is the only great Dhahiri jurist, that preponderance alone confirms that the Islamic State is not Dhahiri. Musa says his friends who had made *hijrah* to the Islamic State reported that judges there were applying Dhahiri methodology, and some called themselves Dhahiri. "[Dhahirism] has had prominence in the past. The seed is now coming back, and is doing away with all this deriving of sources from human logic," Musa said. "It's a beautiful thing." Other Islamic State sympathizers leave traces of Dhahirism in their wake, even when they omit use of the term itself. Israfil Yilmaz, a Dutch fighter, wrote to his friends that the Islamic State takes its authority "from nothing other than the Koran and the Sunna and the *ijmaʿ* [consensus] of the *sahaba* [Companions]."[47] That is the Dhahiri legal methodology in one sentence.

Some policies of the Islamic State make more sense when viewed in a Dhahiri light. The Islamic State's enemies have condemned the group for its war against Syrian and Iraqi Christians. Christians, mainstream Muslims say, deserve protection: one of the earliest caliphs, ʿUmar, entered into a pact with them, and proper Islamic practice requires keeping 'Umar's peace. The famous "Letter to Baghdadi"—the critical rebuke signed by dozens of prominent Islamic scholars—upbraids the caliph on these grounds: "From the legal perspective of Shariah," the letter says, Christians "all fall under ancient agreements that are around 1400 years old."[48] Many Salafis recognize the covenants of Caliph 'Umar as binding after his death, because 'Umar was one of the four caliphs to follow Muhammad directly. That gives them the status of "rightly guided" caliphs, and makes them subject to emulation by Salafis and, indeed, most other Sunnis.

But the Islamic State's leaders have shown no reverence for 'Umar's pact. One of the leaders of Islamic State of Iraq (the immediate predecessor to ISIS), Abu 'Umar al Baghdadi, *canceled* the pact and demanded a new covenant. In May 2014, ISIS unilaterally revised the pact, preserving portions and adding others to serve their needs.[49] To many observers, this selectivity smacked of hypocrisy, or reneging on an eternal agreement between the faiths. To Dhahiris, no contradiction existed: The Islamic State violated the Pact of 'Umar because it was 'Umar's and not God's. If God had wanted Muslims to be bound forever by the dictates of 'Umar, he would have said so.

The Islamic State regularly does things contrary to Dhahiri method. Musa opposes suicide bombings, one of the Islamic State's hallmark practices, on classic Dhahiri grounds: "The Koran says don't kill yourself," he told me.[50] "If it meant that you can kill yourself under certain conditions, it would have said so." Pushing blindfolded homosexuals from the tallest buildings in Raqqah and Mosul continues a practice of Abu Bakr al Siddiq. As a Dhahiri, Musa doesn't approve of these executions, because God didn't give Abu Bakr al Siddiq the last word, and nothing in the Sunna or Koran requires disposal of homosexuals in this manner. Indeed, Ibn Hazm rhapsodized in poetry about the beautiful men he knew. He was famously tolerant of homosexuality, and said the crime should incur only discretionary punishment [ta 'zir], such as whipping.[51]

Musa admits that his enthusiasm might lead him to see Dhahirism even where none prevails. When he heard from friends that Dhahiris had power within the Islamic State, and that influence was confirmed to him directly by his teacher, he got excited. "It's like when there's a beautiful woman, and you find out she likes you," he said. Your attention sharpens. "You're like, 'Oh really?'" Even though the Islamic State is not officially Dhahiri, there can be no doubt about the presence of Dhahiri tendencies among the *Dawlah*'s followers, and the value of its legal minimalism to its project.

One of Ibn Hazm's opponents eulogized him by saying that his only sin was to have forbidden *qiyas,* or analogical reasoning. Other than that, he called Muslims to follow the Koran and Sunna. Who could object? These are the sources that all Muslims follow, and that they agree take precedence over other sources. A pragmatic interpretation of the Islamic State's apparent Dhahiri turn is that it is appealing to the lowest common denominator of the *ummah,* the criteria on which all agree. Dhahirism can claim to bind together diverse Muslims. It is the type-O blood of Islamic jurisprudence, a universal donor.[52]

Perhaps more important still is the mindset to which Dhahirism appeals. There is something in Dhahirism attractive to young people prone to binary, totalizing worldviews. In their most conservative forms, many religions and sects share the trait of inflexibility. But Dhahiris are special. The rejection of figurative or analogical interpretation strikes most mainstream (and Salafi) scholars as preposterous, given how much intellectual effort Muslims devote to interpretation. Through Dhahiri eyes, the same scripture that those scholars see in need of painstaking interpretation is no more complex than the manual for a toaster. Nuances vanish. Dhahiris read the Koran as if it were a software program, and their ambition is to become the hardware that can run it. Over Internet chat, I mentioned to a non-jihadist Salafi friend that Musa is a Dhahiri, and he wrote back a forehead-slapping "LOL . . . I am literally doing the robot dance right now."

Another attraction of Dhahirism is political. Like Sulayman ibn Sih-man a thousand years later, Ibn Hazm worried about the geography of Muslim land, and whether non-Muslims and Muslims could live near each other without compromising the latter's religion.[53] In 1031, Ibn Hazm witnessed the fragmentation of the Umayyad caliphate due to civil war. He felt the burden of chaos and disunity for the rest of his life. He therefore stressed the obligation to declare fealty to a strong individual Muslim leader. A caliph was not just the source of spiritual salvation but a bulwark against the dangers of this world as well. And because Andalusia stood at the frontier of Muslim con-quest and was close to Christian settlements, the question of whether Muslims could settle and live among Christians, or were compelled to create their own state, arose constantly. A literalist of the Ibn Hazm persuasion would likely therefore feel obligated to declare a caliphate before all else. That the caliph would have to satisfy all requirements, including being Qurayshi, is an obvious requirement of Dhahiri lit-eralism.

Ibn Hazm's rulings on this topic may have played a small part in provoking the Islamic State's caliphate declaration in 2014. Long be-fore Baghdadi's pronouncement, the conditions for a valid caliphate had existed, and the Dhahiris knew it. They noted that the caliphal *mise-en-place* was ready, Musa said, and his teacher, Yahya Abu Has-san (whom English-speaking Dhahiris revered as "something of a leader"), began preaching about the declaration of a caliphate as a matter of religious obligation—not merely a good thing to do, but a requirement of Islam.

"[Yahya and I] were talking about Mindanao," Musa told me. "In theory, if one could take power in a certain area and find someone who is a valid *khalifah,* it would be a duty to establish the *khilafah.* This is true even if the *Dawlah* says 'We're going to establish *khilafah* after two weeks.' No. If you can establish it tomorrow, establish it tomorrow. This is your duty." Musa does not say that he planned to do such a thing, and he does not say he had a potential caliph ready. You don't just find a Filipino Muslim with proven Qurayshi ancestry hanging around the food court at the Davao City mall. But he and his teacher contemplated the potential effect of a rival claim. In theory, there cannot be two caliphates; the first would always supersede the second. But the mention of a potential rival caliphate might scare Baghdadi and speed up his plans. "Yahya thought [a potential rival caliphate] could push them to do what they are supposed to do anyway."

Yahya and others, already in Syria, spoke quietly to those in power and said they were ready to take up arms against Baghdadi if he delayed any further. The prospect of a caliphate weighed on the minds of jihadists, and they worried that two dueling caliphates would be worse than none. Yahya and his allies prepared a letter to the emirs of the ISIS provinces, airing their displeasure at the failure to appoint a caliph. "Yahya was like *this* with ʿAdnani [ISIS's spokesman]," Musa said, pressing his fingers together. Weeks before Baghdadi's Mosul speech, Yahya approached ʿAdnani, meeting him in person near Aleppo and warning him that Baghdadi would be in a state of sin if he did not promote himself to *khalifah* immediately. ʿAdnani replied with good news—that a caliphate had already been declared secretly, months before, and that the public announcement would come soon. Yahya shared the update with Musa, who leaked word of a caliphate declaration on Facebook, to skeptical but excited followers.

The figure of Yahya—an English-speaking convert within ISIS, with a direct line to ʿAdnani and enough cojones to challenge Baghdadi to a death match—intrigued me. But Musa didn't elaborate on his identity and used only his *kunya*, or teknonymic alias: Yahya, father of Hassan. He mentioned that Yahya had fallen into bad luck recently, and was being held captive by the Free Syrian Army, one of the secular rebel groups fighting ISIS and Bashar al Assad. Musa didn't, or wouldn't, say more.

He didn't need to. In 2015, a pro–Islamic State Twitter user going by the name Swordsman wrote to me and advised me to contact "Abu Yahya" to learn more. The name resembled Yahya Abu Hassan's closely enough to lead me to believe he was the same person Musa had mentioned. The Twitter user identified him as Greek. "He is on the field [in the war zone] also and part of the IS," the Twitter user wrote. "A great mind and a trustworthy student."

He then shared a link to a website called *Ghuraba'*, a collection of Dhahiri writings by Musa and a few others—including a "Yahya al-Bahrumi." In fluent Arabic and English, Yahya wrote prolifically about many subjects, all in the cause of jihad. He projected calm in his most grotesque opinions. He wore the label *irhabi* ("terrorist") with pride:

> For years past, the kuffar [infidels] have ascribed Muslims with irhab [terror] and, for years, Muslims have sought to shake this nomenclature (often for reason of comfort in dealing with the kuffar). This word ("terrorist") has also been cast as an insult and has been received as such. But irhab itself is something notable scholars have declared obligatory and supported verbatim by the Qur'an itself.

He called for emigration to the Islamic State: "Allah's Messenger even lifted his protection from any Muslim who lives among the disbelievers," he said. (In one of the early Muslim raids on infidel territory, Muslim fighters accidentally killed Muslims who were living outside Muslim territory. They asked the Prophet what to do about this collateral damage, and he said, "I am innocent of their blood.") Yahya wrote:

Allah rejects the wilāyah [allegiance] of those yet to emigrate, a man in dār al-kufr [infidel territory] claiming that giving him the bayʿah [pledge] is obligatory is in direct contradiction to this ayah [verse]; we seek refuge with Allah from such disgrace. . . . The khalifah [caliph] will not be found except among the ranks in jihad or those in open preparation for it.

This disgrace—not making *hijrah* and waging jihad—was a form of apostasy.

Call me extreme, but I would imagine that all of those who willingly choose to live among those with whom Muslims are at war are themselves at war with Muslims—and as such, are not actually Muslims.

Get out if you can—not only in support of your brothers and sisters whom your taxes have been killing, but also to protect yourselves from the punishment Allah has ordained for those who betray the nation.

He called for the death of Muslim leaders who do not institute ISIS-style Shariah:

As for [. . .] dealing with the current situation of political leaders using other than the sharia in their governing of nations and whether or not this constitutes kufr [disbelief], then the answer should be apparent. The response, whether or not it includes takfīr [excommunication] (though the conditions must be met), should be to command virtue and forbid vice, and that can and must include the overthrow of tyrannical regimes—whether those regimes are Muslim or not.

We should recognize that anyone who opposes the Khalifah after his khilafah is established must present his full proof for judgment or be quiet. Otherwise, he is a renegade whose blood is permissible.

Among the worst apostates, he said, were Muslims who neglected the duty of establishing *khilafah* and instead busied themselves with masturbatory discussion of minor issues such as whether kangaroo is halal, or how to go to the bathroom in the ideal Islamic way. These, he said, were stalling tactics to avoid the real business of Islam, which was jihad on behalf of a Muslim state.

> Who are you to criticize anyone for establishing the Khilafah when you found no opportunity to do it yourself?! You claim you were not consulted? Our men, women and children have been bleeding for decades (at least) because of your inaction, because of your endless talks, because of your focus on menstrual blood and "how to perform Hajj correctly," because you lacked the courage to initiate this obligation; or merely because you lacked the actual knowledge of what the Khilafah entails and how its conditions are understood.

In dozens of articles posted over years on the *Ghuraba'* site, Yahya demonstrated knowledge of classical Arabic and familiarity with Islamic sources and history. His Arabic was stunning even to Musa. Musa told me that another Muslim in their Internet discussion group once challenged Yahya's leadership. "Then Yahya did something that shocked us all. He responded to the guy in traditional Arabic poetry that he devised off the top of his head, using the guy's name in the poetry, explaining the situation and answering his objections," Musa says. "I was just taken aback. The guy exited the conversation and never spoke up again."

Like Musa, Yahya bore marks of autodidacticism and was supremely self-confident. Most disturbing, his calm was justified: he knew his texts better than his opponents, and his readings of them—

while unusual—followed a harsh but undeniable logic. For any claim, he could spout textual support, and for any counterclaim, he could undercut the argument with a rhetorical sweep of the leg.

But I still didn't know who this strange figure was. The website included a narrative biography and a small photo. Yahya's mug shot shows a bespectacled young man with a Kalashnikov over his shoulder. He is dressed for cold weather, as if in preparation for a night raid or patrol. He is smiling, and when I saw him I asked myself when I last saw someone looking so content.

As for the biography itself, nearly every word showed signs of careful selection, including his name, "Bahrumi," a neologism. "Bahrumi" is not an Arabic word. It is a portmanteau of two Arabic words: *bahr* [sea] and *rumi* [Roman]. The Roman Sea is the sea Romans called Our Sea, or *Mare Nostrum*. Jihadists often choose noms de guerre that consist of their first names plus their national origin. He called himself Yahya the Mediterranean.

The biography continued:

> Abū Ḥassān Yaḥyā ibn Sharaf ibn ʿAṭāʾ ibn al-Ḥārith al-Ḥuwayrithī. His roots are from the island of Crete in the Roman sea (Baḥr al-Rūm). Born in 1404 [A.D. 1983–4] and raised as a Nazarene [Christian], Yahya then entered Islam in 1422 [A.D. 2001–2]. He traveled seeking knowledge and work in the path of Allah until Allah granted him hijrah to Sham. He now resides in the countryside of Aleppo.

He used only the Islamic calendar. For his full name he gave not only the *kunya* (Abū Ḥassān, father of Hassan) but his patrilineal descent, "son of Sharaf, the son of ʿAtaʾ," et cetera. "Nazarene" for "Christian" conforms to IS nomenclature. (The letter *nun* ن for Nazarene was painted on abandoned Christian houses in Mosul, to mark them as fair game for confiscation.) The transliteration of Arabic words studiously observed standard diacritical markings.

So perhaps he was Greek after all—and from Crete. Now I thought I had enough data to narrow down his identity: a philologically inclined Cretan jihadi convert to Dhahirism. The list of candidates could not be long.

Converts often choose Arabic names that are the equivalent of their birth names. Yahya is Arabic for John in English or Ioannis (Ιωάννης) in Greek, so I began searching online for Dhahiris with these names. I rapidly found a reference to a Dhahiri "Ioannis Georgilakis," and here the trail began to sizzle under my feet. Georgilakis's Facebook page showed photos of the same hirsute young man with glasses, dressed in Muslim garments and playing with his kids. The eldest of these must have been Hassan, whose birth had made Ioannis "Abu Hassan."

The name presented a few clues. The suffix -akis in Greek is Cretan. His first name is formal and stilted—Ioannis, the form that would be intoned at a christening, say, instead of the more relaxed day-to-day version Γιάννης (Yannis). Was the Greek an affectation? Many of his Facebook friends were English-speakers, and few were Greek. "Georgilakis" isn't an especially common surname even in Crete, and given Yahya's apparent creativity in self-naming, I tried a few permutations, including the English "John," and the vanilla, non-Cretan Greek version of "Georgilakis," which would be "Georgelas."

One of the first hits for "John Georgelas" was an August 15, 2006, press release from the FBI. "Supporter of Pro-Jihad Website Sentenced to 34 Months," it crowed. Yahya was an American. At the time of his conviction he lived in the suburbs of Dallas, twenty minutes' drive from the house where I grew up.

YAHYA THE AMERICAN

The pure products of America
go crazy—
      —William Carlos Williams, "To Elsie" (1923)

A good movie for me is one in which the enemy says
something that makes sense.
    —Anne Carson, *The Beauty of the Husband* (2001)

Plano, Texas, is a short drive from downtown Dallas, toward the Oklahoma border. Two decades ago, the Plano of my youth was a flatland of middle-class subdivisions, expanding with the inevitability of a prophesied caliphate. Dallas's old money and its oilmen rarely stopped there. They preferred to drive past it en route to the grassy ranchland where they could shoot, fish, and nap on a porch while listening to the breeze rustle the cottonwoods. Since then, new money—especially immigrants—has arrived; the newcomers have immigrated for tech jobs and share few of these rustic pursuits. Instead they added houses to the rolling pastures, and the subdivisions multiplied. Tolstoy wrote that happy families are all alike. If their houses are also alike, then the infinitely reproduced and indistinguishable mansions of Plano are a sign that God has smiled on this land.

John Georgelas's last known address in this country is an elegant brick house with white Doric columns, a small portico, and a circular driveway. In August 2015, when I first drove up, I could hear the happiness of children. I saw a boy, who looked about ten, bouncing a basketball in the driveway and two others playing nearby. As I approached the front door, I spied a yellow-ribbon decal ("We support our troops") in the window, and behind it a foyer, tidy and richly decorated, and a piano festooned with family photos.

The man who answered the door was Timothy Georgelas, John's father and the owner (with his wife, John's mother, Martha) of the house. Both parents are Americans of Greek ancestry, and when I learned the father's name, yet another element of Yahya's biography made sense. "Timothy" derives from the Greek Τιμόθεος (Timotheos), "honoring God." Yahya called himself "Yahya, son of Sharaf," abbreviating Timothy to Tim—"honor," or *sharaf* in Arabic. *Huwayrithi,* the last in his chain of names, took longer to figure out. It is a diminutive Arabic noun from *harith,* or "reaper": "small reaper." That turns out to be a rough translation of "Georgelakis." The suffix "-lakis" is a Cretan diminutive, and "George" is from γεώ- (geo) for "earth" and -έργ (erg) for "work": small workers of the soil, or small reapers.

Tim, sixty-five, is a West Point graduate and radiologist. He has a full head of gray hair and soft features that betray no sign of the stress of having raised the most prominent American member of the Islamic State. He has, however, no illusions about the life his son has chosen. "He and John [Yahya] are enemies," I was told by someone who knows them both, "until the Day of Judgment."

Tim wore shorts and a T-shirt, and a crisp draft of air conditioning escaped as he said good morning. When I told him I had come to ask about Yahya Abu Hassan ibn Sharaf, he stepped outside and shut the door as if to seal off the house from his own son's name. He slumped in a white wicker chair by the front door, and with a reluctant gesture, he invited me to sit across from him.

He stared at the magnolia tree in the front yard and said nothing. I told him what I knew—that his son John was Yahya, a longtime jihadist now working for the Islamic State in Syria. Tim pursed his lips, and with a shake of the head began to speak. "Every step of his life he's made the wrong decisions, from high school onward," Tim said. "It is beyond me to understand why he threw what he had away." Yahya's two sisters have both earned doctorates, he added, as if to demonstrate that it wasn't failed parenting that led his only son to drop out of school, wage holy war on two continents, nearly achieve martyrdom in Syria, and plot mass murder.

"I think we were too easy on him," Tim told me. "He was always the youngest kid in the class, and always a follower. I have bailed him out so many times—financially, in circumstances with his wife and kids, you name it. I always pick up the wreckage." (The children I had seen playing were three of John's four sons. The youngest was still an infant.)

The Yahya Tim described to me was a sad figure, a sheep who had strayed into a wicked flock. Above all, he was easily manipulated. Tim did not know—or did not want to know—that Yahya had shapeshifted from sheep to wolf, from pathetic follower to leader of men.

Relatively few Americans have made *hijrah* to the Islamic State—only hundreds, compared to thousands from Europe and tens of thousands from the Arab world—and the numbers are not going up fast. According to FBI director James Comey, the number of Americans traveling to Syria fell from six to ten per month in early 2015 to just one per month by mid 2016.[1] Many are Americans of recent foreign extraction, some of whom have spent more time in the countries of their parents' birth than in their own. The number who were raised in America, with no recent ties to another country, is tiny. John Georgelas's facility with technology (one area in which he has never struggled) and his command of Islamic State doctrine have made him dangerous and useful. We know he has been close to the group's chiefs and has fought and been wounded in Syria. Some of those careful, pedantically accurate transliterations of Arabic words in *Dabiq* are John's handiwork, and by the middle of 2016 he had become the Islamic State's leading English-language polemicist.[2]

The parallels between Yahya and another American jihadist, John Walker Lindh, are striking. Lindh joined Al Qaida before September 11, 2001, and went to Afghanistan to fight as a member of Al Qaida's Ansar brigade. In November 2001, United States Special Forces plucked him barely alive from a pile of rubble near Mazar-e Sharif, Afghanistan. After being nursed to health, Lindh stood trial in Northern Virginia and pled guilty to aiding a terrorist group. His timing was either lucky or unlucky: he was caught, and not killed, when he was still young and naive. The judge gave him twenty years, and if his good behavior continues, Yahya Lindh (as he now calls himself) will be free in 2019, at the age of thirty-eight.

Lindh, like Georgelas, was raised in privilege, though in a politically opposite milieu: Lindh's father, Frank, is a gay leftist lawyer in San Francisco, and Tim Georgelas a conservative Republican. Frank defends his son as a prisoner of conscience. "They're political prisoners!" he told me, referring to John's fellow residents of the Terre Haute penitentiary.[3] (Their consciences have led some of them to try to blow up the Lincoln Tunnel.)

Before he converted to Islam, Lindh's hobbies included posting to Internet forums about rap music while pretending to be an angry black man.[4] After Lindh's conversion—precipitated by viewing the Spike Lee film *Malcolm X*—his studies inclined toward Salafism, and ultimately jihad. Like Georgelas, Lindh had no military training—George W. Bush ridiculed young John as a "Marin County hot-tubber"—and felt called to scholarship. He has spent his sentence studying Islam.

The prison where Lindh is incarcerated prevents him from reading the fatwas of Islamic State scholars. I know, because I have tried to send him Georgelas's writing, only to have it returned to me, undelivered, due to the prison's ban on subversive material. Lindh nonetheless thanked me for the attempt.

I asked him his opinion on the Islamic State, and he replied cautiously:

> As you can probably imagine, I am somewhat isolated from the outside world, so I don't think it would be appropriate for me to comment. . . . Considering the attention that the Islamic State has attracted from the media, academics, researchers, and others over the past couple of years, it is striking to me how few appear to have actually visited the Islamic State to see how things really are there and to meet and interview its leaders. I would like to suggest that you visit the Islamic State yourself so that you can pose your questions directly to its officials and leaders.[5]

I told him I would love to go, with their permission, but I didn't trust them not to behead or enslave me.

> I understand your concern about being killed or enslaved, however I believe that your apprehensions are misplaced. Those journalists who have been taken into custody by the authorities of the Islamic State travelled there illegally. Had they gone with the proper documentation, I am confident that the authorities of the Islamic State would have honored their covenants, as required by Islamic law.[6]

I asked him a few more questions about Islam. Eventually he stopped replying and referred me to a colleague whose opinion he trusted: Ahmad Musa Jibril, the Palestinian-American cleric featured on the King's College terrorism researchers' list of the "new spiritual authorities" to whom foreign fighters in Syria look for guidance.

More than a decade in prison appeared to have the same effect on Lindh that thirty-four months in prison were to have on Georgelas: not a softening of jihadism but confirmation of it.

In December 1983, John Georgelas was born into a rich white family with a long military tradition. His grandfather, Col. John Georgelas, was wounded twice in the Second World War and worked for more than a decade on the Joint Chiefs of Staff before founding a successful construction business in northern Virginia.[7] Col. Georgelas's son Tim spent seven years in the U.S. Army, then accepted an Air Force commission to attend medical school. ("The same medical school as Nidal Hasan," the Fort Hood shooter, he told me.) Tim retired as a colonel in 2001 and now practices privately in a north Dallas breast-imaging clinic. He dotes on Martha, a short, dark-haired housewife whose Facebook photo shows her standing proudly in front of the George W. Bush Presidential Library, near downtown Dallas.

The Georgelases moved frequently, as Tim's military assignments required. John entered school at the age of four, while the family was living in England, and he was young and small for his class. He was sickly—he grew benign tumors and had brittle bones—and his infirmities may have pushed him toward religion. When he was eleven, his leg shattered, and he spent a long time out of school, recuperating at the family's home back in San Antonio. Lonely and depressed, his mind turned to God in idle moments, and he became attached to the Greek Orthodox Church, which he hounded his family into attending more regularly.

As the family's male heir and youngest child, John enjoyed a special status in the Georgelas patriarchy. With it came expectations, and therefore disappointment when it became clear he was unsuited for the soldier's life. His body refused to grow into robust, battle-ready form. His temperament wasn't suited for discipline. When he returned to school after his leg injury, he had little interest in academic achievement or following rules—especially the kind of rules common in schools with large numbers of children from military families. His father tried repeatedly to correct his behavior and failed.

John's rebellion took numerous forms, and like many a military brat before him, he experimented with the counterculture. As a teenager, he smoked pot, dropped acid, and ate magic mushrooms. He hated his father for punishing his drug use and hated the U.S. government for criminalizing it. By the time he graduated from Air Academy High School, a public school on the grounds of the U.S. Air Force Academy, in Colorado Springs, his primary interest was the voracious consumption of psychedelics. His grades were miserable, Tim says, but his standardized test scores were higher than those of his high-achieving sisters. John ended up studying philosophy at Blinn College, an open-admission junior college in central Texas. He passed only a few classes.

But he showed intellectual ability: he taught himself to program and built his own computers running the Linux operating system, not the Windows or Mac machines favored by the masses. When he was fifteen, he presented his mother with a birthday wish list that prompted a magnificent harvest of gifts, nearly all books. Hoping to encourage his intellectual development, she bought him a Koran, in a translation by Muhammad Marmaduke Pickthall. Later, in a class on world religions at Blinn, the instructor's cursory lecture on Islam annoyed him, so John sought more information from local Muslims.

Curiosity turned to something more. "I don't hate Muslims," Tim told me, giving the standard preamble to anti-Islam comments. "But I sure hate the religion for what it did to my son." A few days before Thanksgiving 2001, on the first day of Ramadan, John converted at a mosque in College Station frequented by foreign Muslim students from Texas A&M.

Western jihadists find their way to violence by many different routes, but they often fit a broad profile. And that profile fit John like a wetsuit. He came from a middle- or upper-middle-class family; he squandered opportunities commensurate with his innate talent; he recognized that he would not excel in the fields chosen or glorified by his parents and authority figures. Often, a personal crisis—a death in the family, a near-death experience of one's own—triggers existential contemplation, and the meaning-seeking behavior that leads one to religion; in John's case, his childhood frailty might have filled that role.[8] Jihadists are also overwhelmingly left-brained, analytic types. (Musa was studying history at a Melbourne university prior to his arrest. But before his jihadism rendered him borderline unemployable, he worked as a computer security technician.[9])

Whether the conversion was meant to spite his parents, or whether that spite was just an ancillary benefit of his spiritual salvation, it's not possible to say. Nor do we know whether he immediately embraced violent jihadism. But the timing is suggestive. When John finally uttered the Muslim declaration of faith, the ashes of the World Trade Center had barely cooled. Anti-Muslim sentiment in America was reaching new highs, and in central Texas, conversion to Islam would have been a singular act of rebellion, a great glob of hawked-up spit in the eyes of his dad and other authority figures.

John, now known as Yahya, found his parents' lack of curiosity about his conversion insulting. His parents found the conversion itself an insult and a sign of mental weakness. "Every university town in this country has a mosque for one reason," Tim told me. "Kids are away from home for the first time, vulnerable and subject to influence. They hear the message and they're hooked, and that's what happened to John." Yahya quit classes and sold his pickup truck to buy a plane ticket. In December 2001, the family received an email from Yahya announcing that he was in Damascus learning Arabic.

He acquired Hans Wehr's *Dictionary of Modern Written Arabic,* a cuboid volume that is the standard Arabic-English reference work. It is not meant to be read straight through. The typical student of Arabic keeps the Hans Wehr on a corner of his desk and consults it as needed for the rest of his natural life. Yahya memorized it in six months. Then, as a chaser, he memorized *Kitab al ʿAyn,* the ninth-century dictionary of Arabic by al Khalil al Farahidi. He wandered through Damascus, chatting up everyone and learning classical Arabic to a level of proficiency rarely achieved even by educated native Arabic speakers. Here was a task, like building his own computers, that he could accomplish at his own pace, with his own tools, and whose attainment was wholly his own, rather than the result of blindly following his father or his professors.

When he arrived in Damascus, Yahya identified as Sufi, perhaps as a holdover from his counterculture teens. Gradually, though, under the influence of British Muslims who were more rigid in their approach to the faith, he became jihad-curious. They convinced him to follow a Bin Ladenist, Salafi approach instead. Yahya objected to mainstream imams' tendency to tell him to trust the words of scholars ("make *taqlid*"), and not to attempt his own interpretation of scripture and law. Typically Muslim laymen are advised not to derive legal rulings on their own, and instead to follow more experienced scholars. But Yahya maintained a typically American can-do attitude toward his religion, similar to the one many Texans adopt toward their trucks: if he couldn't understand or fix it himself, it didn't feel like his.

He drifted further from his parents and sisters. Later, when counseling other Muslims about how much effort to put into proselytization at home, versus heading directly to the Islamic State, Yahya wrote:

> What about those [Muslims] who are trying to work on their families, but their families insist on kufr [disbelief in Islam]? Should they wait their whole lives in patience, trying to guide someone whom Allah has not chosen for guidance, or should they move on and help their true family: the Muslims?

In the *Symposium,* one of Plato's speakers imagines that each pair of lovers once shared a single body—two heads, four arms, four legs, all awkwardly stuck together—until the gods split them apart. They then wandered, longing for their lost partners, feeling completeness only when reunited. That feeling is love.

This quaint infidel vision may explain the tempestuous romance between Yahya and his wife, two people made, by Zeus or Allah, from the same physical and mental material. Tania Choudhury was born in London in 1983 to British-Bangladeshi parents. Like Yahya, Tania grew up riddled with benign tumors and incorrigibly rebellious. Like many other first-generation British Muslims, she tormented her parents first by doing drugs, and then by adopting with alarming vigor the religion they had neglected in the pursuit of an assimilated English middle-class existence. When she was seventeen, to the astonishment of her family, she draped herself in a full-body covering or *jilbab.* At nineteen, when she married Yahya, she fantasized about packing a bomb under it.

She was a pretty girl, a petite firecracker of mischief. But the mischief would not be the usual disobedience, like dating boys her parents didn't approve of. When her parents suggested that she try to meet boys, Tania hissed that "Muslims don't date," and swore that until marriage no strange man would know anything more of her physical appearance than its cloaked outline. She had a type. Her ideal suitor, the Bieberian heartthrob she swooned over with friends, was John Walker Lindh.

The romance with Yahya began through a Muslim matrimonial site. In some ways their digital courtship was the stuff of banner ads—shared interests, true love, marriage and kids—but in other ways it is the sort of thing Match.com or eHarmony would prefer to keep out of their promotional material. The two fell in love fast, and just as couples might bond over Netflix or jogging or cooking, they bonded over jihad and a shared capacity for bad decisions. After a month of digital flirtation, Yahya flew to London, and they met in person on March 15, 2003. Within three days they married secretly. Tania's family figured out they had wed and told her she had thrown away her life. But they relented, concluding that the scion of a wealthy American family might not be the worst their daughter could do.

After a few weeks in London, Yahya and Tania left for College Station. In Texas they partook of the pleasures of freedom, young love, independence from family, and in Tania's case, from the strictures of a respectable English life. They lived cheaply and happily, embracing as their community the foreign Muslim students at the mosque where Yahya had converted. The mosque threw them a wedding party, and rich Gulf Arabs around the university kicked in money to support Yahya's study of Islam.

The couple indulged, too, in their other shared passion, which was getting high. Islamic orthodoxy considers cannabis an intoxicant, and therefore forbidden. Yahya's practice of Islam was heterodox even then. He rebelled, as usual, in a scholarly way. In a historical essay entitled "Cannabis," heavily footnoted with classical Arabic sources, he made the Islamic case for pot:

> This paper was prepared to counter the claim that cannabis, the plant that produces the oft-smoked product known commonly as *hashishah* [حشيشة] in the East or *kif* [كيف] in the Maghrib, should be forbidden due to its use as an intoxicant. This paper will show, beyond any possible interpreted doubt, that cannabis was not only legal according to the earliest ages of Islam, but it was used to a great extent in Muslim society without harm. . . . The plant should not be forbidden, due to its firstly being a natural creation of Allah without explicit directive for prohibition in the revelation and secondly being a great source of many materials and medicinal uses.

There is evidence, he wrote, that early Islamic leaders taxed hemp. Since Muslims cannot tax forbidden substances, such as pork or alcohol, then they must have considered pot permissible. The Prophet never forbade pot by name, even though it was a substance known to early Arabs and, presumably, to Muhammad himself.

As for psilocybin: A hadith mentioned by Yahya describes the Prophet's having descended from a mountain after meditation and extolled the medicinal properties of mushrooms—particularly as a cure for diseases of the eye. Yahya and Tania took this to mean that God had sanctioned the ingestion of psychedelic mushrooms. Their claim is not as crazy as it sounds: the hadith also says the mushroom turned blue—and a tendency to turn blue when bruised is an indicator that a mushroom has mind-altering properties.[10] So the young lovers blissed out under the Texas skies, shrooming after the example of the Prophet himself.

Tania's Facebook page identified her as "Tania Internationalhobo," and the early years of their marriage generated frequent flyer miles if little paying work. Yahya and Tania lived furtively in Damascus for an extended honeymoon, quietly associating with other jihadists. Their existence mirrored that of many young terrorist tumbleweeds of yesteryear: Black Panthers, Baader-Meinhof gangsters, fin-de-siècle anarchists. They hid from the authorities and lied to anyone who inquired about their activities. When Syrian government spies started asking neighbors about them, they moved on, settling briefly in a town selected because it was prophesied to be the headquarters of the Prophet 'Issa [Jesus] upon his return.

Tania and Yahya often quarreled. Still strong-willed, she wanted to obey only God. But God's words were unequivocal: *Men are in charge over women,*[11] says a Koranic verse that echoes what John Georgelas might have heard in a conservative Christian household. So for most of the ten years before the founding of the Islamic State, Yahya maintained a Rasputin-like control over Tania. He mesmerized her with his confidence, and she repressed her own misgivings whenever she found herself questioning him. Tania has mild dyslexia; Yahya's reading of Islamic texts convinced her, with its fluency and recall and breadth, that he could produce an unanswerable argument about any point on which they disagreed.

As a sickly child, Tania, too, had contemplated God, and had strong views about salvation. She determined that Yahya was a genius with gifts God had denied her, and she accepted her place in the world of jihad. Service to Yahya was her ticket to heaven. She endorsed slavery, apocalypse, polygamy, and killing. She aspired to raise seven boys as holy warriors—one to conquer each continent.

From Syria they returned to London. It was then, and perhaps still is, the world capital for certain types of loudmouth jihadists—the types to have been exiled from their home countries, less often for their odious political views than because they simply would not shut up.

The most colorful characters from that milieu became nationally and then internationally famous for yelling outrageous things. Any journalist wishing to find an angry Muslim to voice an opinion incompatible with liberal values or free expression need only linger outside the Finsbury Park or Brixton mosques and ask the men filing out after prayers if they spoke English and had strong views about, say, Salman Rushdie or the intentional encrustation of the Koran with dog shit by anti-Islam provocateurs. This exercise efficiently screened out all but the wackos and the publicity hounds, some of whom still grace cable-news shows today.

From this menagerie of goons, Yahya chose to follow a Jordanian named Muhammad bin ʿIssa bin Musa al Rifaʿi, known to his followers as Abu ʿIssa. Born in 1959 in the city of Zarqa (whose other hometown jihadist hero is Abu Musʿab al Zarqawi), Abu ʿIssa had fought the Soviets in Afghanistan in the 1980s and circulated among

Maqdisi's jihadist set in Jordan during the early 1990s. In the 1990s, after a prison stint in his home country, he returned to Afghanistan and fought again, this time under the banner of a group called Jama'at al Muslimin (the Group of Muslims).

In all these respects, his jihadist résumé was unremarkable. But Abu 'Issa was special: he was descended from the tribe of Quraysh. Once his pedigree became known, his followers in Afghanistan advanced him as a candidate for caliph, and on April 3, 1993, they swore loyalty to him and created what the French scholar Kévin Jackson calls "the forgotten caliphate," an unsuccessful precursor of the Islamic State.

Abu 'Issa's base during that period was the Pakistan-Afghanistan border. In the 1980s and 1990s, Peshawar, the capital of Pakistan's North-West Frontier Province, served as a proving ground for jihadists, and many present-day jihadists once fought there or supported the fighters who did. In the 1980s, Bin Laden spread his wealth around by paying Arab jihadists to fight the Soviets, and 'Abdullah 'Azzam, the Palestinian jihadist who mentored Bin Laden, was assassinated there in 1989. Even the Blind Sheikh showed up. So many factions arose, particularly on the Pakistani side, that the defining characteristic of the region's jihadists came to be disunity. Abu 'Issa's caliphal claim was intended to bind the factions together.

It did not succeed. "The announcement of the caliphate created a strong reaction against him," Jackson, the French scholar, told me. "They were ridiculed by other jihadis."[12] For all the reasons that Al Qaida today rejects the Islamic State, its predecessors then rejected Abu 'Issa. Few wanted to surrender their power to him, and when he phrased his offer of leadership as a demand, they responded with mockery and then force.

Abu 'Issa consolidated control of his microcaliphate in Afghanistan's Kunar province. There he embraced many practices that the Islamic State would later realize on a larger scale. These include the abolition of infidel currency (the Islamic State's official specie is a locally minted gold dinar) and rejection of nationalism. The total area controlled did not extend beyond a few small towns, and the local Afghans despised Abu 'Issa and his followers. "These are the extreme fringe of the whole jihadi community," Jackson says. They mass-produced enemies. When Bin Laden came to Afghanistan in 1996, Abu 'Issa sent a message to demand his obedience. (There is no record of a reply.) Jackson's description of the microcaliphate fore-shadows some of Yahya's own heterodox views:

> Abu 'Issa issued "sad and funny" fatwas, as Abu al-Walid puts it, notably sanctioning the use of drugs. A nexus had been forged between [Abu 'Issa's group] and local drug smugglers. (The fatwa led one jihadist author to dismiss Abu 'Issa as the "caliph of the Muslims among drug traffickers and takfir.") Abu 'Issa also prohibited the use of paper cur-rency and ordered his men to burn their passports.[13]

In the late 1990s, when the Taliban took over Kunar, Abu 'Issa and his men relocated to London, and it was in that diminished state, preaching to a mostly skeptical jihadi intelligentsia about the obliga-tion of establishing a caliphate, that Yahya and Tania first encoun-tered them. Through Tania's contacts, they met a member of Abu 'Issa's group who styled himself the leader or emir of "the Emirate of Shepherd's Bush." They formally joined the group and gave alle-giance, or *bay'a,* to Abu 'Issa. The caliph himself lived in Maryle-bone, near the fictional home of Sherlock Holmes at 221B Baker Street. For a while, Yahya had the jihadist-dork dream job of tutoring the caliph's son in the subjects of computer hacking and martial arts.

A caliph without territory is not a caliph, though, and eventually Yahya abandoned Abu 'Issa. The Marylebone Caliphate controlled nothing—not even a street—and Abu 'Issa could not serve any Islamic society as caliph. Allegiance, or *bay'a,* takes the form of a contract: the caliph gives Islamic governance, and the subject gives obedience. So

if the caliph cannot deliver his end of the bargain, the contract dissolves and both revert to being ordinary, unpledged people.

What ultimately ended Yahya's association with Abu 'Issa was a
legal dispute. The two men agreed that the charging of interest [*riba*]
was forbidden in the Koran. They fell into discord, however, over
whether those who charge interest or allow it are full-blown apostates or merely sinful. Yahya believed the former, and Abu 'Issa disagreed so vehemently that he convened a meeting and publicly
dressed him down. Yahya and Tania dissolved their *bay'a* and left
London for Manchester. In early 2014, Abu 'Issa died after spending
most of his final years in prison in London.[14]

Yahya, meanwhile, had begun to find his intellectual calling. His time
with Abu 'Issa was not entirely misspent playing online and teaching
the caliph's son roundhouse kicks. At a bookshop in London, before
joining Abu 'Issa, Yahya had found a copy of the works of Ibn Hazm.
Abu 'Issa and his group knew Ibn Hazm's work, and during Yahya's
time with them, he grew more and more attracted to it. The Dhahiri
methodology outlined a legal and theological position that aligned
with Yahya's own logical disposition.

Throughout his life, Yahya had gravitated toward rationality and
mechanical systems. Computers did his bidding. Humans did not. In
his writings, he congratulates himself frequently for the rationality of
his positions, for his insistence on evidence for every claim. On his
personal website, he shared a couple lines of C++ computer code, a
geeky statement of his own hard-line stance:

```
if (1+1+1 != 1 && 1 == 1) return true; else die();
```

Translation: if you believe the Christian Trinity ("1+1+1") is
not monotheistic ("!= 1"), and if you believe in the unity of God
("1 == 1"), then great. Otherwise: die.

Yahya saw confirmation of the Dhahiri method everywhere he looked, even in the writings of Thomas Jefferson ("Laws . . . should be construed by the ordinary rules of common sense. Their meaning is not to be sought for in metaphysical subtleties which may make anything mean everything or nothing at pleasure").[15] He still read the Bible, too. "Remember 1 Corinthians 14:33: *For God is not the author of confusion*," he wrote in one posting. "Certainly, to claim that one must believe in a single God, while saying that God is three distinct persons, is a rather confusing statement."

"Then again," he continued, with Ibn Hazm–like sarcasm, "perhaps my mind is but corrupt by those dangerous diseases: rational thought and logic."

In September 2004, Yahya and Tania returned to the United States, continuing to rely financially on Yahya's parents. They settled briefly in Torrance, California, with Yahya hoping to find work as an imam. His jihadism disqualified him for mosque jobs, however, and increasingly the two sought only each other's spiritual camaraderie. Eventually they stopped frequenting mosques altogether, on the grounds that they were dens of spies.

In 2004, their first son was born in California. They intended to name him Muqatil, which means "killer" or "fighter" in Arabic. It is not a common Arabic name. In the end they settled on Hassan, after Hassan ibn Thabit, a poet and Companion of the Prophet. In English, they called him Michael, for the echo of Muqatil. Their baby needed a non-Muslim name, if he was going to be an international terrorist someday.

Yahya and Tania moved with Hassan back to Dallas, and a year later, Yahya took a job as a data technician at Rackspace, a server company based in Texas. At night, he prowled jihadist forums and offered tech support to Jihad Unspun, a Canada-based Islamist site widely thought to be a recruiting ground for would-be terrorists (and possibly a trap—a "honeypot"—that the authorities used to attract and bust them). During the day, too, Yahya looked for ways to use his position at Rackspace to wage jihad. On April 8, he accessed the password of a client, the American Israel Public Affairs Committee, with the intention of hijacking its website.

As hacking jobs go, it was amateurish. Rackspace found out, and the FBI, aware of Yahya's terror links, moved fast. A SWAT team showed up early in the morning. He and Tania were already awake for dawn prayers. Yahya surrendered peacefully and warned the officers that a child was sleeping inside and that his wife needed to get dressed. The FBI prosecuted him for hacking into a protected computer—this was the source of the Department of Justice press release I found earlier—and sent him away for thirty-four months.[16] He spent much of his term in a Seagoville, Texas, penitentiary. Prior to his arrest, he had planned to travel to Iraq to fight against the Americans, so prison may have saved his life.

Tim says Yahya's arrest caused marital friction of a new sort. With her husband in prison and studying Islamic texts full-time, Tania began asserting her independence. After receiving scowls from neighbors due to her Muslim dress, she told Yahya she planned to wear just a veil, and not a full-body cloak. Yahya, furious, demanded that she cover fully when she visited him in prison, to be sure no one would titter at the immodesty of the sheikh's wife. (He had Muslim acquaintances in prison and was the most scholarly among them.) He told her to leave infidel America to join the group known as the Nigerian Taliban, a predecessor to Boko Haram. She refused and threatened divorce.

But she never left him—even after he got out of prison and took a second wife, a Jamaican-British friend of Tania's. Tania did not approve but also didn't forbid the union. The new bride lived in London, and the groom could not travel without violating parole. Yahya investigated the Islamic legality of a marriage conducted across physical distance. He found precedent: Muhammad married Ramla bint Abi Sufyan, the widow of his brother-in-law, when she was in Ethiopia and he was in Mecca. The Prophet's marriage was contracted by letter. So Yahya and his second wife married over the phone, with Tania present and quietly fuming. (Yahya later divorced his second wife.)

About his crimes, he remained unrepentant. "He can justify anything he does, and he didn't think he did anything wrong," Tim says. "He is just full of himself." During his parole, Yahya stayed in Dallas, took tech jobs, and worked as an IT specialist for a shoe wholesaler. In August 2009, ten months after he left prison, a second child arrived and Yahya and Tania remained reasonably well behaved, though Yahya's colleagues at the shoe company report that the couple occasionally posted politically worrisome items on Facebook.

Among their enthusiasms, at this point, was the libertarian Republican presidential candidate Ron Paul, whose anti-government obsessions and isolationist foreign policy Yahya and Tania both found congenial. The Prophet had endorsed the gold standard, and so did Paul. Yahya and Tania liked pot, and the Libertarians were the closest thing to an anti-Prohibitionist party in the United States. And—finally—Paul's foreign policy suggested a possible disengagement with Israel. "You guys (meaning Americans) need to stop supporting democracy, and just make Ron Paul your king," Tania wrote, only half joking. Yahya wanted revolution. "Tyranny is here," he replied, "and the Tree of Liberty is thirsty."

On October 1, 2011, Yahya's parole expired, and he drove to Dallas–Fort Worth airport with his wife and two children, a free man. When their flight took off for London that day, he left America, for probably the last time. "Muslims in America," he wrote around then, "remember: Hijrah is always an option, and sometimes an obligation."

From London, they flew to Cairo. Since that February, the city had been friendly to Islamists. Hesham Elashry and Musa Cerantonio were broadcasting freely, and a pious long-bearded type could walk the streets without fear. Yahya and Tania lived there for the next three years, at first happily: their two boys turned out to be clever and precocious—YouTube videos show the younger one reading words in English, French, and Arabic before the age of two—and they were joined on Christmas Day 2011 by another boy. The family sailed fe-luccas on the Nile and savored life beyond the reach of the U.S. gov-ernment.

Yahya earned money by translating fatwas from the salaried reli-gious scholars of the government of Qatar. Ever allergic to human authority, he seethed at the banality of those fatwas and the govern-ment clerics' abject servitude to tyrants. None of the fatwas ever mentioned what he considered the core imperatives of Islam, such as the establishment of a caliphate and emigration from lands of disbe-lief. The scholars never discussed slavery or jihad, except to down-play them, and they relentlessly glorified the Qatari royal family. These fatwas were, Yahya claimed, based on *ra'i*—opinion, not evi-dence. In his spare time, he worked on a social-networking website based on the Islamic science of hadith.

Some of his writings from this period are theological, not juridical or political, and one can glimpse in them a subtle intelligence, less violent than it would become. In one essay, he propounded a curious Dhahiri metaphysical position, attributing to God a final attribute, beyond the ninety-nine names ("the merciful," "the avenging," "the majestic," etc.) accorded to him in mainstream Islam.[17] That final at-tribute is *dahr* [time], and Yahya's disquisition on it borders on the mystical:

> Do not curse time, for verily Allah (God): He (It) is time. (Sahih Muslim 5827)
>
> The word in Arabic used for "time" is الدهر Ad-Dahr. Its definition is akin to saying the "concept of time," not a mea-

sured quantity of the effects of time. . . . God being time explains His eternalness, being the First (Al-Awwal الأول) and also the Last (Al-Akhir الآخر), two more of Allah's 99 names in Islam. . . .

Logic necessitates the eternal nature of time, since one is unable to comprehend "before time was" or "after time ceases" since before and after (and past and future) are concepts necessitating time; therefore it is only logical to say the obvious: time is not bound by time; in fact, nothing is bound by itself but is rather bound by something other than itself . . . except time, since time binds everything else, from the rising of the sun, its setting, the coming of seasons, the passage of years, to the things we do, the things we say, what we remember, what we forget, our actions, our thoughts—all of these things are bound by time and that is inescapable. We are already slaves to time, we just need to recognize that and let time govern us. . . .

It is easier to move forward once we realize that Islam does not promote an anthropomorphic father-figure deity nor something that came in the flesh, nor a spirit in the wind or any of that sort. Time is far more deserving of praise and worship than any man, beast, plant, stone or celestial being, since all such things are governed by time.

A man of this temperament is but a few doobies away from a harmless, hippie version of Islam. But metaphysics held less interest than politics, and ultimately the call of jihad and *khilafah* was irresistible.

In Cairo, Yahya met jihadis and became locally respected for his scholarly rigor. One person who knew him then describes him as one of the strongest pre-ISIS pro-caliphate voices, and says the online seminars he conducted in Arabic and English did much to "prepare"

Westerners for the caliphate declaration that would come a few years later. Musa met him digitally, through Yahya's preaching, and has never met him in person. European jihadists even began traveling to Egypt to learn from him. He impressed one sheikh so much that the man declared that it would be sinful for Yahya to expose himself to danger on the battlefield in a conflict like Syria or Afghanistan. "You," he said, indicating Yahya—"your blood is haram [forbidden to spill]."

In his sermons and public statements, Yahya anticipated many of the themes of Islamic State propaganda, including distrust of Islamist movements that compromised their religion by partaking in secular politics. He criticized the government of Sudan, one of the more conservative Islamist regimes. "I doubt Sudan is actively implementing the Shariʿah," he told one friend, "since (a) they are a sectarian state and (b) they do not call for *ghazw* [invasions of non-Muslim territory] or the establishment of a Quraysh-led Khilafah, which are both integral parts of the Shariah."

When dozens died in riots across the Muslim world over the depiction of Muhammad in the short YouTube clip *The Innocence of Muslims,* Yahya stated unequivocally that the filmmaker should be killed, citing Ibn Hazm and Dawud al Dhahiri. Muslims must love their Prophet above all else, he wrote. "If your love for him has not grown to the level that you are willing to sacrifice your own life as well as the life of everyone you love for his sake, then I pray that Allah will put that love in your heart soon."

Yahya idolized Al Qaida's leaders, as he had since not long after his conversion. He considered them soldiers, not thinkers, and forgave their ideological shortcomings. When SEAL Team 6 assassinated Osama bin Laden on May 1, 2011, Yahya posted a solemn eulogy. He counseled Muslims never to speak of martyrs as "dead," at the risk of ceasing to be Muslims themselves. The eulogy quotes the same Koranic verse that inspired Islam Yaken at *istakharah* prayer. Its elegance comes in part from its never mentioning Bin Laden by name:

THOSE KILLED FOR ALLAH ARE ALIVE, NOT DEAD

It is haram [illegal, forbidden] to say the word "dead" when referring to any Muslim who was killed in the Path of Allah, and it is kufr [disbelief, ingratitude] to consider that person to be dead.

Regarding the prohibition against uttering the word "dead" or its translated equivalents, Allah said: *Do not say of those killed in the Path of Allah: "dead"; rather, "alive," but you do not perceive.* (2:154)

As for the disbelief of one who considers them to be dead, then Allah (exalted) said: *Do not consider those who were killed in the Path of Allah as dead; rather, they are alive, with their Lord, being given provision.* (3:169)

Tania, meanwhile, stood by her husband. "It's a real shame no one [in Cairo] is calling for a Qureshi [Qurayshi]-led khilafah," she told her friends. "Why don't Muslims want to see the return of the Islamic golden age?"

But in private she was becoming less thrilled with the idea of a return to Syria, and of dedicating her children's lives to violence. With each child Tania bore, her fervor waned. Yahya reminded her that the Koran judges harshly those who give up on *hijrah*. Angels will rip their souls from their mortal bodies and prepare them for judgment by God:

The angels will say, "In what [condition] were you?" [The wrongdoers] will say, "We were oppressed in the land." The angels will say, "Was not God's earth of spacious [enough] for you to emigrate therein?" For those, their refuge is Hell.[18]

In July 2013, Muhammad Morsi's government fell, and the Islamist moment in Egypt passed as quickly as it had arrived. Yahya and Tania fretted about the possible consequences for them as jihadis, and sought escape. Even as Yahya became more enthralled with the idea of *hijrah* and of running toward the fight, Tania began to demand comforts for the family. Musa, by now back in Australia and trading messages with Yahya, encouraged them to consider the southern Philippines. It turned out to be too rustic. "Look, I'm happy to be in, like, a mud hut," Yahya said to him. "But my wife is very specific and is asking you to take photos of houses." The houses were inadequate, so they scrapped that plan.

But the Syrian civil war had presented opportunities that Yahya couldn't decline. He wrote poetry in Arabic and English, and in a strange, unlovely mix of Arabic forms and English language. It frequently had a martial tone:

> Smite, indict the might: red, blue, white—
> tight, they benight, ignite the bight—
> The weak: bleak, meek, antique but right,
> lost, tossed across terminal zeit . . .
>
> Rise, cut ties: spies disguised in white,
> by the sword, for the Lord of Might
> Defeat the cheat, trite fleet of fright,
> by rod—by God!—by baud, by byte.

For years before the Islamic State's rise, Yahya had said his weapon of choice was the keyboard ("by baud, by byte"). Now that Syria was becoming the battlefield he had dreamed of, he was ready to take up other arms.

When they left Cairo, Yahya insisted on going to Turkey. It was a nominally Muslim country, and its proximity to Syria appealed to him. They arrived in Gaziantep, in southern Turkey, borne aloft by airline tickets supplied by Yahya's parents. But Tania doubted Yahya's intentions. She was pregnant again, and now that they would be living just a short drive from the Syrian border, she worried that Yahya would force them across. He promised that he would not. The trauma of having to flee Egypt—worrying that they would be locked up or worse—further soured her on jihad. She feuded with Yahya and suggested that he wait until their children were older before going to fight. Exhausted and browbeaten, she relented when he reminded her of her wifely obligation.

In August 2013, Yahya put his family on a bus and told them they were going on a trip. He did not reveal their destination until Tania (now five months pregnant) saw the Syrian border. Going across, they posed as Syrians. Yahya reassured Tania that they would meet a few friends and come right back. By then, the Assad government had lost control of large parts of northern Syria, and around Aleppo, factions were working with and against each other. The region had become an anarchic wasteland haunted everywhere by death.

They squatted in a villa, the abandoned residence of a Syrian general, in the town of A'zaz, a few miles inside the border. The windows had been shattered and the plumbing shut off, but the chandeliers were still hanging. Mujahedin groups controlled the territory: the emir of foreign jihadists was, for a time, Abdelhamid Abaaoud, the Belgian national who planned the November 2015 attack in Paris. Yahya spent days with his jihadi friends. He had known some of them only in an online fantasy life, and now they were comrades in arms.

Yahya's connections assured his family a meager supply of food. Tania and the children vomited and developed mysterious infections. She prepared herself for the possibility that government forces or other rebels would overrun their position. But she also still loved the rush, and was curious about the fighting nearby. She wanted to see the action, but because she was a woman, when she poked her head out the window, she was told to be sensible and get back inside. For the children's sake, she wanted to go back across the border.

When she complained to Yahya—"How could you do this to us?"—he cited a hadith: "War," he said, "is deception."[19]

Tania was no victim: she signed up for jihad, and she passed up nearly a decade of opportunities to ditch Yahya and take her kids somewhere—anywhere—far from his dreams of murder and mayhem. Yahya's spell over her was powerful. But she was at least as culpable as Patty Hearst (whose nickname as a member of the Symbionese Liberation Army was, oddly enough, "Tania"), since at least Yahya's wife hadn't been forced into the movement at the point of a gun. Tania loved to be a hellion, until the lives of her children made mischief too costly.[20]

Now her husband had referred to her as the enemy, and she had to contemplate being raped and murdered, and seeing her children sold into slavery. Ten years of this was enough. Tania demanded to take the kids back to Turkey. Yahya could not or would not join them: he had come to fight for ISIS, and he knew the penalty in the afterlife for retreating from the battlefield. But his kids were not mujahedin, so he let them go, with the assumption that the family would reunite when it was safe.

By September 2013, fighting had engulfed the border crossing where they had entered. One day at dawn, Tania and Yahya hired a vehicle to skirt that danger. They were dropped off elsewhere along the border, two hours away from the original crossing, in a grove of thorny trees. Amid signs warning that the area was sown with land mines, they walked for an hour. As they reached the border, a Syrian government sniper fired at them, the bullets kicking up dirt nearby, and the two adults dragged three puking children, a suitcase, and a stroller across the minefield, through a gap in the barbed wire, and into Turkey.

Tania had also begun experiencing contractions and leaking amniotic fluid. Yahya had arranged for a human trafficker to meet them, and when the trafficker's truck arrived, he paid him off with a few hundred dollars, then turned back to the border, again under gunfire, without saying goodbye or waving. The trafficker drove Tania and the kids a short distance into Turkey—then dropped them by the roadside, without food or water, and sped off with the money. Tania carried the children and luggage toward the nearest town. The day ended with the intercession of a stranger on a motorcycle who helped carry their things to a bus station and then to the airport. Tania's amniotic leak stopped spontaneously, and she spent the next weeks recovering in Istanbul and with family in London before returning to Dallas. Six months pregnant, she weighed ninety-six pounds.

Tania told friends that Yahya had promised not to join any terrorist groups and instead to work with British or American aid organizations. These promises were lies. After she left, Yahya trained as a soldier for several months and continued to tweet and write aggressively in favor of ISIS, though he was not yet in ISIS territory.

During combat in April 2014, a mortar blast sent shrapnel into his back, nearly severing his spine. "I was in immense pain," he wrote, "but I at least knew that my reward is with Allah and that comforted me greatly." The lack of medical care in Syria meant having to rush to an emergency room in Iskenderun, Turkey. To cross the border, he again pretended to be a Syrian civilian. After recovering for some time, he began to fear detection. "It would only be a matter of time before someone would inform the Turkish authorities that I was a muhajir [immigrant]," he wrote. Discovery would mean arrest. He went back to Syria, nursed his wounds, and received treatment from Adam Brookman, an Australian who went by the name Abu Sufyan and is now back in Australia and under arrest for alleged terrorism offenses. Yahya posted images of his suppurating wounds and of himself on bed rest, smiling.

Around this time, he began pestering ISIS's leaders—particularly 'Adnani—to declare a caliphate. When the declaration happened, Yahya was living near Aleppo, about a hundred miles from the Islamic State's capital, not far from 'Adnani's hometown of Binnish. "This is the moment I have been waiting [for] for years," he wrote, "and specifically in recent times since the war began between the Islamic State and the Ṣaḥawāt"—meaning the U.S.-backed Free Syrian Army (FSA). He immediately gave allegiance to the caliph and committed to emigrating to Raqqah.

The obstacles remained significant. He walked with crutches, and he had made a friend, a fellow foreigner with worse Arabic than his own, whom he refused to leave behind. Yahya's Arabic allowed him to pass for Syrian, but his friend's would blow their cover quickly. To make matters more urgent, his guarantor in the area—a fellow IS supporter who commanded a brigade and promised to protect him from the FSA—was killed unexpectedly.

On September 24, an FSA-linked group arrested him outside Aleppo, along with "Abu I.," the other foreigner. "Abu I. wore an explosive belt which caused commotion but he eventually took it off due to the presence of women and children," Yahya later wrote of his arrest. Yahya now pretended to be an innocent Greek, but incriminating pro–Islamic State tweets on his computer gave him away. So he stated that he had pledged to Caliph Abu Bakr al Baghdadi. His captors promised to kill him, then discovered his true nationality, at which point they may have plotted to sell him to the Americans. By the time they identified him, though, local Islamist groups (including the Al Qaida affiliate, Jabhat al Nusra) discovered that the FSA held a foreigner, and made it known that they would view the rendition of a *muhajir,* even a pro–Islamic State *muhajir,* to the Americans as an act worthy of reprisal.

Six months passed, and the FSA released Abu I. because they had no evidence that he had pledged to IS. Yahya and another prisoner, a pro-IS Syrian named Abu Subhi, remained locked up and hatched plans for escape. Their intentions were more grindhouse than Steve McQueen:

> We had a few other prisoners we could count on as long as we didn't tell them our full idea. That is, to them we were just going to take an officer captive, get the keys and run; or, take a hostage and negotiate our release. This went well with the others. Abū Ṣubḥī and I wanted a bit more though. We were thinking of taking as many hostages as possible, decapitating the unimportant ones, painting the walls with their blood, and executing any prisoners who deserved execution [for crimes such as blasphemy or adultery]. We had satellite internet and computers in the prison so we thought of recording everything and posting it online. . . .
>
> We had two perfect opportunities for this operation. The first time I wasn't certain so I signaled to Abū Ṣubḥī that we shouldn't go through with it. The second time I was sure but he wasn't. I kind of regret not doing it as we could have killed so many of these clear apostates and wicked excuses for humans. I just pray to Allah that when the [Islamic] State returns to that area these "people" will be executed.

In the end, Yahya was released anyway, on the condition that he renounce the Islamic State and work for the FSA. He lied about the first part and reneged on the second. After a few months of quietly calling local people around Aleppo to support the Islamic State, he burned his U.S. passport, hitched a ride in a fuel-smuggling truck, and in August 2015 finally arrived in Raqqah.

The injuries Yahya sustained in battle have qualified him for the Islamic State's equivalent of a Purple Heart and an exemption from military service. But even if he were healthy, the Islamic State's human resources office would have saved Yahya for other duties. His back may be mangled by shrapnel, but his mind is intact. He remains fluent both in the doctrine and culture of jihad and in the culture and language in which he was raised. It is no surprise, then, that Yahya is now the Islamic State's leading producer of high-end English-language propaganda and, recently, a prolific author for *Dabiq*. Yahya loves poetry, and he is now in the same line of work as another middle-American expatriate fascist polyglot, Ezra Pound—this time in the caliph's service rather than Il Duce's. Pound lived long enough to regret his treason; Yahya may not. As of his last known contact, in October 2016, armed drones were circling Raqqah for the sole purpose of eliminating people like him.

On December 8, 2015, Yahya's voice came through clearly on Al Bayan radio—the voice of the Islamic State. (Like all Bayan broadcasts, it recounted only good news from the Islamic State's military fronts: suicide operations that sent "Nusayri" [Alawite] soldiers fleeing; clashes between "Sahawat [anti–Islamic State Sunni] apostates" and "soldiers of the *Khilafah*.") He continued to tweet under pseudonyms. The profile photo for one Twitter account is a well-worn laptop, with a Browning 9mm semiautomatic handgun resting across the keyboard.

A few months later, *Dabiq* ran the first article that I have been able to confirm was written by Yahya. His subject was Western Muslims who, despite calling themselves Muslims, are infidels. The headline, "Kill the Imams of Kufr [Disbelief] in the West," was only marginally less grotesque than the accompanying imagery: crosshairs over images of Suhaib Webb (a prominent Boston imam), Nihad Awad (founder of the Council on American-Islamic Relations), and Hamza Yusuf (President of Zaytuna College, in Berkeley, California); pictures of various other Western Muslims; and an image of a crouching, blindfolded "apostate" at the moment an executioner's blade enters his neck. As for the text, it stressed the binary nature of Islam—

believer or infidel, 1 or 0. Yahya rehearses the many stories of Mu-hammad and his Companions' harsh treatment of Muslims who lapsed. Hands and feet are severed, eyes gouged out with nails, heads lopped off, and bodies stomped to death.

He names more Western Muslims, ponderously quoting back their words in support of "crusaders" and enemies of Islam.

> Shaytān [Satan], through his cunning and experience with kufr, has always tried to infiltrate the Ummah. . . . He learned all too well that to misguide Muslims, he need not make them change their names or reject the religion as a whole— a single ruling is sufficient.

Do not be fooled by titles, he writes, by eloquent speeches, or by attempts to compromise between the commands of God and the commands of secular governments.

> Venomous imāms have maintained their disunity over Islam while uniting upon Western interests. They are found spout-ing Sūfī and "Salafī" slogans, calling to their madhāhib [legal schools] and "'ulamā'" [scholars], yet reinterpreting any-thing the scholars that even they recognize said about the concepts of tawhīd [monotheism], jihād, walā' [loyalty to Muslims], and barā' [disavowal of infidels] to make them compatible with Western ideology.

One road leads to salvation. And on the way, one should kill any wayward imams one meets:

> One must either take the journey to dār al-Islām [the abode of Islam], joining the ranks of the mujāhidīn therein, or wage jihād by himself with the resources available to him (knives, guns, explosives, etc.) to kill the crusaders and other disbe-

lievers and apostates, including the imāms of kufr, to make an example of them, as all of them are valid—rather, obligatory—targets according to the Sharīʿah, except for those who openly repent from kufr before they are apprehended.[21]

The issue that followed—*Dabiq*'s fifteenth—bore Yahya's fingerprints everywhere. A polemical article about Christianity notes, with a familiar pedantry and some of Yahya's favorite Bible verses, inconsistencies in Christian doctrine and the historical record. Another article more whimsically mocks the secularist claim that humans are created not by God but by natural forces:

> Creation [was split] into two camps, a camp that utilizes its love and hate in submission to its Creator, with faith in His messenger, and another camp that utilizes its love and hate in submission to its desires, with faith in its doubts . . . The camp of sincerity gathered in the Levant and Iraq and spread to other corners of the earth, reviving thereby the Caliphate, which had been absent for centuries, since the collapse of the Abbasid state . . . It is the clash of encampments—"civilizations"—that many saw coming, as it is found in Allah's signs throughout history and current events. And yet the denier claims that all this is the result of mere chaos!

It is signed by Abul-Harith ath-Thaghri, a likely pseudonym for Yahya.[22]

Some articles are clearly his, and others, whether his or not, speak in a voice he has perfected. Unsigned, but likely written by Yahya, is the pellucid "Why We Hate You & Why We Fight You," which avows the religious nature of the war. "We hate you, first and foremost, because you are disbelievers," he begins. "We hate you because your secular, liberal societies permit the very things that Allah has prohibited while banning many of the things He has permitted." The article reads like a distillation of every conversation I had ever had with a jihadist:

> The fact is, even if you were to stop bombing us, imprisoning us, torturing us, vilifying us, and usurping our lands, we would continue to hate you because our primary reason for hating you will not cease to exist until you embrace Islam. Even if you were to pay jizyah and live under the authority of Islam in humiliation, we would continue to hate you. No doubt, we would stop fighting you then as we would stop fighting any disbelievers who enter into a covenant with us, but we would not stop hating you.
>
> What's equally if not more important to understand is that we fight you, not simply to punish and deter you, but to bring you true freedom in this life and salvation in the Hereafter, freedom from being enslaved to your whims and desires as well as those of your clergy and legislatures, and salvation by worshipping your Creator alone and following His messenger.

The Islamic State has staked its survival on creating a revolutionary Muslim mass movement. With Yahya, it lends an American accent to its universal jihadist message, and a speaker whose strengths, weaknesses, personality, and insecurities are deeply American as well. He knows how to speak to Americans, how to scare them, how to recruit them; how to make the Islamic State's war theirs.

Tania made reverse-*hijrah* to Plano, moved into Tim and Martha's house, and gave birth to a boy, her fourth, in January 2014. He is named for his father—or for who his father once was, not Yahya but Ioannis.

She has not left Yahya behind. On social media, she wrote to a big-hearted relative of her husband:

> Where do I begin discussing the 'Ioannis complex'? . . . He's a man torn between two worlds, well actually four or more in his case (East vs. West, religious principles vs. family and happiness). He's not happy with how life has turned out. . . . He seems to always be in a dark and emotionally fractured mood. He only smiles when he sees the children's glowing faces. . . . We made some really poor choices that backfired on us.
>
> Picturing a future with Ioannis would mean to continue living dangerously. One of my worst fears is to see one of my sons grow up, then finding [him] dead on a dirty cell floor of some disreputable underground prison. Ioannis is fixated on changing the hearts and minds of people and changing the course of history. I'm somewhat jealous of the love and devotion he has for Islam over me.

True belief, in Yahya's case, turned out to be impatient, unkind, boastful, and arrogant. Tania explained the attraction, in the clearest possible terms:

> A few people have asked me why does Ioannis care so much about Syria, since he's an American. So I have to explain to them the prophetic narrations claiming that "Jesus (p.b.u.h.) will return to the Levant, primarily to Damascus, to fight the Anti-Christ . . . when the world is filled with tyranny, Syria will be the only safe haven for the believers, etc. etc."
>
> He's hoping that after Bashar [al Assad] falls, the prophecy (from the prophet Muhammad peace be upon him)

will prevail. I on the other hand am hoping never to see that time period. I just don't want to get involved, because war scares me.

In December 2014, Tania petitioned for divorce. She mentioned in the filing that her husband's last known whereabouts were in Syria, and she requested custody of the children. Yahya did not appear in Plano to contest. Since he does not recognize the authority of U.S. law, he presumably still considers Tania his wife.

Her own transformation has been bittersweet. In her discussions with friends online, she now describes herself as an "agnostic Muslim," or elsewhere as "a lost cause to Muslims now." Musa expressed doubt to me that she remains a Muslim at all. "She has drifted off, to say the least," he says with a hint of loathing. "I look at her on Facebook, and she's dating guys, celebrating Valentine's and Christmas." Her Facebook photos show her unveiled, exposed to the world for the first time in her adult life. "I don't like the term," Musa told me, "but she's a coconut"—Muslim on the outside but infidel on the inside.

These days, she looks like any other painted-lady infidel of north Dallas. She dresses stylishly, baring a shoulder now and then, and has highlights in her dark hair. Still in her early thirties, she looks free, even reborn. "Some people would make *takfir* of [excommunicate] me for this," she writes. "But I have hope in God that he understands my weaknesses."

On Mother's Day 2014, Hassan, her nine-year-old son, wrote a note to her in school:

Dear mom,
    You are strong and lovly. You are one of the Best moms in the world including animal moms. Never give up what you are doing. Keep on this path plese. You are on the path to greatness. You will never be let down by your children.

Plese don't be angre with my dad anymore. I know you
have good reson but plese forgive him.

Many would call Yahya's treatment of Tania unforgivable and urge
her to forget him. But the two have, with the exception of Yahya's
prison time and the past couple of years, shared their adult lives, in
difficult and thrilling circumstances. Lives so bound together cannot
split so cleanly. What life could she return to, when the only life she
knows is the wild one with Yahya? After such knowledge, what forgiveness? What alternative does she know? One of Tania's Facebook
posts summarizes the bind:

> I am still so in-love with Ioannis. . . . Nonetheless I'm tired
> of being pushed over the edge by him, and being told,
> "Tania, you're a strong woman! Pick yourself up so I can
> push you over again!" I want my husband back but not on
> those terms.

Yahya's parents have given up. "We've become numb to what he's
doing," Tim told me. He says they haven't heard anything from him
since 2014, and they hadn't heard confirmation that he was with the
Islamic State until I appeared on their doorstep. "He's no one I recognize anymore. I'm not looking out for what he's doing, or how he's
doing, because I'm not sure it makes any difference." Martha, he said,
has taken longer to come to terms with the loss of her son. They don't
think he will return to this country—not as long as he has a following
in Raqqah, and the certainty of incarceration here. "This is the first
time in his life where he's in a position where he might be emulated,"
Tim said.

I wanted to say that he has been emulated for years, and their in-
ability to see his religion as a valid subject of expertise has kept them
from realizing it. They didn't know how evil their own son had be-

come. Like other parents of jihadis, they saw him as they wished to see him—as the youngster who bumbled through classes, sneaked spliffs, and struggled to hold down jobs. There is comfort in imagining that he remains as hapless as ever and that his Islam is another phase. They would be more troubled by the truth, which is that their son, a failure in so many pursuits, has found his calling.

They housed Tania for over a year. She and her landlords disliked each other, even as she liberalized and secularized. In early 2015, they asked her to leave. The grandkids now live with Tim and Martha, who have traded one son to Satan in exchange for four they get to raise for Christ or the Republican Party or both. Having spent most of the last decade as an itinerant incubator of jihadis, Tania lacks the job skills and degrees appropriate to her intellect, so she does not have the resources or career prospects to raise four young children on her own. The kids will grow up in Plano, their safety and education financed by their father's abandoned inheritance.

According to tradition, the Prophet designated men as the heads of families. Many Muslims take that to mean that on the Day of Judgment, God will question fathers about their children's upbringing as Muslims and ask why their progeny were not taught to pray, fast, and fear Him. Since Yahya fears God, he presumably worries about this ultimate interrogation. When he ducked through the barbed wire and back into Syria, he too made a trade, saving his own soul in exchange for the souls of his wife and children. He will be lucky if the questions about that trade are the hardest that await him.

A DREAM DEFERRED

It is always possible to bind together a considerable number of people in love, so long as there are other people left
over to receive the manifestations of their aggressiveness.
—Freud, *Civilization and Its Discontents*

Hear and obey [your leaders], even if an Ethiopian slave is
made your chief and he has a head like a raisin.
—Bukhari

If the Islamic State fielded an army consisting entirely of unconventional bookworms like Musa and Yahya, its caliphate would be one of
the briefest in history. The combined Syrian, Iraqi, and Kurdish
forces would mow them down as they rested on the battlefield for a
joint or a piece of Vegemite-slathered toast, and the soldiers of the
khilafah would expire in the desert with blood, praise for Allah, and
Monty Python quotes on their lips. But support for the caliphate is
broad and diverse—far more complex than the examples of Musa
and Yahya, or indeed Tania, Islam Yaken, and Hesham, suggest.

It is tempting—especially in cases like that of Musa, who never
made it closer to the caliphate than the southern Philippines—to
mock these figures for solipsism or hypocrisy. The only caliphate
many of them know is in their minds. But it is equally true that the
only caliphate anywhere is the caliphate that exists in the minds of

men and women, whether they are fanatics on Twitter, soldiers on the frontlines of *ribat,* or Baghdadi himself. The Dhahiris had one vision, but the Salafis had another, and surely the Syrians, Iraqis, Chechens, Tunisians, and others in Iraq and the Levant each have their own. No two are exactly alike. Long before the Islamic State controlled a single neighborhood, such people were wandering the earth, entranced by a caliphate of the mind, perhaps or perhaps not resembling the physical caliphate that would rule Raqqah and Mosul.

"This all started, essentially, with an idea," Musa once told me—the idea that Islam requires a Muslim government, and that a caliphate is Muslim government in its purest form. In speaking with supporters of the Islamic State, I began to see how malleable that idea was—and how potent and inspiring it could be, even if the precise form it took differed greatly from Muslim to Muslim. I also found a persistent gap between idea and action, a reluctance by supporters to sully their ideas by putting them into practice.

The day before I met Anjem Choudary—the most famous Islamic State supporter in Britain—was the day his most gifted apprentice announced to the world that he had made *hijrah.*

The apprentice, Abu Rumaysah, then about thirty, was a wanted man. Physically unimposing—like Yahya, he had handicaps that made him unfit for combat duty—he had a vicious mouth and had become, under Choudary's guidance, a passionate propagandist for the caliphate. In September 2014, British authorities arrested him on charges of membership in a banned organization. On release pending trial, he gathered his pregnant wife and three children, boarded a bus at London's Victoria Station, and slipped past the British authorities into continental Europe.

It was now almost two months later, and the weather in London made *hijrah* to warmer, drier climates feel downright sensible. Choudary told me to meet him at Nawal, a sweet shop near his home in Ilford, and by the time I arrived, in mid-afternoon, it was already gloomy dark, and despite the cold, so humid that dew beaded on my cheeks. The servers knew I was there to see Choudary; this was his favorite spot for encounters with reporters. He walked in from the rain, dressed in a crisp blue tunic that grazed his ankles. Choudary seized the initiative in our conversation with a gesture of magnanimity, providing an assortment of South Asian sweets for me to nibble while he harangued me. As we sat down, we looked at Abu Rumaysah's latest tweet, posted hours earlier from Syria. "He makes me proud," Choudary said. Abu Rumaysah had a rifle slung over his right shoulder and his newborn son, in a brown fleece onesie, in the crook of his arm. Hashtag: #GenerationKhilafah.

If Islamic State support is a communicable disease, an infection of the mind, then Choudary is its Typhoid Mary. A lawyer by training, he entered the public eye in the late 1990s and quickly became one of the most loathed figures in the United Kingdom by advocating the death, whipping, or subjugation of his fellow citizens. By the mid-2000s, he was the face of British militant Islamism. The previous face had been hideous: Abu Hamza, the imam at the Finsbury Park Mosque, was a thug out of central casting, with a scowl, a glass eye, and hooks for hands. A native of Alexandria, he held all the most retrograde opinions about apostates and blasphemers, and expressed them with the tact and grace of the nightclub bouncer he had once been. Since Abu Hamza's incarceration (he's now serving a life sentence in the United States for supporting terrorism in Yemen, Afghanistan, and Oregon), Choudary has presided over a reinvention of British jihadism as a scholarly, suave, intellectual pursuit as well as a terrorist one. He is well-spoken where Abu Hamza was grunty; he is dapper where Abu Hamza looked slovenly. But when he speaks, he echoes Abu Hamza on most things, and agrees with the caliphate about nearly everything.

Choudary was born in London in 1967 to Pakistani parents. Like many jihadis before him, he devoted his youth to miscreance, particularly during his student days in Southampton. In the early 1990s, he began moonlighting as an organizer for Omar Bakri Mohammed, a Syrian preacher who was banned from the United Kingdom in 2005 and has been imprisoned on terrorism charges in Lebanon since 2014.[1] Bakri, an educated man, spoke refined Arabic and preached a caliphate-focused message of religious revival. Most of Bakri's British followers lacked good Arabic, so he was able to assume a leadership role on the strength of his linguistic prowess alone. In 2002, Choudary quit practicing law—or at least, practicing English common law—to immerse himself full-time in Islamist upheaval. He led, with Bakri, an Islamist group called Al Muhajiroun [the Emigrants], before the British government banned it in 2010. Under related names—including Al Ghuraba' [the Strangers], Islam4UK, Sharia4UK, and Sharia4Belgium, and countless other permutations—Choudary-linked groups have been advocating death for apostates, adulterers, and others, while agitating for the conversion of various landmarks (Buckingham Palace, Nelson's Column) into mosques, caliphal palaces, and minarets.[2]

Choudary's name arouses passion and disdain among most Britons and, indeed, most British Islamists. It is easy to see why: he has a P. T. Barnum–like genius for publicity; he demands sacrifices of others that he himself has not made; he hogs airtime by accepting absolutely every media request that he receives (Fox's Sean Hannity invited him on regularly); and he does all this despite his considerable ignorance. "Anjem's Arabic is a joke," one British Muslim told me, adding that Choudary's entire strategy is to be outraged, outrageous, and hated. When confronted on fine details of Islamic law, his main tactic is to change the subject. "How the hell he passes himself off as a Shariah court judge, I'll never know." His followers number in the hundreds, and other Muslims have embarrassed him by showing up his Arabic or destroying him in public debate.

"I don't like to deal with them," Musa Cerantonio told me, referring to Choudary and his followers. He disagrees with their methods—they accept *qiyas*—and their over-the-top reverence for their imprisoned Syrian leader. (Choudary suggested to me that Bakri is a "*mujaddid*" [renewer], a figure prophesied to come every century or so to purify Islam and steer it back to its correct course.)[3] "They're my brothers, no doubt, but because they're so vocal about [allowing] *qiyas* and the veneration of Omar Bakri, I leave them be," Musa said. He was also critical of Choudary's men's failure to emigrate. "[Al Mu-hajiroun] don't see it as a sin to be in the UK at all," Musa told me. "They're very comfortable there. We say, 'Some of you have got passports! Why are you still there?'"

Those who dismiss Choudary as a clownish figure must admit he is at least a grim clown, more Stephen King's Pennywise than Bozo. They also, I have found, tend to underrate him as a teacher and pros-elytizer, perhaps because in his cable-news performances he plays to type, acting as a howling weird-beard of radical Islam, in the villain-hero dichotomy of pro wrestling, a Muslim heel to Sean Hannity's Christian face. He can be—to use a term he'd surely hate—a ham.

But none can deny that his message has found purchase among impressionable British Muslims. Members of Choudary's group have been linked to twenty-three out of fifty-one recent terrorist events in Britain, including the beheading of the soldier Lee Rigby in Wool-wich in 2013, and the July 7, 2005, bombings of a double-decker bus and three subway trains, which killed fifty-two.[4] The British govern-ment has estimated that Choudary and his followers have influenced or inspired more than a hundred foreign fighters who have gone on to fight in jihad.[5] He introduced me to Mizanur Rahman (Abu Baraa), thirty-one, and Abdul Muhid, thirty-two, two followers in London who have been watched carefully by security services for their asso-ciations with Choudary and Bakri and advocacy of the Islamic State. They are intelligent men, both close friends of Abu Rumaysah. Be-cause each was awaiting trial for supporting terrorism, Choudary,

Abu Baraa, and Abdul Muhid had to meet me separately: communication among them would have violated the terms of their bail. As in any cult, the Manchurian Candidate effect was strong: ask the same question, or utter certain trigger words, and the same rote, catechistic replies come back. Speaking with them felt like speaking with the same person wearing different masks.

But Abu Rumaysah is Choudary's greatest creation. Born Siddhartha Dhar in approximately 1983, Abu Rumaysah converted from Hinduism in his late teens, through acquaintance with Abu Baraa. During the 2000s, while Abu Rumaysah operated a business that rented bouncy castles for children's birthday parties, he also showed a talent for headline-grabbing, outrage-stoking Islamism. He co-organized a group that conducted "Shariah patrols" in predominantly Muslim neighborhoods in East London, prowling the streets and intimidating passersby into submission to conservative Islamic religious and cultural norms. They harassed women into covering their bodies and faces, and poured out men's beers.

After we traded pleasantries and looked at the pictures of Abu Rumaysah, Choudary waited for me to turn on my recorder, then cast down his eyes and muttered in Arabic, "In the name of God, the gracious, the merciful." Then he looked up and began speaking.

He started from a legalistic position. "Maybe eighty-five percent of the Shariah was absent from our lives," he told me. "These laws are in abeyance until we have *khilafah*. And now we have one." Islamic law, he said, cannot be implemented in the absence of a true Islamic government under a caliph. The Koran stipulates the punishment of amputation for thieves: "As for the man who steals and the woman who steals, cut off their hands as a punishment for what they have earned, an exemplary punishment from God."[6] But that Koranic verse does not license just any cleaver-wielding vigilante to lop off thieves' hands. A legal system, with courts and an executive, is necessary.

That executive is the caliph, Choudary says, and he and his judges must provide all the appropriate protections for the accused. He was quick to point out that the procedures for adjudicating guilt are onerous. "In centuries of Islamic rule," he told me, "only a small number of hands were cut off."[7] Choudary's defense of the *hadd* punishments is a common one in Muslim apologetics. The safeguards against false conviction are significant, and historically, many exemptions have been in place to protect even the guilty from punishment. To amputate a hand, for example, a judge must determine that the accused stole only non-perishable goods of significant value and that he is neither too young to understand what he has done nor insane nor very poor. When a guilty verdict is rendered and the sentence is amputation, the Islamic State observes precautions to ensure that the punishment does not exceed its intent: if the guilty party might die from the amputation, the amputation cannot be performed. The sentence is amputation, not death. (As Portia tells Shylock in *The Merchant of Venice* as he prepares to extract a pound of flesh, "Have by some surgeon on your charge, to stop his wounds, lest he do bleed to death." The wielder of the blade "shall have all justice," but "he shall have nothing but the penalty.") Accordingly, the Islamic State's lay surgeons splash the wrist and blade with iodine, and a medic stands by with clean bandages to dress the wound. To ensure a clean cut and no sudden movement, they blindfold the accused and apply tension by pulling the hand with a rope. The blade lands with a thud—sometimes it is placed gently against the wrist and whacked with a heavy steel rod—and severs the hand at the joint.

Choudary paused and looked me over—wondering, I think, why I hadn't yet flinched. I had resolved to deny him the usual journalist reaction of challenge and reproach. That he held outrageous opinions, I already knew; that he took primal, trolling pleasure in observing others' indignation, any YouTube clip of him could show. I let him talk, hoping that he would tire himself trying to provoke me. I think the strategy worked, because midway through our conversation, he ordered that modern elixir for flagging energy, a Red Bull ("I like the taste").

I encouraged him to tell me where all this suffering—not just the amputations, but the mass killing and war—was leading. He nipped at his Red Bull and answered that it was leading to less suffering. That was the true reason for the Islamic State's embrace of terrorism: terror will save lives, in the end, and make itself obsolete. He told me the Islamic State has an obligation to terrorize its enemies—a sacred duty to scare the shit out of them with beheadings and crucifixions and the enslavement of women and children, because doing so hastens victory and avoids prolonged conflict. Submission to God is a condition of peace, and, ultimately, salvation.

Consider the Koran—"Make ready your strength to the utmost of your power, including steeds of war, to strike terror into [the hearts of] the enemies"[8]—but also the example of the Prophet himself. In the Battle of Badr, in 624, a key victory in his conquest of Mecca, the Prophet heard one of his Companions scream a bloodcurdling war cry. He remarked that at any other time, the screamer would earn reproach for this coarse behavior. But in battle, it was not only permissible but genteel. The beheadings and telegenic savagery of the Islamic State occur in just such ennobling circumstances. They are the modern equivalent of a pants-wettingly loud *"Allahu akbar!"* yelled in close combat.

Choudary told me that the revival of the caliphate had awoken these dormant doctrines of warfare. Whereas he and others, such as Abu Hamza, had once phrased their support for attacks on British troops as "self-defense" by Muslims, the existence of a caliphate bound him to support "offensive jihad" [*jihad al talab*], the forcible expansion into countries that are ruled by non-Muslims. These include Turkey and Jordan, since their rulers are judged to be apostates. "Hitherto, we were just defending ourselves," Choudary said. But the waging of war to expand the caliphate is a duty of the caliph.

Choudary's colleague Abu Baraa explained to me that Islamic law permits only temporary peace treaties, lasting no longer than a decade—the maximum duration of the treaties and ceasefires affirmed by the Prophet himself with the Treaty of Hudaybiyah in 628.[9] Accepting any fixed border—conceding that Islam's authority can be finite—is anathema. If the caliph consents to a longer-term peace or permanent border, he will be in error. Temporary peace treaties are renewable, but may not be applied to all enemies at once: the caliph must wage war to expand the domain of Islam, or remove obstacles to its practice, at least once a year. He may not rest, or he will fall into a state of sin.

For its murderous utopianism, the Islamic State has been compared to the Khmer Rouge, which killed about a quarter of the population of Cambodia. But the Khmer Rouge occupied Cambodia's seat at the United Nations, an act of statesmanship that the Islamic State would not abide. "This is not permitted," Abu Baraa said. "To send an ambassador to the UN is to recognize an authority other than God's." This form of diplomacy is *shirk* [polytheism], he argued, and would be cause to excommunicate and replace Baghdadi. Even to hasten the arrival of a caliphate through democratic means—for example by voting for political candidates who favor a caliphate—would be *shirk*. "Stay Muslim," read placards held by pro–Islamic State activists on the day of the British general election in May 2015. "Don't vote."

This context of rejectionism excused and explained all manner of sin. What looks to outsiders like the Islamic State's brutality, Abu Baraa said, is the lingering symptoms of the diseased societies it has replaced. By Choudary's own account, the Islamic State was stoning criminals and cutting off their healthy limbs at a rate hundreds or thousands of times that of previous caliphates. "The Islamic State is new," he said, "and the people living under it have spent many years under *kafir* governments. They had prostitution, pornography, open sale of alcohol." Is it any surprise, he asked, that they would require correction? The secular tyrannies of Saddam Hussein or Bashar al

Assad had made the birth of a Muslim nation painful, and popula-
tions required the forcible readjustment of Muslim norms.[10] Confusing things further, he said, was a faulty understanding of Shariah,
brought on by faux-Islamic societies such as Saudi Arabia that apply
punishments without implementing a complementary set of social
reforms and improvements. Saudi Arabia beheads murderers and
cuts off thieves' hands, just as the Islamic State insists. "The problem,"
he explained, "is that when places like Saudi Arabia implement just
the penal code, and don't provide the social and economic justice of
the Shariah—the whole package—they engender hatred toward the
Shariah." That whole package, he said, would include free housing,
food, and clothing for all, though anyone who wished to work for pay
could do so.

Choudary and his followers once performed petty stunts for publicity. The Shariah patrols of Abu Rumaysah and others (since they
kept changing the group's name, I began calling them "the Choudarheads") may have slapped a few pints out of a few hands. But that was
as far as they went, and they appeared to have no larger purpose. But
now we can see the relationship between those stunts and the grander
vision of today. The patrols reminded Muslims of their obligations,
Choudary insists. They were small steps to a better world. Look, he
said, at what the Islamic State has done since: it has taken the impulse
behind Abu Rumaysah's grassroots morality posse and invested it
with the power of a government. "They have *hisbah* [morality police]
on the street," he said. "They are part of the State, which is fulfilling
its obligation to forbid vice and command right." Abu Rumaysah's
patrols of Whitechapel were a dry run for Raqqah.

There are at least three Anjem Choudarys. One is the Choudary with
whom I spoke: measured, calm, professorial. The staff of the candy
shop—none visibly conservative Muslims—welcomed him as a man
of dignity who has probably brought them substantial business over

the years, in the form of visiting journalists. I later attended lectures given by this Choudary (to a live audience of two dozen at most) at the Ilm Centre, a tiny Islamic education office in Whitechapel. In the classroom, he maintained this persona, more pedagogue than demagogue, skillfully moving from theory to example, from general to specific and back again. A second Choudary is the undignified blowhard available for bookings on Fox News.

A third Choudary is a young man who went by the name "Andy," and whom the other two Choudarys have tried to bury. As a university student, Choudary lived a secular life—which is to say, one that would, at a minimum, get him publicly lashed in the Islamic State, and screamed at by Abu Rumaysah. Photographs from the time, now widely circulated, show him in full lad mode, draining cans of Foster's and leering at softcore nudie mags. Shiraz Maher, one of the jihadism researchers at King's College London, suggested that if I ever returned to one of Choudary's lectures, I should bring a photo of young Andy surrounded by beer cans, and ask what Islamic law had to say about that.

Paradoxically, though, when I asked Choudary about his past, I found myself in greater sympathy with him. I'm sure many of Choudary's followers feel the same. He is not an Elmer Gantry. He did not deny. "I have not always been a good Muslim," he said. "But I have made repentance and come back to Islam, and that is that." It's possible that when he walked out of the candy shop, he removed a false beard and headed straight to the nearest pub for a pint and a smoke. But I doubt it. Are Catholics who sin and go to confession less Catholic than Catholics who stay home and don't sin at all?

His desire, and that of his followers, was not for purity but for *purification*. You cannot purify without being polluted first. Naughtiness is therefore part of the game, and the cycle of moral bingeing and purging is a feature rather than a bug. To focus on the hypocrisy is to misjudge what the Islamic State means to its followers. If one accepts that they might view themselves as fallen creatures in need of permanent rescue, then the Islamic State looks like a mission of salvation. Its followers view it as a disciplining parent, one whose morality police exist not to harm but to correct: the sting of a switch across the backside, and only in the direst cases the bite of a blade into a wrist or neck.

When I met Abdul Muhid, another of Choudary's followers, at the E1 Restaurant in Whitechapel, he sported a Brillo beard and was dressed in mujahedin chic: blue tunic, Afghan cap, and a wallet outside of his clothes, attached to what looked like a shoulder holster. When we sat down, he was most eager to discuss social services. He told me that the Islamic State may have medieval-style punishments for moral crimes, but its social-welfare program is progressive. Health care is free. "Isn't it free in Britain, too?" I asked. "Not really," he said. "Some procedures aren't covered, such as vision." Social welfare, he said, was an *obligation* inherent in God's law. Reports out of Raqqah suggest that this promise is honored at least sometimes. In November 2015, *The New York Times* interviewed a Syrian defector from the Islamic State. She accused the Islamic State of many crimes, but admitted that it paid—sometimes heftily, in cases that required travel to hospitals in Turkey—for health care.[11]

In a remarkable fit of optimism, Abdul Muhid described a utopian state that lavished care upon its citizens. He said nothing about how the state would fund this generosity. The Islamic State does not have limitless economic resources—indeed, its few sources of income (dribbles of black-market oil, a small tax base, and captured spoils of war [*ghanima;* taxed at a rate of twenty percent—called *khums*—by the state]) are vanishing and not being replaced. It could not afford to pay for a Scandinavian-style welfare state even if its revenues tripled.[12] Abdul Muhid eventually conceded that the income would be inadequate to sustain the services he envisioned.

But here he invoked the genius of the moral mission of the Islamic

State. "When you have no alcohol [and] no pornography, you don't have these social ills to combat," he said. How many of the problems of society stem from drunkenness, from louts smashing pints over each other, or whipping out blades to settle beer-fueled arguments?[13] What would happen if the resources that went to fighting these maladies instead went to health care or poverty alleviation? What if prisoners instead worked for a living, and paid *zakat* [charity] as God commanded? A truly Islamic society would cost less to maintain, and be much more productive.

Expanding on this point, Abu Baraa added confident if unpersuasive fiscal insight. Before joining Choudary, he had been an economics student at Goldsmiths, University of London. What, he asked, if the bankers who had so recently nearly wrecked the world economy were forbidden from practicing their parasitic trade? (To stop money from being made idly, Islamic finance forbids the charging of interest and follows a gold standard.) Getting rid of the bankers' drag on the economy, he claimed, would stir the world to levels of wealth production easily capable of funding a robust welfare state.

After listening to a lot of this talk, I realized that the most striking thing about the Choudarheads was not their rejection of the infidel West but their unintentional embrace of it. They were so marked by the country of their birth that their flat Muslim skullcaps might as well have been bowler hats. Choudary, Abdul Muhid, and Abu Baraa were born in England, and all spoke not the Queen's English but a multicultural London variant—something more authentically British, since generations of colonial subjects have studied and mastered the Queen's but only a lifelong London resident speaks the dialect of the street. They were always projecting their idealized roseate social vision of Britain on the Islamic State. All had come of age in a period when the government promised social justice. Where Yahya viewed the Islamic State through his own Texan libertarianism, Abdul Muhid and the others projected onto it the failed ideals of the Britain in which they were raised. Abdul Muhid lamented the lot of the poor in

England—the struggle to feed a family, the inequities of economy and opportunity, the failure of regulation to provide a fair and humane existence for the weakest. When I first met him, he asked whether I was going to go to Syria. I lied and said maybe. "Please take me with you," he said. But when I later asked him what role he envisioned for himself as a *muhajir* in the Islamic State, he said he imagined himself working in *da'wah* [religious outreach]—right back in the UK. In other words, despite saying he wanted to emigrate, he still knew England was his natural habitat.

The economic theories of Abu Baraa, the former Goldsmiths student, would be well received in cerebral precincts of the Occupy movement. Others resemble classical British welfarism. To secure the society the Choudarheads were looking for, they may as well have given *bay'a* to Sir William Beveridge, architect of the postwar British welfare state. I suspect this irony might have occurred to them: their vocabulary and concerns were so thoroughly infused with British norms and expectations that they must have noticed, if only subconsciously, how inescapable their origins were. And that would surely have infuriated them. The feeling that one's mind is prisoner to a civilization one hates is a unique humiliation. These Muslims had thrust themselves into Islam—never realizing how British their vision of Islam had become.

At times, these contradictions became more overt. In my presence, Choudary never said a negative word about the Islamic State, and when he mentioned the name of Abu Bakr al Baghdadi, he followed it with the blessing "May Allah preserve him." But his bravado faded when discussing practices for which no liberal justification is possible. Chief among these was sex slavery.

The Koranic permission for sex with slaves can be found in Surah al Mu'minin, which marks wives and "those whom your right hand possesses" as licit sexual partners.[14] To have sex with slaves, therefore, is not fornication [*zina*] but is permitted by God and therefore incapable of being forbidden in principle, only in practice. Like

Christians and Jews, Muslims can say that sex slavery is not legiti-mate now, at this historical juncture. Many say precisely this. But they cannot condemn sex slavery in theory without contradicting the Koran and the example of the Prophet. Muslim opponents of the Islamic State reckon with the Koranic endorsement of sex slavery in various ways.[15] Islamic scholars (of both genders) in the United States affirm, as do Choudary and Abu Baraa, that the "position of Islamic law" is that masters may have sex with lawfully acquired female slaves. But mainstream Muslims say—against Choudary and the Is-lamic State—that conquering armies can no longer lawfully acquire slaves, and therefore one can never have sex with one.

Choudary expressed a kind of regret about the need for slavery. He at first defended it as Musa did, as an institution of mercy in a violent time. When the Islamic State subdues a town that has fought against it, it takes spoils, including prisoners. Apostate Muslims—Sunni and Shia—must be killed. Christians and Jews who accept the rule of the Islamic State may be freed and allowed to live within it as subjugated citizens, paying a tax called *jizya*.[16] But they may also be killed or enslaved. "What is to be done with widows and orphans?" Choudary asked. "They cannot be left to die in the desert." Given that popula-tions that resist Islamic State expansion may be killed or ransomed, it is magnanimous to take them as slaves.[17] Sexual enslavement in Islam, he says, is unlike the use of sex as a weapon of war in other societies, because the slaves enjoy rights.

Choudary's rueful defense of slavery contradicts in spirit the Is-lamic State's own statements, which treat slavery as a matter of pride.[18] Members of Iraq's Yazidi community, which is the primary target for Islamic State slave traders, told authors of a 2016 United Nations re-port that 5,838 Yazidis had been kidnapped and at least 3,500 re-mained in captivity—the rest having escaped, or been ransomed or killed. The Islamic State does not attempt to hide the practice, and indeed does everything in its power to publicize it. Fighters are promised slave girls as spoils, and the Shariah scholars who justify their enslavement explicitly avow that one reason for the practice is so the Islamic State's fighters can gratify themselves sexually. At a Koran-memorization competition in Mosul in June 2015, the three winners were given sex slaves.[19] The jurists of the Islamic State approached the topic of sex slavery with the same chilling dispassion they applied to other subjects. In acknowledging that fighters' orgasms were a form of compensation for a tough job, they investigated, and found, loopholes that would make the sex-slave economy more efficient. Classical law concerning sex slaves had required an owner to wait a month after intercourse to confirm menstruation and the empty status of a slave's womb [istibra'] before selling her. Relying on a Maliki opinion, the scholars of the Islamic State decided that owners could follow the spirit of the one-month rule simply by forcing the sex slaves to use contraception. Under those conditions, fighters could trade and sell empty-wombed slaves whenever they wished.[20] None of this could remotely be excused as having the best interests of the slave-girls in mind.

Elsewhere the Islamic State goes out of its way to brag about slavery. "We will conquer your Rome, break your crosses, and enslave your women," 'Adnani, the spokesman, promised in one of his periodic valentines to the West. "If we do not reach that time, then our children and grandchildren will reach it, and they will sell your sons as slaves at the slave market." In the pages of Dabiq, Umm Summayah al Muhajirah fantasized about the price Michelle Obama would fetch at the slave market—a third of a dinar (about $40)?[21] Umm Summayah argues that sex with slaves is acceptable even if the slaves were married to others. She expresses concern that supporters of the Islamic State have forgotten the righteousness of sex slavery:

> The [opponents of the Islamic State] dare to extend their tongues with false rumors and accusations so as to disfigure the great Shariah ruling and pure prophetic Sunnah titled "saby" [enslavement of girls]? After all this, saby becomes

fornication and *tasarri* [concubinage] becomes rape? If only we'd heard these falsehoods from the *kuffar* [infidels] who are ignorant of our religion. Instead we hear it from those associated with our Ummah! So I say in astonishment: Are our people awake or asleep? But what really alarmed me was that some of the Islamic State supporters (may Allah forgive them) rushed to defend the Islamic State [by] denying the matter as if the soldiers of the Khilafah had committed a mistake or evil.

She notes that Muslims are commanded to take slaves and lead them to Islam, and that God not only accepts them into Paradise, but loves them especially, "marveling at those who enter Paradise in chains."

Who, she asks, is better off: a sex slave of the Islamic State, or a prostitute in infidel lands?

A prostitute in your lands comes and goes, openly committing sin. She lives by selling her honor, within the sight and hearing of the deviant scholars from whom we don't hear even a faint sound. As for the slave-girl that was taken by the swords of men following the cheerful warrior [Muhammad], then her enslavement is in opposition to human rights and copulation with her is rape?! What is wrong with you?

The softie Muslim strawman she was assailing could well have been Anjem Choudary. When he explained slavery to me, he made constant hedges and was eager to insist it was not as bad as it sounded. The Prophet, he said, forbade the recreational beating of slaves. Choudary insisted that to beat one's slaves would be effectively to free them, since one could not keep a slave one had so badly mistreated. Muslims who own slaves must feed them the same food eaten by the free members of the household. To care for these slaves and teach them about Islam is a command and a blessing. And, he repeated, the sex slavery was not rape, but permission from God for a consensual relationship in the context of the care that a master was required to provide for his slaves.

I was sure he knew I would not let this pass. There may be a compassionate argument for enslaving a woman rather than letting her starve—but what about for then forcing her to have sex with you? That sounded like rape to me. I said so to Choudary, and he denied this strenuously. "Rape is forbidden in Islam," he said. "The master cannot have sex with a slave unless she permits it." I suggested that the power dynamic between a heavily armed Chechen murderer and a prepubescent Yazidi slave girl might preclude her giving meaningful consent. He had no reply, other than to say that if the master harms his slave in any way, he will be compelled to free her.

"So would they just be at an impasse, if he wanted sex and she refused?"

Choudary said he wasn't sure. "Perhaps they could go to a judge, and he could explain things to her." It was the only time I heard him make an argument I was pretty sure even he didn't believe.[22]

Choudary told me that he hadn't made *hijrah* to the Islamic State because as a public figure, he'd have little chance of escaping the UK. His passport had been confiscated, and he was required to check in with police daily. "I'm Britain's most famous Muslim," he protested. "I can't ship myself there in a box." Another member of Choudary's group adopted a more fatalist approach. "We believe that the people who go to [Syria] are chosen by Allah," he told me, "and we believe if God chooses you, nobody will stop you. We pray that God will one day choose us to be among them."

Gradually, the law closed in on Choudary and Abu Baraa both, forbidding them to use electronic devices and, after their trials, sentencing them each to five years in prison for terrorist support in July 2016. The London police asked me to testify against them, due to pro–Islamic State statements they had made to me in interviews. I declined, citing journalistic privilege, but I was also pretty sure the Crown prosecutors didn't need my help to convict men who for years had literally been yelling in public about how much they love jihad and terrorism.

Like Musa, they are now safe from having to act on their commitment to the Islamic State. But given the comfortable circumstances in which Choudary had long found himself—UK tabloids report that he drew £25,000 a year in welfare benefits—many have speculated that his reasons for staying put were less principled.[23] He pocketed his dole money, and most important, never had to face real war, or the potential discrediting of his ideals. He loved London, despite himself. To keep a distance from Syria is a matter of mental self-preservation. If he were to emigrate and have to observe the caliphate's inevitable shortcomings from up close, his dream would crumple like a butterfly's wings, pinched by reality and the burden of being ruled by humans who are not only fallible but evil. From the safety of Ilford, Choudary could easily maintain fantasies of a caliphate in which human rights would reach their apex and where slaves could politely decline the caresses of their masters.

There are hundreds of sympathizers who have visited the Islamic State and returned disillusioned. They are understandably reluctant to describe what led them to leave. One reason for this is that many of them are in legal jeopardy with their home governments. Also, the Islamic State has promised to kill them. During a visit to Mosul in December 2014, six months after the declaration of the caliphate, the journalist Jürgen Todenhöfer interviewed a portly German jihadist, Abu Qatadah (born Christian Emde), and asked whether any of his comrades had returned to Europe to carry out attacks. The jihadist regarded returnees not as soldiers but as deserters. "The fact is that the returnees from the Islamic State should repent from their return," he said. "I hope they review their religion."[24] He was being polite. Many who have attempted to leave have been slain by the Islamic

State, and those who have succeeded in their return home know that their old friends will slit their throats if they get the chance. (Evidence since then points to a strategic effort—small at first, and now formidable—to reverse the flow of immigration, sending trained assassins to Europe while encouraging Muslims already in Europe to stay put and attack.[25])

But defectors are out there. As of August 2015, Peter R. Neumann of King's College London counted fifty-eight people who had defected, for reasons ranging from frustration with particular individuals in the Islamic State (though "practically no one believed that corruption was systemic"), to exhaustion from brutality and violence (against fellow Sunnis, that is—they were largely indifferent to violence against others), to longing for the comforts of their homes in Western Europe.[26] These are the ones who have gone public. There are others who have returned and are trying to stay quiet, often with the cooperation of authorities. In Dinslaken, the Rhineland town that has contributed a disproportionate number of fighters to the Islamic State, city officials told me they knew of one returnee now working at a local restaurant, and that their main concern was keeping him at least minimally employed—better fry cook than suicide bomber.[27]

What is most striking about these public defectors is not that their idealism shattered but how potent it was in the first place. Many had, and continue to have, high moral expectations for Islam and for the Islamic State. Some went to fight against Bashar al Assad, an ambition that could plausibly be described as humanitarian, given Assad's war crimes. Many had been captivated by "the Islamic State's central promise, which is to create a perfect Islamic society," Neumann wrote. "While many were willing to tolerate the hardships of war, they found it impossible to accept instances of unfairness, inequality, and racism, which they said went against everything the IS claimed to stand for."

To learn about this idealism, I sought out one of the most unusual ISIS returnees: a Japanese convert and Islamic studies professor named Hassan Ko Nakata. I became aware of him when he gave a press conference in Tokyo after two Japanese citizens were executed by the Islamic State. Nakata insisted from the beginning that he did not support, join, or recruit for the Islamic State or any other terrorist group. These clarifications were useful, since he had visited the Islamic State multiple times, at its invitation, and online searches for his name yielded a photograph of him looking jolly while wearing a black bandanna and cradling a Kalashnikov in front of an Islamic State flag.

He agreed to meet me in his lawyer's florally scented office in the Shibuya ward of Tokyo. The lawyer observed our conversation, to watch out for her client's interests. Nakata is fifty-five but looks a decade older, because of his stringy gray facial hair. When I entered the room, he stayed seated, wearing loose-fitting clothes, a bit like a tracksuit. His informal dress and refusal to stand struck me as a conscious breach of etiquette—*I stand for no man*—but within minutes of talking to him, I could tell that the informality was unaffected, and any offense inadvertent. (He later apologized for not standing, and said he had medical issues with his legs.) His sense of humor struck me as uncommon among Islamists, and he showed a decency that felt incompatible with any association with a terrorist organization.

The Japanese authorities were mulling whether to prosecute him for terrorism-related offenses. Now and then in our conversation, the lawyer would interject to ensure that his answers couldn't be interpreted to incriminate him. Like others on the fringes of the Islamic State, he spoke openly and intelligently. He disregarded his lawyer's advice to keep silent. At one point, when she told him to consider not saying more about a particular incident, he barged right ahead and kept talking. She complained, "I don't know why I'm here if you're just going to disregard me." He shrugged. "You don't have to be here," he said. "You can go."

Nakata is a strange man. The grandson of a Shinto priest and the son of parents without strong religious feeling, he was born in Okayama, on the southwest end of Japan's main island of Honshu. As a kid, he got along poorly with other students and immersed himself in solitary or intellectual pursuits, such as *shogi* [Japanese chess]. He also followed pro wrestling. Among his favorite wrestlers was Abdullah the Butcher, the "Madman from Khartoum," best known for stabbing his opponents with forks.[28] This comic-book image of Muslim barbarity did not leave Nakata with an unfavorable view of Islam (nor should it have, since Abdullah is a non-Muslim Canadian named Larry Shreve).

Nakata attended Nada High School in Kobe, and then Tokyo University. Each is considered the best school of its kind in Japan. He studied Christianity and Judaism at the university, and in his third year, he became one of the first students in its new Islamic studies program. He had expected a highly textual approach, reading the Koran to understand the religion. "In fact, there were few lessons like that," he later wrote in a short memoir. "My disappointment must have shown in my attitude. I took to correcting the professors in class and became unpopular."[29]

He converted at the end of the school year, at the age of twenty-two, for reasons that will sound familiar. He considered Islam "logical," "following a clear set of detailed laws." It required none of the complicated, hand-waving explanations that he encountered in Christianity. Everything made sense, he says, and was "easy." He was not particulary pious and allowed himself un-Islamic indulgences right up to the eve of his conversion. Before heading to the mosque in Kobe to make it official, he writes, "I went out for a meal of my favorite *tonkatsu* [deep-fried pork cutlet] and drank a glass of port."[30] A Filipino imam then witnessed his conversion and gave him the name Hassan. To that point, he had spent little time among Muslims. In the more than three decades since the university began teaching about Islam, Nakata says, he is still the only student to have converted. He moved from Japan to Cairo and earned a doctorate from Cairo University in the political thought of Ibn Taymiyyah. In the early 1990s, he worked for the Japanese embassy in Riyadh, and then he returned to Japan to teach Islamic studies at Doshisha University, a Protestant institution in Kyoto.

Although Nakata's early commitment to Islam was casual, in time he devoted himself to the religion—and, finally, to the idea of a caliphate. Highly influential in his thinking was a group known as Hizb al Tahrir [the Party of Liberation]. Founded in Jordan in 1952 by Taqi al Din al Nabhani, Hizb al Tahrir proposed a massive reordering of the politics of Muslim-majority countries. At the time, the ascendant political forces in the Islamic world were socialists—including the Baath Party—and fragmented Islamist groups, including the Muslim Brotherhood. Nabhani thought a unified Muslim entity could wash away the region's royal lines and authoritarian regimes, and leave a single Muslim government.

Hizb al Tahrir's template was, and continues to be, a caliphate. But in contrast to Musa, members of the group are easygoing about classical aspects of what a caliphate entails. They ignore the Quraysh requirement.[31] They look back on the (also non-Qurayshi) Ottoman caliphate—which ended in 1924, extinguished by the secularist republican Turkish government of Mustafa Kemal Atatürk—as legitimate, even though the last caliph, Abdülmecid II, was definitely no Qurayshi warrior-king. He reacted to his ouster not by raising an army, but by retiring to a life of beard-grooming and nude portraiture in Paris. (The fifteenth volume of *Dabiq* denies that any caliphate has existed since the last of the Abbasids, in 1258.[32])

Where Musa and the Islamic State relentlessly look to Islam's classical period for justification, Nabhani sometimes looked forward and sometimes back. He mixed positions that were retro (including a fondness for Dhahiri jurisprudence) with an embrace of modern convenience and technology. He called for Muslims to select their caliph with broad participation, via a secret ballot open to all, and his organization strategized to infiltrate and co-opt student movements throughout the Muslim world in a long-term bid for power.[33]

After Nabhani died in Beirut in 1977, Hizb al Tahrir continued pushing the caliphate—with the sole fixed criteria that the Muslims be unified under one leader, and governed in a borderless Muslim state. Hizb al Tahrir rejects nationalism, including Palestinian sovereignty and the "Islamism in one country" approach taken by Pakistan and the Muslim Brotherhood. In 1979, when the Ayatollah Ruhollah Khomeini looked poised to return from exile in France and seize power in Iran, Hizb al Tahrir sent a delegation to France to propose him as caliph. Even a Shia caliph would do—anything to unite the Muslims under a single banner and begin the process of covering the earth in Islam.

In 1992, in Saudi Arabia, Nakata met a covert member of Hizb al Tahrir and fell hard for its message. (The group is banned in the kingdom.) "In Muslim countries, it's forbidden to teach about the caliphate," he says, but in Japan, he was free to say whatever he liked, with little fear that the Japanese people or government would care, or have any idea what he was talking about. In 2009, in a book called *The Mission of Islam in the Contemporary World*, he called for "the liberation of the Earth and all its creatures through the reestablishment of the Caliphate." He argues that "the real meaning of the caliphate is not a dictatorship, as many non-Muslims and even Muslims believe." It is a benevolent political arrangement, a sort of Islamic anarchism. The caliph should monopolize political rule, and leave his subjects— Muslim and infidel—free to obey their consciences and practice religion as they please.[34] In achieving this multicultural wonderland, the caliph would be emulating and surpassing former caliphates, which were more tolerant than Christian societies of the same eras.

Nakata became a regular on Hizb al Tahrir's conference circuit, delivering lectures on the caliphate in fluent, if Japanese-accented and lispy, Arabic. "The teaching of Islam is that people should live equally under the same law," he told me. "Europeans don't talk about freedom of movement much, but it's the most fundamental of human rights, and a caliphate would protect it." Again one man's caliphate of the mind was being refracted through the lens of his original culture. "The Caliphate," he wrote, "is [. . .] the opposite of a police state." Like the Choudarheads' instinctive welfarism, Nakata's vision seemed to rest upon the traditional Japanese distinction between *honne* [private feelings or beliefs] and *tatemae* [public ones]. Islamic law so strictly respects private space, Nakata insisted, that if a lawman hears or smells the merrymaking of drinkers, he must move on past the window of the offenders' house, as long as it takes place inside.[35] Education would remain a private prerogative, again with freedom for parents to teach what they like. Overall, Nakata concluded, the caliphate should be "secular, anti-totalitarian, and pluralistic." Its arrival is so important that all Muslims have a duty to spread it "to the whole Earth, even with resort to military power if necessary." In his optimism, internationalism, and cultishness, there are echoes of Trotskyism.

Nakata followed the civil war in Syria from afar until 2012, when he made the first of five visits to check on the progress of Islamist movements there. Friends he knew from Egypt provided introductions, and he returned to Japan between trips to teach in Kyoto. He kept up with intra-Islamist discussions of the war, in part by reading online bulletin boards such as Abu Muhammad al Maqdisi's *Minbar al Tawhid wa al Jihad* [*Pulpit of Monotheism and Jihad*], the preeminent online clearinghouse of jihadi ideology. There is no evidence he fought during his trips, but he viewed the caliphate as so important that he could celebrate its potential rise even under violent circumstances.

By 2014, Nakata says, he detected signs that Abu Bakr al Baghdadi was preparing to declare himself caliph. "His followers had begun to call him '*amir al mu'minin* [prince of the believers],'" Nakata says, noting that the title attached to the historical office of the caliph. (Similarly, anyone who proclaimed himself "Head of the British Commonwealth" or "Defender of the Faith and Supreme Governor of the Church of England" would soon be expected to declare himself King of England.) Others had taken the title "prince of the believers" before, though, including Mullah 'Umar of the Taliban and King Muhammad VI of Morocco, so Nakata reserved judgment. He contacted a friend serving as the local ISIS commander in Idlib, Syria, and asked if Baghdadi was claiming to be caliph, and the friend assured him that he was not.

In the winter of 2014, Nakata escorted a Japanese journalist into ISIS territory and introduced him to Armenian Christians living there as subjugated citizens. He found the prospect of a caliphal declaration exhilarating, and in describing those early journeys to me, he sounded like a man both repelled and attracted. On one hand, he hated the violence. He had written of a caliphate arising peacefully and organically, like the fall of the Berlin Wall. But he admitted that the ISIS caliphate would be legitimate as long as it abolished borders and ruled by Islam—and it promised to do both.

Nakata learned about Baghdadi's declaration on Twitter, while at home in Kyoto. "I was surprised by how fast it happened," Nakata admits, still processing the experience. Not everyone gets to see his utopia made real. But for a brief while, he did. His theory of the caliphate was about to be tested by reality.

. . .

In the summer of 2014, shortly after Baghdadi's declaration, Nakata received a WhatsApp message from a fighter known as Omar al Gharib—"Omar the Stranger"—requesting his presence in the Islamic State as a guest of the caliphate. The population of Japanese caliphate activists is probably only slightly larger than the population of Islamist Shinto priests, so when the Islamic State wanted a Japanese specimen, it is not surprising they turned to Nakata.

"We have a Japanese journalist, and we're going to put him on trial," said the message. The "journalist" turned out to be Haruna Yukawa, a troubled forty-four-year-old nomad who may have been fighting with the Free Syrian Army. Yukawa had suffered a string of misfortunes—an unhappy childhood, the death of his wife from cancer, and financial ruin—and responded by indulging in extreme self-harm. Before coming to Syria he had attempted suicide by castrating himself. Since then, he had reinvented himself as a security consultant and moved to Syria to fight alongside rebels. The video of Yukawa's capture shows him disheveled and bleeding, surrounded by Islamic State fighters. He repeats the word "doctor," either pretending to be one or begging for one. After that video, he disappeared.

Nakata saw reason for hope. By inviting him to act as a translator, "the Islamic State wanted to show that they were having a fair trial, to show they have a good side." They told Nakata to bring a journalist to observe. He says he figured that the Islamic State might be using him to publicize and validate their murder of a Japanese citizen. But there was also a chance that they wanted the largest audience possible for a grand gesture of mercy.

In August, he showed up on the Turkish border near Tal Abyad with a Japanese video journalist. He had Omar's number and was supposed to call him once he arrived in the Islamic State. "There were several dozen foreigners going in just as I did," he says. "Most were Arabs—Egyptians and others—and at least three were Uighurs, who had no passports at all." They huddled in a makeshift waiting area, and when the Turkish border guards looked away, the whole mass of them filed through a gap in the barbed wire and into Syria. There they waited for a bus to Raqqah, about an hour away, where American bombs had recently begun falling.

"When I entered, there were no checks of any type," Nakata says. "We did not show our passports, and there was nothing at the border." The Islamic State had effaced the border as it said it would, and a rainbow coalition of Muslims from around the world was immigrating. "Everybody had their own reasons," Nakata says. "My Egyptian friend wanted to be in a caliphate, and the Europeans and Algerians and Tunisians often said they had had bad experiences in their home countries." Many, he said, were not fighters: they were disabled, or women. His lawyer piped up as Nakata began sounding a little wistful. As for him, he said, he was there not out of devotion or allegiance, but solely because he "was invited to go there. But no one else was aware of this."

Buses came and fetched people, and he caught one of the last of the evening. It was a free shuttle: no payment was requested. The Islamic State greased the path in and obstructed travel out. On arrival in Raqqah, he said, everyone signed a sort of guestbook, and he wrote "Hassan al Yabani," Hassan the Japanese.

The bombing had left Raqqah in disarray, with most communication networks down, including all phone lines. Many who had just arrived lacked local contacts, so the state accommodated them in a school and fed them communally. "We usually ate the usual Arab food," he said, "but the cook was Indian, so he sometimes made a very good curry." Nakata couldn't get in touch with Omar, so he sent a messenger to track him down. Meanwhile, everyone split into groups of one to two dozen and they were assigned housing—again, living communally.

And, Nakata says, happily. The new arrivals were promised a monthly stipend from the Islamic State of about $30, later upped to $50. "People seemed to be really enjoying life there," Nakata says, and they preferred it to the homes they had fled. "One time, a guy stopped me at a checkpoint. His face was covered, and he had a gun. He asked, 'Where are you from?' I said 'Japan.' He said 'All right then,' and gave me a chocolate."

I didn't know how to react to these scenes of fraternity and kindness. Nakata volunteered not a single grotesque or regrettable detail—nary a public whipping or the tutting of a *hisbah* officer over his wispy Japanese beard. "At the moment, the Islamic State is in a state of war, and any place in a state of war is going to have a lot of security concerns," he said. "But life was not bad." Indeed, from everything he said about communal living and the diversity of immigrants, I could imagine how solidarity might emerge even if it hadn't existed to begin with. A French jihadist has described Raqqah as having "Englishmen, Bosnians, Somalis, Japanese, Chinese"—"it's the Euro Disney of mujahedin!"[36] What cosmopolitan could resist the scenes Nakata describes? A Japanese wrestling enthusiast breaking bread with a kid from the *banlieue* on his left and a Chinese Turk on his right; an Islamic nanny state promising, and for the time being delivering, comfort and security; radical equality, and constant expressions of mutual love and respect for everyone, whether sick or well, young or old. The presence of a common enemy adds an extra dose of solidarity. A kibbutz in 1967 would not have felt so different.

But Nakata did not stay. In the chaos of the bombing, his contact had disappeared, and the messenger came back with the one thing Nakata's very Japanese sense of order could not abide: news of a delay. "When the messenger finally found the guy, he told him I'd have to wait another week. But I was due to come back to Japan," Nakata said. "I was annoyed." He sent back a message. "I came here because you told me to come, and then you left me waiting all this time. Next time keep your promises." Nothing could be done, so he left Raqqah to attend to a previously scheduled meeting with the Taliban, in Qatar.

.   .   .

Back in Japan, the government raided Nakata's house and confiscated his passport—thus putting him in the same convenient or inconvenient limbo as Musa and the Choudarheads. In October 2014, the journalist Kenji Goto traveled to Syria to try to win Yukawa's freedom. In January 2015, Goto and Yukawa appeared in an Islamic State video. Wearing orange jumpsuits, they knelt in front of the executioner Muhammad "Jihadi John" Emwazi. He demanded a ransom of $200 million. The Japanese government asked Nakata to send a message to his contacts, refusing to pay ransom. Nakata thought the proposed message would get both men killed, so he refused. They were killed anyway.[37]

Nakata is now spared having to decide whether the caliphal obligation to which he has devoted his life is one that he needs to fulfill. In common with Musa and the others, he seems to like his home country, although in his case he is open about it. In one interview, he made the remarkable assertion that "all Japanese people will go to Paradise," because God will judge only Muslims and those who heard and rejected the message of Islam. The Japanese are so ignorant of the religion that they will get a free pass. The free pass will not apply to him. I did not give him a free pass, either. "Was it all you wanted?" I asked about his brief holiday in utopia. "Was it a valid caliphate?"

He said first that the caliphate contained many Syrian and Iraqi Baathists, and that many had "converted" to Salafism, but still had wicked secular minds. As for the true believers, they also misunderstood the mission of Islam. ("Make sure you don't get yourself assassinated," his lawyer said, exasperated, as he continued to elaborate—and, from the Islamic State's perspective, probably flirted with apostasy.) "A lot of the Salafis have just read through a few pamphlets and don't know about the true importance of the caliphate," Nakata said. "They think growing a long beard and wearing a certain type of hat is adequate. To me, the end of borders is the essence of the caliphate."

"Do you think yours is a view of the caliphate that is shared by many others?" I asked.

"No, I don't think so," he said, laughing.

But he continued to defend the partisans of the caliphate against those who rejected the institution altogether. In the war of fatwas between the Islamic State and scholars from mainstream universities and government-sponsored mosques, the caliphate's scholars were winning, he said. "The level of argument against them is much lower than that of the people arguing for them," Nakata says. "I can't say the Islamic State's scholars are the highest level of scholar," he added. But they were not losing the argument.

This still felt evasive. His fellow Japanese might be saved by ignorance, but he had educated his own soul into a hazardous state. He could still try to leave Japan; he could still give allegiance to the caliph—who, after all, controlled territory and publicly demanded obedience.

Thomas Aquinas advised: "When you meet a contradiction, make a distinction." Faced with a caliphate of savages, Nakata created a distinction—without classical precedent—between two types of allegiance [*bay'a*]. The first, he says, is *bay'a* that creates a caliphate and fixes it in place. This is reserved for the innermost circle of scholars, the "people who loosen and bind" [*ahl al hall wa al 'aqd*]. Only then, once those scholars have ratified and endorsed a caliphate, does the obligation to give allegiance reach others, including him. "We are still in the stage of fixing or creating a caliphate, and there is no fixed law or quorum that says when that is done," Nakata says. He couldn't say for sure when he would be obliged to act. But he seemed to think it was not yet, and that his own life was likely to end due to natural causes before he would be forced to decide.

By this time I knew the objections of an Islamic State loyalist like Musa well enough to hear his Aussie accent howling in my ears at these equivocations. "You say you want *khilafah*?" Musa once asked fellow Muslims who supported a gradualist path to *khilafah*. "Well, how are you getting it? You're saying the *Dawlah* is invalid because of one certain point? Go and help them! The best chance is right in front of you. Don't you at least want to go live under Shariah?"

Considering that Nakata still fondly remembered his last pork cutlet and glass of wine, I had to consider that the secret answer to this last question might be no. I could think of few more destructive actions than to convince him otherwise.

As an organization, Hizb al Tahrir has officially opposed the Baghdadi caliphate, even as certain figures at the fringes of Hizb al Tahrir (followers of Choudary, Omar Bakri, and others) have made *hijrah* to join it. I reached out to leaders of Hizb al Tahrir, and they refused to talk to me. But some of their supporters were more forthcoming, and not all were as idiosyncratic as Nakata-*san*.

In early 2015, a Twitter user going by @GleamingRazor sent me a series of tweets and online notes critical of my writing. He gave his name (I am not making this up) as "Da Masked Avenger." Over several exchanges, he answered me courteously and intelligently, while never letting the mask slip to reveal his true identity. He alluded in his writing to Christopher Marlowe and Thomas Hobbes, and his diction suggested Western higher education—and, I hoped, another view of *khilafah* to complement Nakata's. He described himself as "Islamist." He hated apostates and Muslims who gave comfort to apostates. He said Ayaan Hirsi Ali, the Dutch parliamentarian and author of the anti-Islamist books *Rebel* and *Heretic*, was "risible," and he suggested her murder might not be a bad thing. When Malala Yousafzai, who as a fifteen-year-old schoolgirl was shot in the face by the Taliban and later won the Nobel Peace Prize, came out with a movie critical of conservative Islam, he tweeted that he would "rather be raped by a rutting rhino" than go see it.

He refused to tell me his real name, though he claimed the "[Brit-

ish] security services know" his identity anyway. "I have my reasons," he wrote, and I left it at that. After brief negotiation, he agreed
to meet me in person. When I arrived at our meeting point—the
Starbucks on the fourth floor of the London department store
Selfridges—I spotted a South Asian fellow sipping tea and wearing a
blue sweatshirt. He appeared to be in his late thirties, and his hair
and cropped beard were lightly flecked with gray. If he was nervous,
he didn't show it, and at no point did his eyes dart about, despite his
paranoid insistence on a ridiculous pseudonym. He had a standard
London multicultural accent, more refined than the Choudarheads'
but not posh. About his own biography he offered nothing, and he
told me in advance that certain topics would be out-of-bounds. "I
won't talk about jihad, because if I did I'd fall afoul of terrorism stat-
utes quickly."

The stereotype in the British Islamist community, he told me over
our teas, is that the proles go for Salafism, and the educated middle
class goes for Hizb al Tahrir, as Nakata did. The Avenger wouldn't say
whether he was a member of Hizb al Tahrir, but he recommended
that I speak with the group, and everything he said followed their
party line.

Rank-and-file Islamic State supporters "are not the intelligentsia of
the Muslim *ummah*," he said. "We're talking about thugs." He paused,
biting his tongue. "I mean, I don't mean to be disparaging about them,
especially [when talking] to an infidel. They're my brothers." But disparage them he did. They were, he said, ignorant of caliphates and
Islam, and spoke loudest about the matters they understood least.
Choudary, he said, deserves extra ridicule and censure, because he's
smart enough to know better yet leads dozens of others into sin. "He's
not a fool," he said. "Because of his intelligence, he gets less intelligent
people to follow him. And that is why I hate him so much."

He objected to Muslims—from Dhahiris on down—who view

scripture in narrowly literal or legal terms. "They think of Islam as a code of laws, a set of dos and don'ts. And there are, in fact, things that are set in stone: the *hadd* punishments cannot be revoked," he said. But other than these elements of divinely ordained criminal code, the religion transcended law and should be considered a "methodology," he said, with various values to be weighed—including custom [*'urf*] and public interest [*maslahah*].

This shaped his views on slavery. "Islam permitted slavery," the Avenger said, matter-of-factly. "There is no *ayah* [Koranic verse] or hadith that bans it. But Islam does not *command* the taking of slaves." Custom, and the best interests of Muslims, had made the practice of owning humans inapplicable to the present. "In old times, when you went to war and defeated your enemy, you could seize their baggage, and that included women. Now, when the French and Germans go to battle, they don't bring their women along." Slavery, in this understanding of scripture, is about as relevant to present-day battle as catapults and triremes. "Custom says we don't do this, so *maslahah* and *'urf* lead us to say [slavery] is forbidden." Salafis, he said, pretend these considerations don't exist, and they believe all that is permitted is also commanded.

Equally anathema, though, to the Avenger is the effort of "modernists" to take these mitigating considerations too far and pretend that Islam commands nothing at all—no *hadd,* no *bay'a,* no subjugation of Jews and Christians. Overused, custom could license Muslims to scrap whatever elements of their faith didn't conform to a fashionable, infidel-friendly view of human rights and international order. The most extreme of these modernizing Muslims were atheists and pseudo-theists like Ayaan Hirsi Ali and Maajid Nawaz, founder of London's Quilliam Foundation. (He said he knew and was friendly with Nawaz's brother.) Both Hirsi Ali and Nawaz identify as Muslims but link arms with non-Muslims to call for reform and liberalization—the Avenger would say abolition—of Islam. "Because of them, Choudary uses ' *'urf* ' like a swear word," the Avenger complained. Salafis and "modernists," he said, formed a dialectic of ignorance that left groups like Hizb al Tahrir abandoned in the middle.

And that brought him to what he considered the real solution to the problem of the Baghdadi caliphate. "You hang out with interesting people," he told me. I thought he meant supporters of the Islamic State, but he went on to say he was referring to more sinister company, such as the Center for Strategic and International Studies and the Council on Foreign Relations, two think tanks where I had recently lectured. "You talk to these people," he said. He looked pained. "Can you please tell them, finally, that they will not be able to tell Muslims how to live our lives forever?" I wondered whether he was seriously suggesting that I had power over the policy titans who run these institutions.

He repeated the point, but this time as a threat. "If they don't let us choose our own government, things will only get worse," he said. The Islamic State horrified him, but it existed because U.S. hegemony had thwarted Muslims' dreams. The present conflict could have been averted if the U.S. had stepped back and allowed a true caliphate to take root and lead the *ummah*. It would be a caliphate obedient to God's law, but learned and careful rather than brutish and brash. "I'm not going to pretend Islam will never fight with you, or that we'll live in harmony forever," he said. "Expansion is part of Islam, and eventually we will subjugate you. But can you not see that to let us rule ourselves is at least better than having groups like [the Islamic State]?"

Muslim self-rule could happen only through a caliphate, he said, and I should prepare myself for that—either through the Islamic State or other, milder means. I preferred the second option but was curious about the first. "Could you ever imagine giving *bay'a* to Baghdadi?" I asked. At what point would he accept the Caliphate of Ignorance?

He thought for a while. Like Nakata, he was torn between a utopian dream to come and a dystopian nightmare already under way. And he knew that he was, in theory, obliged to swear an oath to any valid caliphate. Islamic State supporters' standard criticism of Hizb al Tahrir is that as soon as a caliphate exists, they start attaching additional requirements to avoid having to recognize it. "They say it has to be big," Musa told me, incredulous. "Well, how big? Five times the current size? They're just making things up." The excuse the Avenger gave me sounded distressingly arbitrary in that context. "It still isn't a state," he said. "Too small, too disorganized."

"But what if it kept growing and took Baghdad, Damascus, or Amman?"

He thought longer. "Then I would have to reconsider," he said.

DISSENT

They will pass through Islam like an arrow through its prey.
—Bukhari

If they were right, one would have been enough.
—Albert Einstein,
after publication of *100 Authors Against Einstein*

Most of my interview subjects have been well-spoken. Plenty of other Islamic State recruits, like plenty of normal people, are dullards and goofballs, incapable of articulating the beliefs that rule their lives. At best they are proficient at parroting them, with the same brain-shrinking effects apparent in Hare Krishna followers when they sing their two-syllable mantra for the ten thousandth time in a day. The Islamic State mantras are familiar. "Revival of the caliphate." "Purification of Islam." "*Kuffar.*" "Application of the *hadd* punishments." "End of the world." They know these things because they've been taught them, and not because they have crafted their own ideologies or studied classical Arabic. "The average recruit is intellectually submissive," Thomas Hegghammer says. "He knows what he's supposed to believe, and he probably believes it. But he's easily led."[1] Aimen Dean, a former Al Qaida member who now consults for the British government, said something similar to me and others at a conference in Qatar. "A confused militant is an ineffective militant."[2] Confusion is not hard to sow. Rank-and-file Islamic State supporters don't need to be convinced that they are wrong—just convinced that they might not be right.

Convincing hard-core ideologues is trickier and has higher stakes. Curious how one might make the case, I went to meet the two most prominent Muslim scholars in the United States today: Hamza Yusuf and Yasir Qadhi. Yusuf is the president of Zaytuna College, in Berkeley, and Qadhi teaches at Rhodes College, in Memphis. "If you go to an ISNA [Islamic Society of North America] convention," one Islamic studies professor promised me, "those two guys are the rock stars. They have entourages. They have groupies. Standing-room-only audiences to hear them talk about *fiqh* [Islamic law]."

He oversold them a tad. For pure rock-star bad-boyism, the Islamic State is unbeatable: Turki al Bin'ali does the Islamic equivalent of smashing an electric guitar and kicking over an amplifier every time he steps up to the *minbar*. Hamza Yusuf and Yasir Qadhi, by contrast, are soft rock at best. They are mild, learned men, and their groupies seek them out not because they are renegades but because they have submitted to tradition—Sufism, in Yusuf's case, and a version of reformed Salafism, in Qadhi's. These traditions are at odds with each other—the Salafis accuse Sufis of idolatry, and the Sufis accuse Salafis of intolerance and anti-intellectualism—and the two men disagree fiercely.

They are united, though, in having been marked for death by the Islamic State. *Dabiq* has written about them twice—the second time in an article by Yahya Abu Hassan, pronouncing them "valid—rather, obligatory—targets" for assassination.[3] Their ultimate sin, Yahya wrote, is collaboration with "Crusaders" against Muslims, which in itself invalidates their Islam. Yusuf, as Yahya and others have pointed out, met with George W. Bush to advise him early in the Afghanistan war.[4] Qadhi's Salafi orientation places him closer to Islamic State–

compliant views. Originally schooled as a Wahhabi, Qadhi has transformed into a flag-waving American patriot.

In mid-2015, Musa Cerantonio fielded followers' online questions about Qadhi and Yusuf and expressed sentiment similar to Yahya's— putting the followers on guard for the slightest wavering in their own belief:

> Some might be fooled by their outer appearances since
> [Qadhi and Yusuf] present themselves as teachers of Islam
> when they are in fact callers to the Fire. Do not let these ap-
> pearances deceive you, as we know that even a single word
> of *kufr* [disbelief] may cause someone to have all of their
> other acts nullified. . . . Knowledge and education alone will
> not save us from falling into disbelief or deviance as many
> with more knowledge than us have strayed due to the evil
> hidden in their hearts.[5]

Musa knows Qadhi personally—they appeared together on at least one panel, at a Salafi conference in India in 2008, and he says Qadhi once suggested that Musa write for Qadhi's website. (Qadhi reminds me that Musa had not yet expressed jihadi views at that point.) But any sense of camaraderie has vanished. Qadhi told me Musa is "crazy" and "just some guy in Australia." Musa fantasizes about meeting Qadhi again. "I hope I see him face-to-face again. He will run away," he told me. He said that Qadhi is guilty of *'irja,* belief that one's Islam is in the heart, and not revealed by pious action and jihad. He gave another translation of *'irja* in case I didn't understand: "Yasir's a little pussy."

In 2015, after they were first mentioned in *Dabiq,* I met Qadhi and Yusuf on separate occasions. I approached them because I was frustrated by other Muslims' accounts of the Islamic State's relationship with Islam. The problem was not, and has never been, a failure of mainstream Muslims to condemn terrorism, or to denounce the Islamic State. The problem is their reluctance to seriously acknowledge or engage with the Islamic State intellectually. Instead, their defense of Islam is typified by the refrain "Islam is a religion of peace," combined with happy-talk about mercy and love. They do not address the scriptures the Islamic State cites about war or hate. Such apologism is the photonegative of sweeping claims that Islam is essentially harsh and murderous. It is every bit as simplistic and pointless. And Yusuf, at least, has tired of it. During Ramadan 2016, as the Islamic State unleashed a wave of terrorist attacks, he wrote:

> What we need to counter this plague are the voices of scholars, as well as grassroots activists, who can begin to identify the real culprits behind this fanatical ideology. What we do not need are more voices that veil the problem with empty, hollow, and vacuous arguments that this militancy has little to do with religion; it has everything to do with religion: misguided, fanatical, ideological, and politicized religion. It is the religion of resentment, envy, powerlessness, and nihilism. It does, however, have nothing to do with the merciful teachings of our Prophet, God's peace and blessings upon him.[6]

After so much denialism by others, Yusuf's words counted as bluntness.

Mainstream Muslims are in a bind. The Islamic State professes that there is one God, and that Muhammad is his last and greatest prophet. Denying the Islamic State's faith and its supporters' status as Muslims—excommunicating them because you disagree with their version of Islam—is to concede the match. After all, *takfir* is the official sport of the Islamic State, and if you practice it, you become one of them. For Muslims who hate the group, the Islamic State's claim that there is no god but God, and Muhammad is his prophet, is a statement of faith that forces a painful admission: the Islamic State is a Muslim phenomenon. Wicked, perhaps; ultraviolent, certainly. But Muslim, by definition.[7]

No one wants the most well-known practitioners of his religion also to be its most fanatical and bloodthirsty. Most religions have zealots that the mainstream would prefer to make disappear, and the Muslim bind is not unique. Protestants will reluctantly admit that members of the Westboro Baptist Church—who picket funerals of U.S. soldiers, bearing signs that say "God Hates Fags"—are Christians who spend huge amounts of time in Bible study, or that they accept Jesus as their savior. Jews cringe at Neturei Karta, the ultra-Orthodox cult that sends delegations to Holocaust-denial conferences, but admit that they are Jews. Burma's 969 movement is very Buddhist, despite preaching an unenlightened message of ethnic hatred against Muslims. Mel Gibson thinks the pope isn't Catholic enough, and that may qualify him as crazy—but as a crazy *Catholic*.[8]

The Islamic State is as Islamic as the above are Protestant, Jewish, Buddhist, or Catholic—which is to say, it is thoroughly Islamic, even though it is, by its own proud admission, a minority sect.[9] Whether it is "legitimate" is a question other believers answer for themselves, overwhelmingly in the negative. But these questions of legitimacy are a matter of opinion and dogma: the fact that the majority believes the Islamic State to be deviant does not make them objectively deviant, any more than many Christians' view of Mormonism as deviant makes Mormonism "illegitimate," or a "perversion of Christianity." The same could be said for any other religious minority, including progressive ones; being in a minority (violent or not) does not equate to being illegitimate. Being in a minority means being in a minority.[10]

Muslim critics of the Islamic State are then compelled to acknowledge that the group is led and supported by Muslims, albeit Muslims with whom they vociferously disagree. The mortification is compounded by the discovery that the Islamic State consults the same texts as other Muslims, and dips into the same Sunni historical tradition. The Islamic State's scholars do not cite Marx, the *philosophes,* the laws of Manu, or Paul the Apostle. They cite Koran, hadith, and carefully selected thinkers within the Islamic tradition. Their fanaticism is a Muslim fanaticism. It takes astonishing levels of denial to claim, as uncountable Muslims and non-Muslims have, that the Islamic State has "nothing to do with Islam," merely because the group's heinous behavior clashes with mainstream or liberal Muslim interpretation.[11]

Yasir Qadhi's interpretation of Islam may be mainstream, but it is not liberal, except in comparison to his earlier work. Born in 1975 in Houston to Pakistani-American parents, Qadhi received a degree in chemical engineering from the University of Houston, then an Islamic education in Saudi Arabia at the University of Medina, the Harvard of Salafism. His early work included a scholarly close reading—a fan's notes, almost—of works by Muhammad ibn ʿAbd al Wahhab, the spiritual godfather of Saudi Islam and a favorite scholar of the Islamic State. Qadhi focused on Ibn ʿAbd al Wahhab's understanding of *shirk* [idolatry], the assigning of a "partner" to God and thereby denying His oneness and unshared lordship.[12] His commentary on Ibn ʿAbd al Wahhab is patient and measured, and compliant with Wahhabi austerity, including the need to remove all adornment from graves and do away with singing and the veneration of saints. He also flirted with anti-Semitism and Holocaust denial, claiming at one point that "Hitler never intended to mass-destroy the Jews" and that the Holocaust was a "hoax."[13]

Qadhi's return to the United States in 2005 began a transformation that has led to his shedding the "Salafi" and "Wahhabi" labels, although he acknowledges that Ibn ʿAbd al Wahhab had some good points. He repudiated his earlier comments about the Holocaust[14] and complemented his religious training with an equally rigorous secular one, completing a Ph.D. in religious studies at Yale University, where I teach. Yahya is correct when he accuses Qadhi of American patriotism. Qadhi does not mind adorning his website with American flags and proudly living by the U.S. Constitution. Some Salafis shake their heads and wonder what happened. But for each enemy he has made among the *shirk* patrol, he has acquired several admirers from the community of Muslims seeking to live a pious, Shariah-following life in their own more tolerant way—perhaps more like a Muslim Brother than a Salafi.

His writing since his return to the United States is notable for internal conflict about his metamorphosis—as if the voice of Ibn ʿAbd al Wahhab still sometimes whispers in his ear, and he is not sure how to answer. In 2008, while at Yale, Qadhi attended a class taught by Tony Blair. In a sententious essay for his website, he describes grappling over whether it was "morally and ethically allowed for me to take a class with someone whom many were actually viewing as a potential war criminal." Could he contain the "force and vigor" of his hatred? He confronts Blair about the morality of the Iraq invasion and receives an unflustered answer.[15] (Musa thought this was pathetic. "[Qadhi] says he did his job as a Muslim by asking Tony Blair a question," Musa complains. "That's it? Really? I'm not saying he should have slit his throat. But still! I call him Yasir Gandhi.")

In February 2015, Qadhi returned to Yale for a short visit, and his doctoral adviser, Frank Griffel, held a dinner in his honor upstairs at Mory's, an unofficial faculty club across the street from the main university library. It was the coldest night of the year, and when I arrived, bundled up and a few minutes late, Qadhi and a cadre of graduate students were already cozy in a wood-paneled private room, surveying the menu's steaks and risottos.

Qadhi and I shared a frosty handshake. He was familiar with my writing about the Islamic State and opposed my view that the Islamic State is very Islamic, and that it has intelligent Muslim intellectuals tirelessly issuing fatwas justifying (among other things) the assassination of Yasir Qadhi. I sat next to him, and he was cordial as he explained his disagreements.

"The problem is not what you say"—that the Islamic State is Islamic—"but what you didn't say, and what needs to be said," he told me. The American public needs to know the Islamic State's origins as the product of a bellicose American foreign policy with a near-psychopathic fixation on bombing and despoiling Muslim lands. The public does not need to dwell on its place in Islamic history and thought. Americans think that the Islamic State "hates us for our freedoms," he said, and that we are "angelic" and have somehow waged decades of war in Muslim lands without moral blemish. To describe the Islamic State's arguments and their religious basis was not wrong, he said. But it was politically disastrous, because even if the Islamic State is Islamic, describing it as such buttressed the arguments of those who already identify the Islamic State with Islam and were already threatening him and other Muslims. He mentioned Pamela Geller, a vicious anti-Muslim bigot and activist, as an example of a fan of my writing.

Journalists like me, he said, should take care to note the sources of authority in Islam. They are not people like Musa Cerantonio and Anjem Choudary—"fringe cartoon characters [who] don't have mosques or any kind of institutional presence, let alone authority, in the Muslim community," he wrote in an intemperate blog post about my work a few days later. (He compared me to "another Wood," Clint Eastwood—director of *American Sniper*—for my role in "riling up" anti-Muslim sentiment.)[16] The real authorities, he told me, were degreed scholars, professors, and people who had devoted their lives not to coffee-shop ranting but to perseverance with the long and difficult tradition of Islam.

Since I had such a scholar in front of me, I asked him: Is the Islamic State Islamic? He answered emphatically, if evasively: "They are Muslim," he said, but they defied teachings at the core of the religion. These included, he said, injunctions to show mercy and humility, and long historical and legal traditions designed to prevent the very excesses the Islamic State revels in. Then he repeated what he viewed as the real root of the problem: the sins of the U.S. government—not just its foreign policy but its prison system, its militaristic culture, its drone strikes, and its failure to remove money from the political process.

I scraped the last peas off my plate and began a gentle rejoinder. I conceded, happily, that the invasion of Iraq in 2003 created the power vacuum that the Islamic State filled (although the Syrian civil war and the long history of predatory government in the region were hardly attributable in full to American foreign policy). That the Islamic State exists within a political world was not news.

What amazed me, I said—to Qadhi's visible irritation—was that a distinguished Muslim theologian would respond to the Islamic State's theology with a lecture on campaign finance reform. Even if money in politics can be implicated in the rise of a neoconservative American foreign policy, did he have nothing to say about the group's theology, its scriptural interpretations, its legal methodology? Could he not meet the likes of Musa Cerantonio on his own terms? Qadhi was replying to Musa's religious claims not with religious counterclaims but with political claims—and political claims with which Musa would agree! The Islamic State's story of its own origins acknowledges that the Crusader George W. Bush's blunder into Iraq set the conditions for *khilafah*. They count Bush's foreign policy as a blessing.

I tried to outline what I understood to be the Islamic State's gripes about Qadhi's theological views. Qadhi was clearly disgusted at the idea of having to reply to Musa (channeled through a latter-day Clint Eastwood) as if Musa were a scholar. The extent of the Islamic State's error, Qadhi seemed to be saying, was so great that Mory's busboys would be turning off the lights and kicking us out before he could get started explaining. Even his blog post three days later did not broach any theological subjects. The only point he made at dinner that marshaled Muslim text or history was a reference to the Kharijites, a seventh-century sect that went to extremes in its practice of excommunication and murder of fellow Muslims. That sect, he said, had been condemned by Muslims both Sunni and Shia, and the Islamic State, as its modern incarnation, should be condemned in the same terms.

The dinner ended with a handshake icier than the one that began it. I had succeeded in provoking a reply from Qadhi that skirted all the issues that I had come to learn about. I am sure he was just as exasperated. It was hard to fault him for his frustration: as a conservative Muslim who had spent his early career thinking about the vice of *shirk,* he now had to distance himself from a group that he despised, but that was no less obsessed with *shirk* and, by his own account, was definitely Muslim. To criticize someone who disagrees with you about so little is not easy—especially when someone like me will not stop pointing out the similarities. The differences, though small, ensured permanent mutual enmity between Qadhi and the Islamic State. But the similarities were enough to make that enmity awkward to explain.

When Qadhi does confront the Islamic State's religious claims directly, his points are worth considering. His claim about the Kharijites—the early schismatic sect to which he and others have compared the Islamic State—is one of these cases.

The history of Kharijism is brief and bloody and Muslim sources tell a partisan tale about the group's misdeeds. In 657, a quarter century after the death of Muhammad, two rival claimants to leadership of the Muslim community fought the Battle of Siffin, in present-day Raqqah. On one side was ʿAli ibn Abi Talib—cousin of the Prophet, husband of his daughter Fatima, and Muhammad's rightful successor according to the Shia—and on the other was Muʿawiyya, who was not from the Prophet's household but was favored by the Sunni.

The battle was bloody, killing 25,000 of 'Ali's men and 45,000 of Mu'awiyya's in three months of intermittent fighting. Eventually, the rivals spared their armies further slaughter and agreed to arbitration.

A third group then arose from within 'Ali's camp. Called the *qurra'*, or reciters of the Koran, they came from the Tamimi tribe of Iraq and were well-known as dangerous idiots. They opposed the arbitration because they believed debating the issue at all displaced God's will with human judgment. This group left 'Ali's camp to follow an obscure tribal leader named 'Abdullah ibn Wahb al Rasibi, also known as "the callused one" [Dhu'l-Thafinat] for the thick pads of skin on his forehead and knees from intense prayer. Because of this exodus, history remembers them as "those who departed" [*Khawarij*], or Kharijites.

They are now among the most despised groups in the history of Islam. Opposing both Sunni and Shia, they unleashed a wave of killings across Arabia. Edward Gibbon described it in *Decline and Fall of the Roman Empire*:

> In the temple of Mecca, three Charegites [Kharijites] or enthusiasts discoursed of the disorders of the church and state: they soon agreed, that the deaths of Ali, of Moawiyah, and of his friend Amrou, the viceroy of Egypt, would restore the peace and unity of religion. Each of the assassins chose his victim, poisoned his dagger, devoted his life, and secretly repaired to the scene of action. Their resolution was equally desperate: but the first mistook the person of Amrou, and stabbed the deputy who occupied his seat; the prince of Damascus [Mu'awiyya] was dangerously hurt by the second; the lawful caliph ['Ali], in the mosch of Cufa, received a mortal wound from the hand of the third. He expired in the sixty-third year of his age, and mercifully recommended to his children, that they would despatch the murderer by a single stroke.[17]

Slaying ʿAli, a rightly guided caliph, during his prostration before God is an impressive trifecta of sin. Being ornery bastards prevented the Kharijites from making alliances and friends, and both Shia and Sunni leaders killed them when they got the chance. The Kharijites ruled isolated pockets of Arabia, dispensing a harsh justice to those who chose to immigrate to their land, or who happened to live there. The most extreme among them—followers of a Kharijite warrior named Nafiʿ ibn Azraq—treated all non-Kharijites as infidels, and stressed the obligation of all Muslims to make *hijrah* to the Kharijites' small territory in southern Iraq and western Iran. According to one source, making *hijrah* to join the Azraqites entailed a brutal hazing ritual that required each aspirant to slaughter a non-Kharijite Muslim. Their command to piety brooked no failure: if a Muslim sinned, he could be considered an apostate even if the sin was minor, such as drinking. The Kharijites took a literalist approach to scripture and worship. Instead of praying five times daily, as all other Muslims do, they pointed to Koran 11:114 ("establish prayer at the two ends of the day") and prayed only twice.[18] Within a century they were reduced to a few minuscule communities that had given up on recovering worldly power.[19]

The slur "Kharijite" has recurred many times in Islamic history, usually as a catch-all term for "Muslim who does not get along well with other Muslims." As an insult, it associates any irritable pietist sect with sin. In fact the Kharijites followed a fairly specific and idiosyncratic program, almost universally regarded as deviant by Muslims ever since. They shed blood freely—according to some sources, they would split people in half and vivisect pregnant women—and did not distinguish in battle between soldiers and civilians. Their cavalry attacks and guerrilla tactics made them famous for blitz-like seizures of towns, before authorities could prepare themselves.

Few Muslim sources pay these fanatics any compliments. But to remember them only for their irascible bloodlust risks forgetting appealing aspects of Kharijism, which no doubt account for the success it briefly enjoyed. Later sources may disparage them, but in some ways the Kharijites were preserving the earliest impulses of what became Islam. They stressed reading of the Koran, *hijrah,* asceticism, *takfir,* and *al wala' wa-l bara'* [loyalty to Muslims and disavowal of infidels]—all core principles and practices of the early religion. Muhammad had come to power as a unifier of warring tribes—the Ansar originally welcomed him to Medina as a mediator—and by the time of the Battle of Siffin, Mu'awiyya and 'Ali had come to resemble squabbling hereditary kings. The Kharijite emphasis on piety promised to re-abolish the importance of tribe, race, and lineage. (They even denied that their caliph needed to come from the tribe of Quraysh.) Kharijites believed in equal opportunity—opportunity to lead, to get beheaded, to assume responsibility for one's soul. The hadith about following your emir, "even if he is an Ethiopian slave with a head like a raisin," has long been taken as a Kharijite slogan of racial equality.[20] Most Muslims may revile the Kharijites of history, but aspects of Kharijism are inescapably modern. To those who believe in the equality of man, the evil of despotism, and freedom to determine one's own fate, the Kharijites offer much to appreciate.

The common bonds between Kharijism and the Islamic State scarcely require explanation. Both groups rejected authority and created chaos; they urged revolt against unjust rulers as a matter of principle, despite a general preference in Islam for obedience, even to unjust leaders. The Kharijites practiced mass excommunication; the Islamic State cuts off the heads of "apostates" daily, and it declares whole classes of Muslims (e.g., the Shia) infidels. The Kharijites broke off or departed [*kharaja*] from the Muslim mainstream; the Islamic State has stated that it defies mainstream Islam (and thus returns to real Islam). Most of all, both groups are just really mean.

One consequence of calling the Islamic State modern Kharijites is to affirm that they are also, by implication, Muslims: the Kharijites

tried to cast other Muslims out of the religion, but most of their enemies did not return the favor.[21] Second, because the Prophet is supposed to have prophesied the emergence of a Kharijite group and
commanded his followers to fight it, as soon as anyone calls others
Kharijites, he implies that he must fight them. It can't be just an insult. Because they are Muslim, however, infidels should not be the
ones to fight them: that is the job of Muslims. At dinner, Qadhi as-
sented to both points: the Islamic State is a Muslim group, not infidel,
and Muslims must denounce and fight them. He would be happy to
see the Islamic State defeated by Muslims, just not by a non-Muslim
army.

The Islamic State's supporters deny that they are Kharijites. Turki
al Bin'ali rejected the comparison point by point, in a recorded sermon. "We don't excommunicate people for major sins" such as
drinking alcohol or theft, he said. The Kharijites would take alcohol
consumption as evidence of apostasy. But the Islamic State has not
executed anyone for drinking, eating during the Ramadan fast,
smoking, or stealing. Nor, he said, does the Islamic State "practice
mass excommunication on the basis of false assumptions." Instead
they judge people as apostates only if they have individually committed clear acts of disbelief, such as fighting against Muslims, or other
classic Wahhabi faith-nullifiers. Then he anticipates the next point
on which the Islamic State's enemies claim it is Kharijite—isn't "fighting against Muslims" what the Islamic State does every day? Again,
Bin'ali says no. "We don't consider it legitimate to rebel against a
leader who is Muslim and monotheist," he says. The Islamic State has
fought only against non-Muslims and polytheists.[22] (This point is
valid only if one accepts his expansive category of people who are
apostates.)

Other defenders of the Islamic State point out that the Kharijites'
egalitarianism included abolition of the Quraysh requirement for
the caliph. The Islamic State, by contrast, has observed and emphasized that requirement—therefore they cannot be Kharijites. They

did not, these defenders say, revolt against an unjust ruler or "leave" Islam. Instead, they seized uncontrolled land and remained in the religion, strengthening it. They note that the Kharijites partook in other odd heterodoxies—such as requiring women to pray while menstruating, changing the daily prayer schedule, and editing certain verses out of the Koran—that no one accuses the Islamic State of doing.[23] Periodically the Islamic State claims to discover and punish Kharijite sects within its own ranks.[24] Finally, the Islamic State attempts to hoist its Muslim enemies by their own petards: those who say "the Islamic State are not Muslims" are themselves committing *takfir* on Muslims—which is something a Kharijite would do.

As a rhetorical move, calling the Islamic State "Kharijites" hits its followers hard. They compare themselves to the Companions of the Prophet; instead, their opponents say, we should compare them to the first goon squad in Islamic history. But the Kharijite accusation also concedes to the Islamic State the idea that modern disagreements are best resolved by appealing to theology or ancient history, rather than to basic decency or a shared modern morality. On the other hand, the accusation infuriates the Islamic State, so many Muslims continue to fling it around on that basis alone.

Hamza Yusuf, many people told me, would have strong opinions about the Islamic State and a smoother delivery than Qadhi. The two are not close: Qadhi is still seen as Salafi-influenced, and Yusuf as Sufi. Sufis vary widely in political outlook and religious practice. Some focus on reading texts, and others on dancing (e.g., whirling dervishes), devotional music, or other practices. Because of Sufis' veneration of saints and graves, and their strong emphasis on following senior scholars, Salafis tend to view them as aficionados of *shirk*, and perhaps poets and pantheists in Muslim disguise. Sufis view Salafis as intolerant and obtuse, and liable to burn every Sufi book and steamroll every Sufi shrine on the planet, if given the chance.

In early 2015, I wrote to Yusuf and received an invitation to meet. The ideological claims of Islamic State supporters and non-Muslims' claims that the group might have religious legitimacy left him "deeply disturbed," he said. ISIS "is a religious problem and not merely a political one, but the ins and outs of that fact are complicated." And he reminded me that the Islamic State had recently sentenced him and "another Muslim intellectual"—he didn't say Qadhi's name—to execution.

Hamza Yusuf was born Mark Hanson in 1960 and grew up in Marin County, where John Walker Lindh would be raised two decades later. As a teenager, he nearly died in a car crash, and during his recovery, he found a Koran, met Muslims, and converted to Islam. Still in his teens, he moved to Norwich, England, to follow a Sufi sheikh, and then to the United Arab Emirates for further study. He spent years studying in Algeria and Mauritania before returning to California in 1988 to train as a nurse and minister to the poor and sick. However, he found himself more in demand as a Muslim orator and scholar than as a physical healer. Audiences in the United States, Europe, and the Middle East loved his mastery of Arabic, his compelling tales of peregrinations in exotic foreign lands, his joyful and learned command of sources in Islamic history as well as Western philosophy and literature. Now firmly established as a major figure among American Muslims, he gathers crowds and commands large audiences at religious gatherings.[25]

Yusuf invited me to his home in the San Ramon Valley, over the hills from Berkeley. He answered the front door of his town house and greeted me with strong eye contact. He wore a small turban and a trimmed beard. His face was taut and youthful, and except for the turban he looked not so different from other Berkeleyites who had traded a drugged-out, tie-dye lifestyle for rude spiritual and physical health. He led me into a carpeted room with a whole wall covered in books, in front of which he sat, amid a small number of students, including a faculty member at Zaytuna and a doctor from Michigan who had recently settled nearby. Throughout the afternoon, he referred to the books frequently and often took long pauses to retrieve them and look things up. They were not ornamental, nor were they placed to intimidate. They were a life-support system.

To Yusuf, the Islamic State's scholarship is the thinnest of veneers. "Outwardly, [the leaders of the Islamic State] look very impressive," he says, "because they can quote Koran and hadith and can really make people think that they know what they are talking about. But if you sit with them for five minutes, you can expose their ignorance very quickly."

Consider, he said, the Islamic State's justification for burning to death the Jordanian pilot Mu'dh al Kasasbeh—namely that since the pilot had burned people alive and crushed them with rubble, he must suffer the same fate, under the doctrine of reciprocal punishment, or *qisas*. "First of all, *qisas* is never applied in *fitna* [social discord] or war. That's by the consensus of scholars: no *qisas* in war." Instead, he said, *qisas* is restricted to civil punishment, a literal eye-for-an-eye administered in times of peace by a proper court to settle disputes between two citizens. The Islamic State was applying an established doctrine, but only after plucking it out of a context that had been considered essential for centuries.

Second, he said, in burning Kasasbeh they acknowledged the scriptural command not to use fire as an instrument of torture—only God may punish with fire[26]—but they treated that command as subordinate to the use of *qisas* by Abu Bakr al Siddiq and others. Traditionally, however, historical examples are considered the weakest category of authority, and inadequate for the taking of a life. "No scholar would ever use a piece of *historical* tradition as *legal* evidence," Yusuf said. "You are dealing with gross amateurs, not jurists."

He counted the Islamic State's endless harping on the need to establish a caliphate as equally laughable. The establishment of a caliphate, he said, is an optional element of Islam, and one that the Islamic State has implemented incorrectly. "The caliph [is supposed to] represent all the Muslims," he said, exasperated. "[The Caliph] ʿUmar said that if anyone claims to be caliph, do not take *bayʿa* [allegiance] with him." That is, a unilateral, contested declaration of a caliphate is always impermissible, because a caliph is caliph only with the consent of all Muslims. Therefore all rival claimants are illegitimate, by virtue of their rivalry. "I can't just claim to be the *khalifah*," he said, waving his hands around in the air like a mad sorcerer. "'I'll just declare this is my caliphate! You guys are my subjects!' It's just stupid."

As for warfare against infidels, Yusuf admitted that war is a component of jihad, and not a minor one. But he noted that jihad "is the prerogative of a [valid] state. [To declare jihad] is a legal ruling that pertains only to political authority. You cannot have vigilante justice," just as it would be bizarre for an Arizona border militia to "declare war" on Mexico and attack it. In Muslim traditions of just war, jihad also requires examination of the likely outcome. To declare war against the entire rest of the world would be idiotic, he says, since Muslims would be annihilated. "If somebody calls for preemptive jihad in the modern world with [the infidels], we [Muslims] declare him insane."

I tried to listen to Yusuf as his enemies would—with Musa's penchant for excommunication, Choudary's pugnacity, and Hassan Ko Nakata's romantic caliphal idealism. First they would attack his methods and conclusions. "How dare he limit *qisas*!" Musa would say. "By what authority? This is something Allah has permitted. When did he say that it is not allowed in war?" That Muslim scholars agree about its wartime inapplicability would not faze an Islamic State supporter. Nor, I'm sure, would they be impressed by Yusuf's claims about jihad, which again rely on a scholarly consensus that the Islamic State simply does not recognize.

Others would resort to ad hominem attacks. "These are scholars for dollars," Choudary told me, dismissing Yusuf and others as tools of existing states, including the Gulf monarchies and, yes, America. Yusuf's association with George W. Bush is considered damning, as is the fact that his beloved teacher, Abdullah bin Bayyah, is a professor in Saudi Arabia. I asked Choudary about the document signed by more than a hundred Muslim scholars—a "Letter to Baghdadi" informing Baghdadi of his error and the disapproval of Muslim intellectuals.[27] "Look at them," Choudary seethed. "They are in palaces. And where are our scholars? In prisons or in Syria."

When I mentioned these likely responses, Yusuf was as annoyed as Qadhi had been. Yes, Yusuf's preaching had brought him fame and prosperity, but he had also been studying Islam for the past forty years. This is longer than Turki al Bin'ali has been alive. He spent that time immersed in the classical traditions of Islam, including years of text memorization. He was not going to throw these traditions away because a gang of desert lunatics said he should. The Islamic State's scholars could not possibly know what they were discarding, much less develop arguments that could counter 1,400 years of accreted consensus. There is not enough time in a human life to learn all that the consensus consists of, let alone whether it should be abandoned.

This argument wouldn't have moved Musa and his friends. "The proof of your education is in what you *say*," Musa once told me. "It does not matter if you are a seven-year-old child or the best-educated scholar in Saudi Arabia." But, as Yusuf said, the callow ignorance of people like Musa made them impervious to argument. How do you convince someone that he has thrown out the best parts of his tradition, if he refuses to look at what he has chucked away? Sa'adia Gaon, the great rabbi of tenth-century Baghdad, described his critics in similarly scornful terms:

> [The critic] would fail to recognize the truth even if it should
> by chance occur to him or he should happen to come upon it.
> He is thus like a creditor who does not know the art of weigh-

ing, or even the nature of a balance and weights, nor yet how much money is due him from his debtor. Even if his debtor were to pay him his debt in full, he would be uncertain whether he had paid it.[28]

The problem remained: Yusuf could claim that the Islamic State's supporters did not possess the knowledge necessary to judge whether they were right or wrong. But that still did not mean they were wrong. So I continued to press him for arguments against the Islamic State that relied only on the texts of revelation, without reference to the opinion of scholars.

But the task I gave him was an impossible one in his eyes—not least because the texts of revelation do not read and interpret themselves. They need scholars. I felt increasingly embarrassed by my persistence. It felt like asking the pope what he thought of some random schismatic Catholic sect in rural Kansas. The questions were becoming an assault on Yusuf's dignity. He, too, evidently felt chagrined by this line of questioning, because eventually he sprung up from the carpet and walked over to the wall, pointing to a short Arabic document in a modest frame. He didn't answer my question. "Come here," he said, "let me show you." I unfolded my legs, stiff from sitting for so long, and tottered over to read.

"This is my *ijazah* [permission]," he said—a letter signed by his teacher, authorizing him to teach and listing the chain of teachers who preceded him, and through whom his knowledge had been transmitted. I read the letter silently to myself until Yusuf began to read it aloud for us both. The bulk of it consisted of a list of the names of scholars, starting with Abdullah bin Bayyah, then Bin Bayyah's teacher, then his teacher's teacher, and so on. For more than a minute, Yusuf read the chain of authority, until it ended with Muhammad, the Prophet of God. "These are all real people, people who lived," he said. "This is our tradition, and this is how we ensure protection of the tradition. They don't have this—they don't have scholars, they don't have teachers." The jihadists do, in fact, have teachers, and scholars like Maqdisi, who has issued an *ijazah* to students he trusts. (Bin'ali's, issued by Maqdisi, is posted online.) But the point stands: the Islamic State's thinkers tend not to have institutionalized scholarship on their side, culminating in pieces of paper framed on their walls.

For the first time, Yusuf sounded desperate. How impressed did he expect me to be by this list of names, which, for all I knew, might have come straight from a Mauritanian phonebook? (I later told Musa about Yusuf's reading his *ijazah* aloud, and he laughed. "I imagine that he then told you: *Now bow down and kiss my ring.*") Yusuf represents the current generation in a long line of scholars, and he is more patient than the hotheads of Raqqah. But in the end, he was offering an appeal to authority—more than a thousand years of authority, but authority all the same. The Sufi tradition of West Africa, in which Yusuf trained, stresses following a senior scholar and learning at his feet. When he spoke of his teacher, Abdullah bin Bayyah, his voice contained real wonderment, even love. He loved his sheikh, but the Islamic State loved no one, so that love carried no weight for the people he wished to defeat with it. More important, Yusuf could not point to an instance where the Islamic State was flat-out, verifiably wrong. Religion does not provide many occasions for conclusive arguments of that sort.

Before I left Yusuf's house, he told me how dire the life of a Muslim in America had become. In the short term, he worried most about threats he had received from the Islamic State. He had seen the Facebook page of an Islamic State fan living in Fresno. That guy could have lunch, drive up to Berkeley, spray Zaytuna College with bullets, and be home for evening prayers. But Yusuf was nearly as worried about anti-Muslim militiamen. "I was accused in a book of being a 'Muslim mafia don,'" he said, and I tittered at the idea that this Marin County bibliophile would put a hit out on someone. More likely Yusuf would invite his enemy over for lunch, engage him in learned conversation, and accidentally crush him with a bookcase. "You can laugh, but this is real," he said. Conspiracy theorists believed he might be a sleeper agent of the Islamic State, and no one could predict how they would react. Right-wing militia types were organizing just up the road in Dublin, California. "I've got five kids, you know. And I wonder how the Jews [in Germany] felt in 1933, when the first anti-Jewish laws came in. I just wonder what they were thinking. A lot of them got out when they saw they were being demonized. And I really feel that now."

Yusuf avoided saying the name "Yasir Qadhi" during our conversation. But he did imply, in dark terms, that even typical Wahhabis could be implicated in the rise of groups like the Islamic State. Yusuf bemoans the influence of Salafis and blames them for causing stress and strife for Muslims by constantly berating them for supposed *shirk,* and implying that many are infidels. "Wherever they go, that's all they ever do. Every single place they go. And when you add the political dimension to it, it becomes deadly." Yusuf regarded Salafism as a spectrum disorder, with quietist Salafism at one end and jihadi Salafism disconcertingly close at the other. He said he "does not oppose" quiet Salafism, but the spirit of intolerance is often still present. "I don't think they are really [that different from the Islamic State], in the end," he told me. "They just draw the line at a different point." Later, after the deadly attacks during Ramadan in 2016, he called the death and destruction "the bitter harvest of teachings that have emanated from pulpits throughout the Arabian Peninsula."[29]

I had now met people from several Muslim factions opposed to the Islamic State: Yusuf, devoted to his slow-cooked Sufi scholarship; Hassan Ko Nakata and the Avenger and their competing caliphal visions; Qadhi and his political rabble-rousing. Of these, only Qadhi could ever have been described as Salafi. And he appeared to have fallen away from the Wahhabi line. The irony, though, is that despite

Yusuf's insinuations, Salafis are in some ways the group best positioned to debate the Islamic State. Most Salafis are not jihadists, and most reject the Islamic State. Unlike Sufis, they can engage jihadists on issues of shared concern. They are not shut out of the conversation before it begins.

The differences between jihadi Salafis and quietist Salafis are partly a matter of timing. Salafis are committed to expanding Dar al Islam, the land of Islam—even, perhaps, with slavery and amputation—but not necessarily right now. The quietists' first priority is personal purification and religious observance, and they believe anything that gets in the way of those goals—such as causing war or unrest that would disrupt lives and prayer and scholarship—is forbidden. For their radical interiority, quietist Salafis are accused of resembling an early Islamic sect called Murji'ites—those who "postpone" judgment of other Muslims. The Murji'ites opposed the Kharijites. The Kharijites claimed that failure to pray, or commission of sins such as drinking or fornication, could remove one from Islam; the Murji'ites believed that Islam is an affair of the heart, something that can be invisible to outsiders and does not require outward performance of religious duty. (Some draw the line at prayer: anyone who totally and willfully neglects prayer is not a Muslim.) Murji'ites say that you would need a window into a person's soul to see whether Islam is strong within him—and therefore execution for apostasy could never be justified.

No one calls himself a Murji'ite today: it is agreed that Islam is not *entirely* an interior affair, so strict Murji'ism is regarded as heresy.[30] But near-Murji'ite stances at least free the believer to take hard-line, intolerant positions without assuming the duty to force them on others. If Hamza Yusuf represents a response to the Islamic State that calls for a Sufi-oriented, tolerant Islam, the quietist Salafi Murji'ites represent a response that doubles down on an intolerant reading of text. The quietists still accuse others of *kufr*. But they come to political conclusions opposite those of the Islamic State. The strongest evidence for the compatibility of this sect with Western societies is that they already live in Western societies, without serious rancor or disruption.

In late 2014, I first visited the Philadelphia mosque of Breton Pocius, then twenty-eight, a quietist Salafi imam who goes by Abdullah. His mosque is on the border between the crime-ridden fringe of Northern Liberties and a gentrifying area that one might call Dar al Hipster. His beard allows him to pass in the latter zone unnoticed. He passes culturally as well. After months of chatting in person and over Twitter, he became fond enough of me to confess that he wanted to be the Salafi David Letterman and host a show where he could call people to Islam and interview Muslims about their faith. His ideal first guests would be two new converts, Tracy Morgan and me.

After a Polish Catholic upbringing in Chicago, Abdullah converted as a teenager. He denies that he is a scholar, but he talks like an old soul, exhibiting familiarity with ancient texts, and a commitment to their study motivated by the conviction that they are the only escape from hellfire. When I met him at a Northern Liberties coffee shop, he carried a work of Koranic scholarship in Arabic and a book for teaching himself Japanese. He was preparing a sermon for the 150 or so worshippers in his Friday congregation, and the topic was the obligations of fatherhood.

Abdullah told me his main goal is to encourage a halal life for Muslims. That includes forbidding practices common to Philly (eating pork, drinking beer) or that many Muslims misguidedly consider integral to their spiritual life, such as music, celebrating holidays dedicated to saints, and mysticism. These prohibitions put him at the far conservative end of the Muslim legal spectrum, but they do not have obvious political implications. The rise of the Islamic State, he says, has forced him to confront political claims that he, like most quietist Salafis, never previously considered, and greeted with skepticism when he did. "Most of what they'll say about how to pray and how to dress is exactly what I'll say in my *masjid* [mosque]. But when they get to questions about social upheaval, they sound like Che Guevara."

When Baghdadi appeared on the scene, Abdullah adopted the slogan "Not my *khalifah*," and in our conversation he derided the amateur jurists of the Islamic State as "garage-band Dhahiris." "The times of the Prophet were a time of great bloodshed," he told me, "and he knew that the worst possible condition for all people was chaos, especially within the *ummah*." Accordingly, Abdullah said, Salafis should not sow discord by factionalizing and declaring fellow Muslims apostates.[31] Instead, Abdullah—like a majority of Salafis—believes that Muslims should remove themselves from politics entirely.

Quietist Salafis like Abdullah agree with the Islamic State that God's law is the only law, and they eschew practices like voting and the creation of political parties. They interpret the Koran's hatred of discord and chaos as requiring them to fall into line behind just about any leader, including manifestly sinful ones. "The Prophet said: As long as the ruler does not enter into clear *kufr* [disbelief], give him general obedience," Abdullah told me. The classic books of creed—including those by Ibn ʿAbd al Wahhab himself—all warn against causing social upheaval. Quietist Salafis are forbidden from dividing Muslims from one another, for example by mass excommunication. Living without *bayʿa*, Abdullah said, does indeed make one ignorant [*jahil*], or benighted. But he suggests *bayʿa* need not mean allegiance to a caliph, let alone to Abu Bakr al Baghdadi. Under this interpretation, *bayʿa* might resemble acknowledgment that one lives in society, and not as a Unabomber-like figure, isolated and detached. It can mean adherence to a social contract and commitment to living in a society of Muslims, ruled by a caliph or not.

Quietist Salafis believe that Muslims should direct their energies toward perfecting their personal lives, including prayer, ritual, and hygiene. Just as Jews might disagree about whether it's kosher to tear off squares of toilet paper on the Sabbath (does that count as "rending cloth"?), the quietists spend an inordinate amount of time—even more than Hesham—ensuring that their trousers are not too long, that their beards are trimmed in some areas and left shaggy in others. Through this fastidious observance, they believe, Muslims will win God's favor, be rewarded with strength and numbers, and see a legitimate caliphate rise. At that moment, Muslims will achieve glorious victory over the Crusaders in an apocalyptic showdown. But Abdullah joins Hamza Yusuf in claiming that a caliphate cannot come into being except in a precise, orderly fashion, through the will of God.

The Islamic State would agree, to an extent. But they say that the will of God is written on the battlefield and in the survival and flourishing of Baghdadi. Abdullah's retort amounts to a call to humility. He cites ʿAbdullah ibn ʿAbbas, one of the Companions of the Prophet, who sat down with dissenters and asked them what gave them the gall, as a minority, to tell the majority that it was wrong. Violent dissent is forbidden, wherever it causes bloodshed or splits the *ummah*. Even the manner in which Baghdadi established his caliphate runs contrary to what Abdullah said Muslims expected, based on prophecy. "The *khilafah* is something that Allah is going to establish," he told me, "and it will involve a consensus of scholars from Mecca and Medina. That is not what happened. ISIS came out of nowhere."

The Islamic State loathes this talk, and its fanboys tweet derisively about quietist Salafis. They mock them as "Salafis of menstruation," for their obscure judgments about when women are and aren't unclean, and other low-priority aspects of life. "What we need now is fatwa about how it's haram [forbidden] to ride a bike on Jupiter," one tweeted drily. "That's what scholars should focus on. More pressing than state of Ummah." In July 2016, when Saudi government scholars inveighed against the phone game Pokémon GO, an Australian alleged Islamic State supporter condemned them, and not because he wanted to play the game. "Your governments are complicit in aligning with the kuffar in massacring Muslims, scholars are rotting away in prison cells, women are being raped and you want to talk Pokémon? Then they question why the youth no longer respect their scholar-

ship."[32] Anjem Choudary says that no sin merits more vigorous op-
position than the usurpation of God's law, and that extremism in
defense of monotheism is no vice. It is therefore obligatory to rise up
against unjust leaders.

This quarrel is irresoluble. It does, however, show that a literalist,
conservative reading of Islamic texts can yield nonviolence as well as
violence. The people who come to the faith spoiling for a fight cannot
all be dissuaded from jihadism, but those who are searching for an
ultraconservative Islam can find their alternative here. It is not mod-
eration; most Muslims would consider it extreme. But those seeking
a literal-minded version of the faith would not instantly find Abdullah's interpretation hypocritical, or blasphemously purged of its in-
conveniences, as they might find Hamza Yusuf's. His California
Sufism would never persuade a Muslim looking for the meanest,
most extreme interpretation on the market. This other version of
Salafism—rooted in an inflexible, literal reading of text that aggressively seeks to perfect the inner self instead of punishing others—
might.

For that hardened segment of the Muslim population, the only
plausible diversion tactic I've heard comes from Yahya Michot, a professor of Islamic theology at Hartford Seminary. Michot—born Jean
Michot in 1952—converted to Islam and began his career as a scholar
of Avicenna, the eleventh-century Persian philosopher and scientist.
He moved from the study of metaphysics to the more political terrain
of Ibn Taymiyyah, the Damascene polymath quoted constantly by
the Islamic State. Michot suggests that the Islamic State's own favorite
scholar be turned against it. He argues that Ibn Taymiyyah has been
misused, and that more careful assessment will prove—even to the
most likely foot soldiers—that the Islamic State's theology of jihad is
bogus.

Michot describes himself as a "compulsive" translator of Ibn Taymiyyah. Translation is like a medication. He has to render a bit of Ibn
Taymiyyah into French every day just to stay sane. He says he was

initially impressed, if not by the depth of the Islamic State's analysis of Ibn Taymiyyah, then by the breadth of material they quoted. "I thought, 'Wow—where did they find that?'" Michot says. "They had really done their homework, and I wondered whether they had used my translations."[33]

His compliments ended there. They had quoted Ibn Taymiyyah accurately, Michot says, but they hadn't read him closely enough. Ibn Taymiyyah, he said, despised idolatry, just as the Islamic State claims. But he left individual idolaters off the hook. Take, for example, the Shia. "They were the hippies of his time," Michot says, derisively. "They weren't following any religious prescriptions or social conventions. And Ibn Taymiyyah did indeed say that they were nonbelievers." But rather than condemning them directly, he adopted what Michot calls "a sociological approach," and claimed that the disease of nonbelief was best treated systemically, rather than through individual *takfir*. Shia scholars had failed to educate the people about sources of theological error. Cure the scholars and you cure the disease. As a fellow scholar, Ibn Taymiyyah said, his job was to say that dancing or talking to God was a form of disbelief. "But when it came to having to deal with a particular individual, he said 'We cannot condemn, fight, or kill'" unless it became clear that the offender knew of his error and had no justification for his ignorance. He argued that potential apostates needed a thoroughgoing investigation of the sources of their error—the process called *istitabah*. If the accused had a sheikh who misspoke or hadn't been clear or convincing, that might be grounds for mercy and sending the accused back for remediation. "Many people may be growing up in places and times in which many of the sciences of prophethood have faded," Ibn Taymiyyah writes. Such people "shall not be accused of unbelief."[34] Michot smirked. "In other words, good luck [carrying out a sentence for apostasy], because you will always be able to find circumstances that would make it impossible for the rule to be applied to individuals."

Elsewhere, Ibn Taymiyyah quotes a hadith about a man who

"never did a good deed," and who told his family to burn his body and scatter the ashes on land and sea, with the blasphemous purpose of disassembling his corpse beyond God's ability to reconstruct and punish it. God forgives the man, because the cause of his blasphemy was fear of God. Again, the lesson appears to be that God dispenses mercy freely, if unpredictably, and accusations of unbelief should be made with great caution.

Ibn Taymiyyah condemned the Mongols—who had overrun the Levant and killed the Abbasid caliph—as non-Muslims, despite their claims to the contrary. But in that case, too, his judgment was not as broad as commonly supposed. It applied only to the Mongols—not to any Muslim ruler who could be said to be sinful. We know that he meant the Mongols specifically, because he left other rulers (even rulers he thought to be in error) unaccused of disbelief. "He would never—and did never—call for armed rebellion against [his own] Mamluk rulers," even though the Mamluks refrained from fighting the Mongols, as Ibn Taymiyyah wished. Later jihadists removed that anti-Mongol order from its context and took it to justify rebellion against a larger range of targets, including Sadat, the Saudi monarchy, and others. This "Mongolization" of Muslim leaders runs counter to the precision targeting of Ibn Taymiyyah's writings—and Michot claims that Osama bin Laden, a fan of Ibn Taymiyyah, knew it. When Bin Laden, a Saudi national, informed the Saudi royals that they were ruling in a state of disbelief, he did not threaten them with overthrow. "He made a smaller and more obedient step," Michot said. "He asked them to please submit their resignation." (In fact, Michot says, Bin Laden considered the Americans to be the modern Mongols.)

The solution Michot proposes, then, is not to claim for Islam a false tolerance, along Sufi lines, which pretends that the borders of the religion are fuzzy, or to maintain that a believer would never stray into disbelief except on purpose. Better, he says, would be to teach potential jihadis that if they dislike their Muslim leaders, their own favorite texts counsel them to shut up and tough it out. Be hard-nosed and resilient—even if that means going to jail, as Ibn Taymiyyah did. But do not revolt against your leaders by picking up weapons. "You have with Ibn Taymiyyah all the texts of civil disobedience and self-sacrifice you need. Of course those texts are not read," he says.

The question remains: Why, if Ibn Taymiyyah would have made a kindred cellmate of Thoreau or Martin Luther King, do so few of his interpreters realize it? The stoic nonviolence of Ibn Taymiyyah is less familiar than the cruelty, as when he clamored for a Christian to be hacked to death for slandering Muhammad. The person responsible for this lopsided interpretation may be Ibn Taymiyyah's most influential follower, Ibn 'Abd al Wahhab. The Saudi cleric obscured Ibn Taymiyyah's tolerance by removing the excuse of ignorance in selected instances of apostasy and excommunication. Ibn Taymiyyah, in Michot's account, insisted on *istitabah*. Ibn 'Abd al Wahhab declared that everyone had fair warning about polytheism and idolatry. Even laymen could be expected to know about the indivisibility of God and his monopoly on lordship. If they didn't hear the message right the first time, their apostasy would have to be willful. Another cause of Ibn Taymiyyah's apparent obstinancy is that until recently, much of his oeuvre was inaccessible. Ibn 'Abd al Wahhab read and quoted him. But he likely did not go to Damascus, the repository of the largest Taymiyyan manuscript cache, and he definitely did not have access to the texts anyone can find online today. A full edition of his fatwas was not compiled until the 1960s.

Michot therefore proposes a bibliographic solution to a bibliographic problem. He taught Islamic studies for several years at Oxford; when the British prison authority asked him how to deal with radicalization in its cellblocks, he replied: *Make Arabic compulsory for all Muslim prisoners. Equip every library with an Arabic library with the works of Ibn Taymiyyah.* Violent interpretations cannot survive contact with the full range of text. "Sufism has been promoted as the [Islamic] antidote to terrorism: 'Let them dance, and they will not plant bombs anymore,'" he says. This will not do. Better to let them think hard about *kufr*. "Islam has to be understood as a middle way between the spiritual cancer of ISIS and the spiritual diabetes of Hamza Yusuf."

Most of the recruits to the Islamic State are, alas, immunized against dissuasion. As Yusuf said, they do not know about what they do not know—and moreover, they would distrust it, especially if it were being fed to them by Oxford professors or "ex-Muslims" like Aimen Dean now working for the infidels. For those still dissuadable, other mental barriers remain. Learning enough Arabic to read Ibn Taymiyyah takes years for a patient, scholarly person; for a semiliterate hoodlum, it could take a lifetime. Recruits want instant gratification, and the Islamic State's anthology of decontextualized Taymiyyan slogans makes much easier reading than volume 17 of Ibn Taymiyyah's *Majmua ' al Fatawah*.

And the fact remains: Islam is not science but religion. It is highly—though not infinitely—malleable, with no definite conclusions. And hard though it is to admit, the Islamic State's claims often fall within the bounds of rational, if not decent, debate.

Hamza Yusuf has called Baghdadi "pathetic" and his ideological lieutenants "lousy." But once in our conversation he paid them an unintended compliment. Islam was perfect from the start, he said. "That makes it difficult to 'reform' Islam. But what you can do is help people understand the vastness of the tradition, and know that within the tradition itself are all the tools needed to navigate the most difficult of times for Muslims." He said his reverence for tradition, and his insistence on the primary role of scholarly institutions in Islam, made him a "Catholic Muslim," analogous to those loyal to the Church of Rome who resisted the Reformation in Christianity.

The early Protestants, too, saw themselves as wrecking balls for a corrupt system—in their case, a system corroded with the sale of indulgences, and a clergy that neglected northern Europe. The Islamic State sees the same rot in Saudi Arabia and Muslim institutions of higher learning like Al Azhar University in Cairo, and refuses to listen to scholars it deems corrupt.

The Islamic State derides Hamza Yusuf and other Muslim dissenters for making *taqlid,* that is, following a senior scholar instead of using one's own legal judgment (a process called *ijtihad*). *Ijtihad* is like handling plutonium, according to most Muslim clerics. One shouldn't do it without proper training.[35] The reforms of Martin Luther (and the Kharijites) democratized freedom to interpret the religion. If Yusuf were a Catholic cleric in the time of Luther, he would have been upset and disturbed by Protestants who presumed to throw away a thousand years of institutional safeguards and wisdom, only to replace them with their own individual knowledge, or lack thereof. Mass illiteracy once protected religion from amateurism. But now the gates to the nuclear facility have been breached, and hobbyists and high school students are playing with the fissile material.

The Protestant and present-day Islamic State reformations have also both been fueled by massive technological disruption. Luther's revolution was sped along by the printing press, which put religious and political texts in the hands of ordinary people, not just an educated priestly elite. Literacy among Muslims has risen quickly in the last hundred years—and now social media and the Web have given masses of Muslims the confidence to read texts for themselves, and not always to reach the same conclusions as the scholars. I have talked to many Islamic State supporters who have ended our conversations by urging me to "let YouTube be your sheikh"—to search for videos of jihadist preachers like Anwar al ʿAulaqi and others, and skip Al Azhar or Yusuf's own Zaytuna College. Traditional authorities rightly feel threatened.

Islam is not Christianity on a five-century time delay, and its reformation may well take a different shape.[36] Jonathan Sacks, former chief rabbi of the United Hebrew Congregations of the Commonwealth, pointed out to me that the first two Abrahamic monotheisms suffered spells of violent extremism at roughly the same stage in their histories, roughly 1,500 years after their foundings. This moment of adolescent rebellion occurred for the Jews with the Maccabean revolt in the first and second centuries B.C. and for the Christians with the Protestant Reformation in the sixteenth century. Now it's happening for the Muslims, and the incarnation of the reforming impulse is the Islamic State.

These similarities are unsettling, and the conclusion to which they point is less favorable than Yusuf may wish to admit. The Protestant Reformation *succeeded*. Only the most dogmatic Catholics or Protestants today would argue that their side completely vanquished the other in intellectual combat. The European wars of religion ended not with one side convincing the other that one reading of scripture was correct and another wrong, but with a decades-long orgy of violence that left the continent soaked in blood and exhausted. The current horror show in Syria is, at best, the beginning of another cycle of religious war.

THE WAR OF THE END OF TIME

My hand grasps the killing power in Heaven and earth;
To behead the evil ones, spare the just, and ease the people's
  sorrow.

The uncivilized and border peoples offer tribute,
And all the barbarians are submissive.
No matter how vast the territory,
All will eventually be under our rule.
> —Hong Xiuquan, leader of the Taiping Rebellion

Hong was one of those people who believe it is their mission to make all things "new, for the surprise of the sky-children." It is a central agony of history that those who embark on such missions so rarely care to calculate the cost.
> —Jonathan D. Spence[1]

The Islamic State craves an all-out civilizational war. Conducted with modern weaponry, that war would leave billions of people burned to death, crucified, beheaded, or shot in the back of the head, all over an irreconcilable dispute about the nature of God. Many of the Islamic State supporters I met openly longed for this war. Most also had friendlier hopes, for me at least, and invited me to join them in their struggle, because they feared for my well-being if I did not. Both the bloodlust and the concern were real. These men lived lives no less contradictory than the rest of us—they too switched between love and hate, mundane concerns and spiritual ones, complete confidence in their future and anxiety about it.

This last tension best exposed their strange psychology. They *knew* that events would support their theory of the world and its end, and that in time they would be vindicated. But they couldn't sit back and wait for the I-told-you-so moment. Instead, they were desperate—as if the preordained apocalypse might be canceled by their inaction. The contradiction did not bother them, at least not that I could see. They had found a mental state that contained both possibilities.

The ability to accept two opposing eventualities reminded me of Yahya's deification of *dahr* [Time] and of Musa's comment about the Islamic State's law, which he said did not attempt to look back to the seventh century but *up* to an eternal law. They saw time as illusory yet supreme. What happened in the seventh century is happening now; what is happening now will determine the Hereafter. This attempt to live under the aspect of eternity put them out of joint not only with mainstream Islam (think of Abdullah Pocius's concern over Philly Muslims' consumption of pork-heavy soul food) but with life, as lived by people like me who think tomorrow will be different from today. Their perspective could seem cruel or unhinged. It was not so different from the perspective that religious leaders have urged for thousands of years: suffering is an illusion, as is joy; what happens now happens forever; prepare for a kingdom that is not of this world.

One afternoon in Oslo, I had a pizza lunch with a delegation from Profetens Ummah [the Prophet's Community], a Norwegian Islamist group of perhaps a hundred members that is linked with the Choudarheads.[2] (As usual, none of the members explicitly stated their support for the Islamic State. But many posted images from Syria on their social media sites, and their comments were invariably consistent with the Islamic State's ideology.) After an hour discussing beheadings and enslavement, a white-bearded man named Abu Aisha—who had come to Norway from Algeria in 1989 at the age of twenty-four—touched my upper arm in a fond gesture. "When you say you don't support the Islamic State, we respect you," he said. "But why? Is it because you have seen the media—because you have seen what people say about them?"

I said there were many reasons.

"What is the main one?"

"Killing, slavery, amputation," I said. I added that I could go on.

"I understand," he said. "You think this is too much, and you are not the only one. The Prophet himself said people would oppose him. This is a war—and not a war we chose. We do not do this because we want to hurt you. We do this because we want to offer you something." He turned his palms up, in the universal gesture of giving. "We want to see all human beings in Paradise. This is not a greedy religion. We want to see you there with us."

Time was running out, he told me. "When the Prophet was alive, Allah gave him miracles," Abu Aisha said. "Allah opened for him the ability to see everything, until the Day of Judgment." That day is approaching. "We must always look to ʿasharat saʿa [the Signs of the Hour]," he told me, citing the hadith literature about signposts leading to the end of time. God was not unreasonable, he said. He told us all we would ever need to know to recognize the final hour.

"Why do we believe in the Islamic State? Because the Prophet said it is coming." The era of caliphs will pass, and be replaced with the era of kings, and the era of kings will give way to the era of caliphs, and by then the signs of the End would proliferate. "There is an authentic hadith that says there will be a khilafah ʿala manhaj al nabuwa [caliphate on the Prophetic methodology]," he said, echoing the Islamic State slogan. "It will be like the time of the Prophet: if you steal you will lose your hand. The United Nations might not like it, but that will be how it is."

Abu Aisha then listed the Signs of the Hour—events that were foretold in prophecy and have been slowly fulfilled over the past thousand years. These include an embargo of Iraq (fulfilled in the 1990s under Saddam Hussein); leadership of Muslim nations by unworthy people (such as the current so-called apostate leaders); and a war between Muslims and Jews (check). The pre-Islamic deity Lat—one of the Meccan idols smashed by the Prophet himself—will find worshippers again. (*Dabiq* calls the Lebanese Shiite party Hizbullah [Party of God] "Hizb al Lat" [Party of Lat].[3]) The Muslims will ride horses and use swords—as they do in many Islamic State propaganda videos.

Many of the predictions deal with fading morals and standards. There will be many writers and critics—"That's you!" Abu Aisha said—and fools will hold forth on matters of great importance. (Also me? He was too polite to say.) There will be widespread ignorance, rampant fornication, and the drinking of alcohol, says one tradition. There will be music, says another, and people will fornicate out in the roads, like donkeys.[4] (This may be the only prophecy of a major religion that could be fulfilled by the Gathering of the Juggalos.)

"Barefoot naked shepherds will compete to build tall buildings," says another hadith. Abu Aisha suggested that the sport of building needlessly tall skyscrapers in the Gulf fits this prophecy, because the princes and emirs who do so are only a generation or two out of desert poverty. The prophecies also predict the mass importation of non-Muslim servants to Muslim lands, as well as an abundance of money. With oil wealth and guest-worker programs attracting hundreds of thousands of Westerners, Filipinos, and Chinese to the region, these signs are incontrovertibly fulfilled.

To Abu Aisha, my stubbornness would have been funny if it were not tragic. He looked ready to grab me with both hands to try to shake me awake. Were these signs—to say nothing of the perfection of the Koran, and the example of the Prophet—not enough to rouse me from the hypnosis of *kufr*? "We are here to make Islam easy for you!"

I pointed out to him that most Muslims didn't share his view that the world was soon to end. He replied, in effect, that the world was changing, and that Muslims were snapping out of a hypnosis of their own. "The first generation [of Muslims] that came to Norway was very poor and illiterate," he said. They had fled countries that controlled their religious and political lives. "They'd do nothing but work, drink milk, and go to sleep. But this [second] generation was born free. The government was naive if they thought the offspring would behave the same way."

We talked a short while longer, and Abu Aisha asked me, "You have a place to stay tonight? Are you safe?" He was following a Prophetic command: if an infidel comes to you and asks about the religion, answer his questions and let him go safely. I assured him I was safe. (Is anyone unsafe in Oslo?) Profetens Ummah paid for the pizza.

The particulars of the end of the world are not a mainstream concern in Islam. As in Christianity, when your neighborhood clergyman starts talking all the time about the apocalypse, the natural reaction is to consider finding a new clergyman. The average Sunday homily does not include detailed speculation about the Whore of Babylon, the Mark of the Beast, and the Four Horsemen of the Apocalypse. Serious Christian theologians find other more appealing subjects. Too much about the future is obscure, too much unknown. The prophecies are at once vague and lurid, and with little applicability to everyday life.

But in both Islam and Christianity, eschatology—the study of the end of days—is part of the religion. And curiosity about the end of days is as high among the laity as it is low among the clergy. The Islamic bookshops in Whitechapel, or around Couronnes in Paris, all stock extensive apocalypse sections—shelves and shelves, in multiple languages, compiling the diffuse and fragmented statements of the Prophet about the end times. The covers tend to feature skyscapes of lightning and fire, and an aesthetic, perhaps not coincidentally, familiar from the *Left Behind* books and films in the evangelical Christian literature. Amid many titles about dull topics (lives of the caliphs; moralistic treatises on purity; manuals on prayer), these books recount dramatic and sensational stories of final battles between good and evil, supernatural powers, the ultimate rise of a Muslim elite, and plagues and bloodshed.

Jean-Pierre Filiu, a professor of Islamic studies at Sciences Po in Paris, told me that Muslims tend to learn these stories not through formal education but through whispers, rumors, and tales passed down from generation to generation. "The doomsday story is one young Muslims are told before bedtime, and even Muslims with low levels of knowledge have heard part of it," he says. "It is not something discussed in the *khutbah*s [sermons]. It's what you chat about outside the mosque afterward."

Meanwhile, the imams and community leaders either say nothing or utter outright denials that the apocalyptic hadith exist. The head of the Council on American-Islamic Relations, Nihad Awad, professes ignorance of Muslim apocalypticism. "There is no apocalyptic bloodbath in Islam," he told a website after I began writing on the subject.[5] There most certainly is a bloodbath, as many better educated or less embarrassed Muslims could have informed him, citing canonical hadith collections.[6] These reports are ghastly, and the setting of many of the worst events is Sham, the area of Syria and Iraq that the Islamic State has taken as its base.

The street-corner preachers of the Islamic State don't share the mainstream scholars' discomfort with the subject matter. "For the mass of recruits [to the Islamic State], if you say 'end times' and 'Sham,' they understand immediately," Filiu says. Since the mid-2000s, the apocalyptic currents in jihadism have surged. "Al Qaida was toxic enough, with mass murder and genocide. Add the apocalypse, and it becomes unbearable," he says. Al Qaida acted like an underground political movement, with worldly goals in sight at all times—the expulsion of non-Muslims from the Arabian peninsula, the abolition of the state of Israel, the end of dictatorships in Muslim lands. Bin Laden rarely mentioned the apocalypse, and when he did, he implied that he would be long dead when it arrived. "Bin Laden and Zawahiri are from elite Sunni families who look down on this kind of speculation and think it's something the masses engage in," says Will McCants of the Brookings Institution, the author of a book about the Islamic State's apocalyptic thought.[7]

As with many recent developments in jihadism—virulent anti-Shiism, revelry in gore—the change began with Abu Mus'ab al Zarqawi. "Zarqawi injected the apocalyptic message into jihad," McCants says. During the last years of the U.S. occupation of Iraq, the Islamic State's predecessors saw signs of the end times everywhere. They were anticipating, imminently, the arrival of the Mahdi—a messianic figure destined to lead the Muslims to victory before the end of the world. A prominent Al Qaida judge in Iraq approached Bin Laden in 2008 to warn him that the group was led by millenarians who were "talking all the time about the Mahdi and making strategic decisions" based on when they thought the Mahdi was going to arrive. "Al-Qaida had to write to [these leaders] to say 'Cut it out,'" McCants says. Instead, they have reaffirmed their commitment to the end times narrative.

The signs Abu Aisha mentioned are among the "Lesser Signs," and some might argue that their fulfillment was less remarkable than it might first appear. "A slave will give birth to her master," says one prophecy. The Islamic State's revival of slavery makes that possible: the child of a free Muslim man is a free Muslim and inherits the rights of his father—including the right of ownership over his own mother if she is a slave. But these rules have long applied, so slaves have given birth to their masters many times in Islamic history. The emirs of the Gulf do compete to build towers, and their forebears were penniless and perhaps barefoot. But they themselves are filthy rich, fully clothed, and often wearing Ferragamo shoes. So they are not barefoot shepherds. (Then again, if even one of them was, that would be enough to check the box and fulfill the prophecy.) Panic over loose morals is perennial in all cultures, and those looking for fulfillment of the moralist prophecies could probably have found it in any era, including in the time of the Prophet himself.[8]

More unsettling—and impressive, should it come to pass—is what comes next. These are the so-called "Greater Signs," which will initiate the end of the world, are the omens in which the Islamic State invests its desires, and which shape its beliefs about how its grand experiment will end—badly, it turns out, for almost everyone.

Before the Greater Signs comes what is technically the last of the Lesser Signs: namely, a battle at Dabiq, a town in northern Syria, that kills one-third of the world's Muslims, followed by another battle known as "the Great Slaughter." Once the caliphate is revived, Islam will enter a period of discord, during which false prophets and deviants will proliferate. According to the prophecy, the Muslims will face an enemy united behind eighty banners. "We're counting your banners, which our Prophet said would reach eighty in number," says the unnamed narrator of one Islamic State video.[9] That enemy will be, or be led by, an entity called "Rome" [rum] in scripture, but whose present-day identity remains contested. As the battle looms, an army of Islam's finest will assemble and march to Sham from the city of Medina. (A large number of Islamic State fighters come from Saudi Arabia.)

Looking for a guide through this portion of the prophecy, I turned to my old friend Musa Cerantonio. After my last visit to Australia and before his arrest, Musa wrote and published a pamphlet speculating about the identity of "Rome" in the apocalyptic hadith. He agrees with the dominant interpretation that at the time of the Prophet, "Rome" meant the Byzantine or Eastern Roman Empire. The Byzantines had their capital in Constantinople until it fell to the

Ottomans in 1453. There are no more Byzantines, so the present-day meaning of "Rome" is obscure. Some Islamic State interpreters have implied that "Rome" now means any Christian army. Others specify Italy, NATO, Russia, or the United States.

Musa says it refers not to any of these but to modern Turkey. The Ottomans were replaced by the Republic of Turkey—the same republic that ended the last self-identified caliphate, ninety years ago. "Rome," under this interpretation, has gone through two costume changes, first into the Ottomans and now into the Turks. Here the eighty flags come into play: a coalition of nations will rally against the Muslims at Dabiq and will—according to most interpretations—be defeated. Dabiq will also ruin the Roman army, throwing geopolitics out of balance and ushering in a new world disorder. Musa was more circumspect. The source "just says there will be a great battle," he said. "It doesn't say it will be a victory." In the course of the battle, a third of the Muslims will flee, a third will die as martyrs, and a third will survive to lead an assault on "Rome." Musa reads a hadith ("They would fight a fight the likes of which had never been seen, so much so that even if a bird were to pass by their flanks, it would fall down dead before reaching the end of them") as prophesying heavy aerial bombing.[10]

Around this time, the world will begin facing unfathomable natural disasters and other weird phenomena. The Euphrates will divert itself and reveal mountains of gold. Believers should not touch the gold or should take "only a small amount." The twelfth issue of *Dabiq* quoted these prophecies on its back cover, adding that in squabbles over the gold, "Ninety-nine out of each one hundred will be killed, but every man amongst them will say, 'Perhaps I myself will survive.'"[11] The earth will open up and swallow people, and smoke will appear.

After the battle in Dabiq, the caliphate will sack "Rome." In some interpretations, the city falls back to the Crusaders. A battle resembling World War III will take place—*al malhama al kubra* [the Great

Slaughter], which pits the remaining Muslims against everyone else. Some believe Mecca and Medina will fall to the caliphate's forces—possibly before the Dabiq battle[12]—and a Bolshevik-style coup will extinguish the royal line of the House of Saud. Some believe the caliphate will then cover the entire earth, but Musa suggests its tide may never reach beyond the Bosphorus. At that point, once the war has turned in the Muslims' favor (or perhaps even been won by them), the first of the Greater Signs will appear: the Anti-Christ.

Who is the Anti-Christ? "We believe that he is alive and currently chained up on an island in the Red Sea," Musa says. During the time of the Prophet, a group of Muslim seafarers, led by a Christian convert, Tamim al Dari, lost their way and went ashore on an island. "They saw someone who looked strange: hairy, and so ugly that you couldn't tell his rear end from his face." That man directed them to a monastery, and inside they found a gigantic man in chains—the Anti-Christ. He asked them whether the Prophet had conquered Mecca yet. They replied that he had, and the Anti-Christ said, "Good. My time is almost here."

The Anti-Christ is known in Arabic as *al masih al dajjal* [the False Messiah], or just Dajjal. "His skin is sometimes described as reddish," Musa says. "One of his eyes is defective, and the skin partially covers it. He's blind in that eye. It protrudes and looks like a grape, as if to say there's no color." Written across his forehead is كفر, the root letters (K-F-R) of the word *kafir,* or infidel. Every Muslim, even children and the illiterate, will be able to read and understand these letters.

Several omens will precede Dajjal's arrival. One-third of the earth will go without rainfall for a year, and the next year two-thirds will go without. (Climate change, understandably, is a topic of speculation for Islamic State supporters.) And then the Anti-Christ will appear, mysteriously, and present himself as the savior of the world's starving masses. Millions or billions will fall at his feet in gratitude. God will grant him miracles. "Crops will fail, meat will be rare, and he will come with mountains of meat and food and whatnot," Musa says. He will summon rain at will, and he will appear to raise the dead. "If your parents pass away—and I hope they don't—they will appear to come back, and they will say, 'Oh dear son, this is Allah. He has given us life. Follow him.'"

Not everyone will be impressed. "A young boy will appear before him, and [the Anti-Christ] will ask: 'Do you not believe that I am Allah?' He will then chop the boy in two and walk between the two parts, then put him back together, and yet the boy will remain alive." But the boy will say, "Now I'm more sure than ever that you're *al masih al dajjal!*" The Anti-Christ will try to strangle him. God will protect his neck with a lead collar, so the Anti-Christ—now frustrated—will pick him up by the arms and legs and fling him into what looks like Hell. The vision of Hell will be an illusion, though, and the obstinate kid will be in Paradise.[13]

The Anti-Christ will raise an army, and people will be drawn to it, especially women and Iranian Jews. The army will wander the planet, killing and conquering and sending Muslims into hiding.

"What would you do if you saw him coming?" I asked Musa.

"Leave immediately," he said. "The Prophet says you should not fight him, because you will lose." But he will find and kill many, many people, including Muslims who have tried to run away.

Then, at long last, five thousand Muslim fighters will be cornered by the armies of the Anti-Christ in Jerusalem. They will take refuge within the gates of the city. At that point, their leader will be the last of the caliphs, Muhammad ibn 'Abdullah al Qahtani, known as the Mahdi or "guided one." Their destruction will appear assured.

But salvation will come from the heavens, in the form of Jesus. Muslims deny Jesus's divinity, but they believe he did not die on the cross and instead ascended bodily to heaven. In this dark hour, they expect him to return. Wearing saffron robes, he will be borne down by two angels onto the white minaret of the Umayyad Mosque in Damascus. On arrival, he will make haste to Jerusalem and appear in the ranks of the Muslims at dawn prayers. Traditions say his hair will appear wet and will be long and curly. The merest whiff of his breath will kill infidels.

The precise choreography of what happens next is of particular interest to the Islamic State and is mentioned several times in its propaganda. The Muslims will identify Jesus as a stranger, and in hushed voices they will work out that he is Jesus himself. Then the Mahdi, about to lead prayers, will offer to let Jesus lead them instead. (In the story, the Mahdi sounds a bit like a young singer-songwriter who sees Bob Dylan in his audience and tries to persuade him to come onstage, borrow his guitar, and sing a song.) Jesus will refuse and will then take a place behind the Mahdi to pray, like any other Muslim. This brief pas de deux serves as evidence that Jesus will return not as a prophet (Muhammad was the last of these) but as a man. "Jesus and the Mahdi will be like Batman and Robin," one Muslim told me.

Jesus will then call for the gates of the city to open, exposing the Muslims to the forces of the Anti-Christ. Before the fighters rush in to finish the Muslims off, Jesus—armed with lethal halitosis and a spear—will run at the Anti-Christ. The Anti-Christ will flee and, in his ignominious scramble, will melt away, like salt in water. But before he disappears, Jesus will catch him and pierce him fatally with his spear. Jesus will then raise the bloody spear above his head, and the Anti-Christ's forces will surrender and submit to the Mahdi's rule. The return of Jesus as a Muslim will spell the end of Christianity, and—since Christ himself will rebuke the Christians and direct them to follow Islam—also the end of the option of living as a *jizya*-paying Christian or Jew under Muslim rule. Those who persist in disbelief will be annihilated, and the Jews in particular will face harsh comeuppance, with the stones and trees themselves crying out to Muslim warriors to reveal any Jews cowering behind them, vainly wishing to escape death.[14]

What happens next, as Musa admits, is foggy. The Islamic State will already have been reduced to a few thousand fighters. But then, under the Jesus-Mahdi partnership, the rule of Muslims will be glorious. For forty years they will reign—and then everything will get worse.

According to scripture, two fearsome peoples known as Gog and Magog [*ya'juj wa ma'juj*] are currently confined by an iron wall inside a mountain in Central Asia, as they have been for thousands of years. The people who make up these groups are depicted sometimes as large and sometimes as small, but they are always numerous and subhuman. They will break free during the second tour of Jesus on earth and will kill many people, ravaging the world and depleting its resources. They will invade Iraq and Palestine like a pestilence. Their thirst will drain rivers and the Sea of Galilee, and their hunger will consume crops. Many, many people will die, before God will command an insect or worm to burrow into the necks of Gog and Magog and kill them. Various other tribulations will take place. The corpses of Gog and Magog will rot, and the fumes will engulf the planet before God washes the mess away with heavy rains. Even believers find this sequence dreadful to imagine. A Twitter follower asked Musa whether he'd follow up his pamphlet on the identity of "Rome" with another on Gog and Magog. Musa replied that any such pamphlet would be "very short and consist mostly of the words *Allahu 'alim* [God knows—i.e., 'beats me']."

By the end of all this chaos and misery—wars among men, demons, and subhumans—few Arabs will survive, and most of the survivors will be "Romans" (in Musa's telling, Turks). The course of events that will lead to this moment will be unimaginably awful. "I pray that [I] never learn how this comes to be," Musa writes. One creepy hadith says that during the apocalyptic decades, "whoever passes by a tomb [will] say: I wish to God that I were in the place of the one buried there."[15]

The remaining unbelievers—who will somehow not have figured out that Islam is the winning team—will still have a chance to submit to God. Humanity will be surrounded by fire. At the end of time, even the Muslims will die, their lives taken by a horrendous wind.

On the last day, the sun will rise in the west, and God will stop accepting repentance. The world will end. And that will be the story of us all.

It is little wonder that policymakers have struggled to know what to make of these stories. In 2015, a European intelligence official told me that he was sure Islamic State fighters "aren't motivated by all this religious twaddle," and that the apocalyptic thinking couldn't possibly be genuine. Bernard Haykel of Princeton, who otherwise takes the Islamic State's religious claims seriously, has expressed similar sentiments. He told the U.S. Senate's Committee on Homeland Security and Governmental Affairs to discount the end times talk:

> This aspect of the ideology is used for purely propaganda and recruitment purposes and is not to be taken seriously. Why is the Islamic State's English language magazine called *Dabiq*, a place in Syria in which one of the battles of the apocalypse takes place, whereas no such allusions are made so explicitly in its Arabic publications? Also, and more important, why does the Islamic State expend effort and funds in building state institutions, as it has been doing in both Syria and Iraq, when the end is nigh?[16]

I shared this skepticism until the evidence against it became overwhelming.[17] Haykel is correct that the apocalyptic narrative is a recruitment driver, and that references to the apocalypse are less common in Islamic State sources in Arabic than in other languages. But the references to apocalypse are present and prominent in Arabic too: the leading Islamic State news source in Arabic is the A'maq News Agency, which is named for the A'maq Valley, site of another prophesied apocalyptic battle. In 2014, the group celebrated when (at great cost) it conquered Dabiq's strategically unimportant plains. It is there, the Prophet reportedly said, that the armies of Rome will set up their camp. The armies of Islam will meet them, and Dabiq will be Rome's Waterloo or Gettysburg. If the Islamic State did not invest that location with immense importance, it would not have worked so hard to conquer it. (In October 2016, Turkish-backed Syrian rebels stormed Dabiq. The Islamic State had, however, already prepared its fighters for the loss by reminding them that Mecca and Medina would fall before the real Dabiq battle took place.)[18]

Moreover, recruitment by reference to the apocalypse would not be successful if supporters were not already predisposed to apocalyptic thinking. Abu Aisha was not even one of the more apocalypse-obsessed people I encountered. Virtually everyone brought up the end of the world and invoked the apocalypse. My experience was not unique. Jürgen Todenhöfer, the German writer who visited Mosul and Raqqah in December 2014 in the company of Islamic State fighters, says that of the hundred-odd people he interviewed there, nearly all mentioned apocalypse. "I got this story from almost everyone— Swedish people, German people, all types," he says. Their sincere belief, he said, was useful to the Islamic State. But it was belief nonetheless. "They are told this every day. It helps them to do cruel things and find reason for brutality."[19]

But the most persuasive evidence of all is the words of Islamic State leaders themselves. Baghdadi and 'Adnani, speaking in Arabic, have regularly referred to the Apocalypse. In May 2015, Baghdadi mentioned several apocalyptic hadith in one paragraph in a speech. He referred to the final day, when the sun will rise from the west and all who remain outside Islam will be doomed; to the use of horses in the final battles; and to the return to earth of Jesus ['Issa], the second-most revered prophet of Islam:

> God's Messenger (peace be upon him) said, "[. . .] Repentance will not cease [to be accepted] until the sun rises from the West." He (peace be upon him) also said, "Goodness—

reward and booty—will be in the forelocks of horses until the Day of Judgment." He (peace be upon him) also said, "There will not cease to exist a group from my nation fighting upon the truth, manifest until the Day of Judgment. Then, Jesus son of Mary will descend, and [the leader of the Muslims] will say [to Jesus], 'Come and lead us in prayer.' So [Jesus] will say, 'No. You are leaders over one another as an honor from God for this nation.' "[20]

The Islamic State's emphasis on building institutions is consistent with the group's proposed apocalyptic time frame. (Even if it were not, consider this hadith: "If the Resurrection were established upon one of you while he has in his hand a sapling, then let him plant it."[21]) The Islamic State suggests the world might end in decades, not months. We know that this hypothesis has penetrated to the inner sanctum, and on this schedule, because of essays written by Turki al Bin'ali himself. In 2014, Bin'ali released an essay about a hadith that predicted exactly twelve caliphs in history.[22] He interpreted the twelve caliphs as meaning twelve *just* caliphs, and proceeded to cross out historical caliphs who didn't descend from Quraysh or rule according to Shariah. That left only seven, give or take, with Baghdadi rounding out the lineup as number eight. By that logic, the Islamic State would be only three caliphs away from the last one—the Mahdi—and the end of the world. Appointing caliphs is therefore not just the right thing to do, but a way to speed up the apocalypse. If talk of the apocalypse were meant cynically, just to dupe recruits, Bin'ali would not have written about it in the esoteric forum where his essay was posted.

But as a source of mass appeal, the drama of apocalypse is undeniable. In the official English-language propaganda, it is a constant theme. The recruits love it. "Dabiq is basically all farmland," one Islamic State fanboy tweeted. "You could imagine large battles taking place there." The Islamic State's propagandists drool in anticipation of this event, and constantly imply that it will come soon. Every issue of *Dabiq* takes as its tagline a quote from Zarqawi: "The spark has been lit here in Iraq, and its heat will continue to intensify . . . until it burns the crusader armies in Dabiq."

"Here we are, burying the first American crusader in Dabiq, eagerly waiting for the remainder of your armies to arrive," said a masked executioner in a November 2014 video, showing the severed head of Peter (Abdul Rahman) Kassig, the aid worker whose life Stanley Cohen had conspired with Maqdisi to save.[23] During fighting in Iraq in December 2014, after mujahedin (perhaps inaccurately) reported having seen American soldiers in battle, Islamic State Twitter accounts erupted in spasms of pleasure, like overenthusiastic party hosts at the arrival of their first guests.

When the Sinai affiliate of the Islamic State announced it had shot down the St. Petersburg–bound Metrojet Flight 9268 out of Sharm al Sheikh on October 31, 2015, it promised the Russians that it would await their counterattack "at Aʿmaq." It encouraged them to hurry up. A few weeks later, Al Hayat Media Center released one of its flashiest videos. This one was directed at all the world, and it crescendoes prophetically: "Bring it on, all of you. Your numbers only increase us in faith, and we're counting your banners, which our prophet said would reach 80 in number, and then the flames of war will finally burn you on the hills of Dabiq."[24]

The Islamic State's apocalypticism continues to bewilder the uninitiated. In February 2016, after Pope Francis criticized Republican presidential candidate Donald Trump for being "not Christian," Trump warned the pope that someday His Holiness would wish for a Trump presidency, because the Vatican is "ISIS's ultimate trophy."[25] In addition to its hasty assumptions about the identity of "Rome," the Trump statement suggested that the Islamic State was focusing its efforts on far-off apocalyptic prizes, when its near-term goals, both apocalyptic and not, remain in the Levant.

Equally dangerous is the assumption that the Islamic State's apocalypticism will lead the group to undertake transparently irrational actions because of its confidence in divine intervention. If they want a showdown at Dabiq, some say, the United States should send ten thousand Marines (plus Turkish special forces, just to make Musa happy) and slaughter all Islamic State fighters foolish enough to stand their ground. But nothing in the prophecies requires Muslims to go about fulfilling them stupidly. They might instead prefer to delay the confrontation and build up strength: that is exactly the interpretation the Islamic State favored when Dabiq fell. As in all matters, the room for creative interpretation of scripture is vast.

But knowledge of the Islamic State's apocalyptic game plan can, at the strategic level, provide clues about why they do what they do—and what they may do next. Certain events must happen, and certain events must not, in a particular order. Emphasis on this order may inform strategic priorities. For example, the return of Jesus and his triumph in Jerusalem is the first major appearance of Israel in Muslim apocalyptic chronology. Israel does not get wiped out before then, and that may be one reason the Islamic State spends less time complaining about Israel and the Jews than any other jihadist organization of the same scale. Another reason is that the Islamic State considers the leaders of Palestinian resistance, namely Hamas and Fatah, apostates. Given these groups' popularity throughout the Muslim world, to emphasize the desire to behead their leaders would alienate potential followers.[26] Knowledge of the group's apocalyptic commitments also helps explain its strategy of divisiveness. The final battle is just that: an armed conflagration, not a gentle prodding to follow the one God. All followers of the Islamic State are led to believe that they are among the few. So if the vast majority of self-described Muslims reject them, this is not a sign of error but of truth.

Of course many Muslims will fail to resist the siren call of the Anti-Christ. Nothing could be more natural or predictable.

Most important, though, is the appreciation of how the apocalyptic narrative moves the hearts of the group's followers. No other recent jihadist group—Al Qaida, the jihadists of Afghanistan in the 1980s, or followers of the Muslim Brotherhood agitator Sayyid Qutb—has captured the romance of the Islamic State, or its visceral appeal. To die on the gallows, as Sayyid Qutb did, or in a suicide attack on a NATO convoy in Kabul, makes one a martyr. But the martyrdom of an apocalyptic fighter is special. This war is the main event in human history, not a skirmish decades away from the end. As Magnus Ranstorp, a Swedish analyst of jihadism, put it, joining the Islamic State is better than getting tickets to the World Cup. It's like getting to play in the championship match and score a goal.[27]

As the mujahedin lace up their cleats in Sham, we should tremble not because they might be right about the end of the world—the history of messianic movements is a history of failure—but because apocalyptic conviction rarely disappears quietly and often ends in mass death. Martin Luther believed that the apocalypse was imminent, and the sixteenth-century wars of religion that killed huge numbers of Europeans were doomsday wars. In 1850s China, the messianic cult of Hong Xiuquan led to a civil war that killed *tens of millions* of people—more than the Syrian civil war will claim if it kills every man, woman, and child in Syria. In 1890s Brazil, in the dirt-poor backlands of Canudos, an ascetic preacher known as Antônio Conselheiro ["the Counselor"] convinced the peasants that the end was near, and led a revolt against what they perceived to be an uncaring, predatory government. Between five thousand and twenty-five thousand died as the revolt was crushed.

In many cases, messianic fervor emerges from dire conditions. Despair penetrates the recesses of the soul, taking away love and hope, everything but the promise of deliverance beyond the grave. The Syrian civil war has prepared people to embrace this fervor, and the fervor resembles that of Christian apocalyptic projects of previous generations. Anguish is constant, and seeking solace in an imagined world is only human. In the medieval period, the grind of peasant life, with its plagues and hunger and predation, combined with social change to make the world feel dangerously, hopelessly askew. Millenarian thinking was an attempt to right it. Norman Cohn, the historian of European apocalyptic thought, wrote that the eleventh-century peasants in this "state of chronic and inescapable insecurity" were the perfect perpetrators of apocalyptic self-slaughter:

> The resulting phantasy [. . .] became a coherent social myth which was capable of taking entire possession of those who believed in it. It explained their suffering, it promised them recompense, it held their anxieties at bay, it gave them an illusion of security—even while it drove them, held together by a common enthusiasm, on a quest which was always vain and often suicidal.
>
> So it came about that multitudes of people acted out with fierce energy a shared phantasy which though delusional yet brought them such emotional relief that they could live only through it and were perfectly willing to die for it.[28]

Musa and Yahya, of course, were not driven to apocalypse as their only solace in a soulless world. Nor were most of the other foreign supporters of the Islamic State, who lived either in England or Belgium (with their cushy social-welfare benefits) or in Egypt and Tunisia (which are poor, but hardly war zones). At worst, the foreigners could claim alienation from their home environments, a feeling that their Englishness or Norwegianness could never be adequate, and their destinies would remain forever unfulfilled. Many, such as Musa and Yahya, couldn't claim even that. What they lacked was meaning, perhaps, or purpose—things that their suburban existences could not provide, and that they could not manufacture for themselves with the tools of modern life. They loved apocalypse for itself. They chose death—and not, in most cases, for themselves, but for the people whose distant land was the canvas for their dreams.

Christian messianism has been, historically, a more deadly disease than Muslim messianism. But the latter has recurred in recent decades in increasingly virulent forms. The Islamic State's ultimate precursor was also an apocalyptic movement. In the 1970s, a former Saudi national guardsman named Juhayman al ʿUtaibi (1936–1980) led a group of vigilantes in attempts to rid Saudi Arabia of vices such as alcohol, music, and the use of mannequins in store windows. They considered the bulk of the conservative Saudi religious establishment misguided and sought (and received) blessing from certain clerics, including ʿAbd al ʿAziz bin Baz, later the grand mufti of Saudi Arabia. They adopted eccentric, minority practices, such as the wearing of sandals during prayer (as did Musa and his followers at the Footscray YMCA), and they argued that the Saudi royal family's non-Qurayshi lineage, its collaboration with infidels, and its failure to wage jihad invalidated its rule. Finally, they emphasized the pious monotheism of "*millat Ibrahim*" [the people of Abraham]—a phrase employed prominently in Islamic State propaganda and the name taken by one of the most prominent of the European jihadist groups that have made *hijrah* to fight for the Islamic State.

By the end of the 1970s, Juhayman and his followers were hatching plans for a caliphate. Rather than take a place in line with the twelve righteous caliphs, they skipped directly to the last, the Mahdi. They compiled from prophecy a list of his foretold characteristics, including his name, the size of his forehead, and the existence of a birthmark on his cheek. Incredibly, Juhayman found a suitable candidate with all the correct traits: his brother-in-law, Muhammad ibn ʿAbdullah al Qahtani.[29]

On November 20, 1979—the first day of the year 1400 on the Islamic calendar[30]—about three hundred plotters concealed a large cache of weapons in coffins and smuggled them into the Grand Mosque in Mecca. After prayers, Juhayman seized the microphone, sealed the mosque, and declared his brother-in-law the Mahdi, giving him bay'a before a baffled audience of mostly non-Arabic-speaking pilgrims. The fighters expected, as per prophecy, an enemy army to march on their position from the north, and then to be swallowed up by the earth en route to the battle. Their handheld radios revealed no such events. Instead, Saudi security forces attacked, and within four days of fighting, the Mahdi was killed (he had been picking up the Saudi forces' live grenades and throwing them back, possibly convinced of his own invincibility). After two weeks, the Saudis stormed the mosque and cleared the network of tunnels beneath. About five hundred people died, most of them government soldiers, and on January 9, 1980, the survivors of Juhayman's group—including Juhayman himself—were beheaded publicly in eight cities around the kingdom.

Cole Bunzel, the Princeton scholar, characterizes Juhayman's as an "apocalypse now" movement—a group that thought the end was in motion at that moment. He contrasts it with the Islamic State, a mere "caliphate now" movement.[31] But the ties between them are clear. Threads of intellectual descent connect the groups through Abu Muhammad al Maqdisi—once a young admirer of Juhayman—and his student Turki al Bin'ali. In the early 1980s, Maqdisi met Juhayman's followers in Kuwait, and his subsequent writings adopted their intransigent, jihad-focused ideology, including the concept of *millat Ibrahim*, which Maqdisi took as the title of a 1984 book.[32] Bin'ali has learned from Juhayman both by positive and negative example. Appointing a Mahdi may have been an overreach, but reviving a caliphate could be a happy medium of Prophetic fulfillment.

What is most astounding about Juhayman's stunt is that its complete failure hardly extinguished its emotive appeal for Muslims from a range of backgrounds and dispositions. Osama bin Laden spoke positively about Juhayman. Prominent Saudi scholars wept over the deaths of Juhayman and his followers, who were not washouts and wingnuts but their serious and dedicated students.

In 2014, before the Islamic State officially declared him an apostate, Yasir Qadhi called Juhayman's group "one of the most scary and dangerous movements in our recent history."[33] But he acknowledged that he had trouble discerning the heresies in Juhayman's writings. Juhayman was orthodox and zealous, just at the "fine line between fanaticism and righteousness." The next year, on the thirty-sixth anniversary of Juhayman's death, Qadhi wrote that the vision Juhayman proposed was "so beautiful and sweet. Yet, their actions proved them to be worse than their enemies."[34] The Islamic State has tapped into this same millenarian vein, and inspiration continues to pump through it, even after Juhayman's group's signature act—the naming of a Mahdi—literally blew up in its face.

And that is the final note in this apocalyptic song. One might imagine that the failure of prophecy might prompt reassessment by those who have sown such carnage in the prophecy's name. *Why not just defeat them at Dabiq, and show them that they're wrong?* This suggestion is born of the same naive view of religion that imagines its followers as bound, inevitably and automatically, to interpret text and history in just one way.

In his classic study of a UFO cult whose doomsday hour passed uneventfully on December 21, 1954, Leon Festinger hypothesized that true belief, when falsified by events, sometimes reacts by getting stronger and more committed. He concluded that refutation would *harden* beliefs that were held with conviction by people who were emotionally, spiritually, socially, and materially invested in their truth.[35]

The followers of the Islamic State have utterly diverted their lives, and they take great care to isolate themselves in a social setting that supports continued belief and punishes doubt with the sword. Even as their caliphate crumbles around them, their leaders and propaganda offer excuses, fortify their resolve, and strain to explain why a resounding defeat is a step toward vindication.[36]

And for some who leave the Baghdadi caliphate, it will survive in their hearts. They need not be violent, and they may acknowledge their error and rejoin society. But I suspect few will truly repent. They will be like those gray-haired lefties who were at the fringe of the counterculture of the sixties and remember it as the period of their lives that gave them the most meaning. They raised fists with radicals before they went back to school and became dentists. But they still break out the beads and sandals on weekends.

When the Peruvian novelist Mario Vargas Llosa visited the backlands of Brazil in 1979, researching his novel about the failed Antônio Conselheiro uprising, he found a shoeless, sunburned old woman in one of the villages Antônio founded. This was eighty-one years after Antônio's death. "Antônio Conselheiro?" she asked. "He isn't dead. I hope to see him, and I hope he gives me advice before I die." For people like her—abandoned by the world, or alienated from it—

> he spiritualized their orphanhood and gave reasons to carry on living and face death bravely. He did all this by reworking the only culture within reach: the religious. Curiously, by opting for the strictest orthodoxy and trying to bring the faith he had been brought up in to its logical conclusions, he was seen as being in rebellion against all institutions of society, and was persecuted and exterminated like a rabid dog.[37]

Abu Bakr al Baghdadi will not and should not be remembered with the same detachment or fondness. His cynicism and brutality disqualify him. But his followers believe. And that is a guarantee that the movement will, in one form or another, live on.

AFTERLIFE

The Germans had come to understand that [. . .] the production of lawlessness was an appropriate way to find murderers who could be recruited for organized actions. Within weeks they grasped that people liberated from Soviet rule could be drawn into violence for psychological, material, and political reasons.

—Timothy Snyder, *Black Earth*[1]

In early October 2016, the Iraqi Army was hovering at the edge of Mosul. The recapture of the city, which the Islamic State had taken in June 2014, by now looked inevitable. Long delays had left many Mosulis cynical, but by now the Islamic State itself appeared resigned to its fate. Their propaganda was no longer saying that they would occupy their strongholds forever. They promised only survival. Complete eradication would be "impossible," said an editorial in the Islamic State's Arabic weekly newspaper, and they'd live on to "conquer Rome" and fight alongside Jesus. This was not the first time the Islamic State had tried to manage expectations. Less than a year before, Baghdadi had promised in Churchillian tones:

> O Muslims, do not be amazed at the gathering of the nations and religions of disbelief against the Islamic State, for this is

the condition of the victorious group in every era. This gathering will continue and the trials and tribulations will intensify until the two camps are completed, such that there does not remain in this camp hypocrisy, and there does not remain in that camp faith [. . .]. The more the nations increase in their frenzied mobilization against it, the more it increases in its certainty of God's victory and that it is upon the straight path, and the more severe its tribulations become, the more it casts out the enemies and hypocrites and the more pure, firm, and steadfast its ranks become.[2]

Abu Muhammad al ʿAdnani, the group's charismatic spokesman, had been trying to rationalize defeat for some time now. His last encyclical, dated May 2016, seemed to anticipate his own assassination by a drone strike three months later. "Do you think, O America, that victory is by killing one leader or another?" he asked.

Or do you, O America, consider defeat to be the loss of a city or the loss of land? Were we defeated when we lost the cities in Iraq and were in the desert without any city or land? And would we be defeated and you be victorious if you were to take Mosul or Sirte or Raqqah or even take all the cities and we were to return to our initial condition? Certainly not![3]

In 2008, Iraq and the United States paid Sunni tribes to eject the Islamic State's Al Qaida forebears from cities and towns in Anbar province and forced them to hide in the countryside. They had rebounded from setbacks graver than the loss of Mosul, ʿAdnani said, and they would do so again.

While the Iraqi forces prepared to mobilize, I was more than five thousand miles away, standing next to a pile of coconuts that nearly reached my chest. With me were the elders of Butril, a village in a remote section of the Philippine island of Mindanao—the presumed destination of Musa Cerantonio and the wayward sailors of Footscray. About a year before, Butril had been the site of an operation by Philippine Marines that killed eight members of Ansar al Khilafah, an Islamic State–linked jihadist group hiding out in the area's jungles and mountains. If Mosul's fall was certain, I wanted to see where the Islamic State might go next. And this was it.

The air was sultry, and no breeze stirred the palm and banana trees. In the time-honored traditions of upper management and the press, the village elders and I were standing around watching a laborer sweat. The laborer, who didn't give his name, looked about thirty and had the spindly, lean physique of a man whose body was channeling every calorie he consumed into physical labor. His body was so defined that it could have been used to teach anatomy to medical students. He husked coconuts for a living, at fifty cents per hundred, and the village elders had asked him to show me how the village supported itself, by processing the coconuts and selling their dried meat in town.

Musa had once told me that love of the *Dawlah* [Islamic State] reached levels in the southern Philippines that he never experienced elsewhere. In Butril, I saw no evidence whatsoever of caliphate appreciation. The men who emerged from the mosque after noon prayers observed none of the rules of dress or grooming that the Islamic State forces on its subjects, and the people noted with pride that the teachers at their local school were Christians. Everyone, including the Marines who had accompanied me to Butril and were prowling the streets while I spoke with the elders, acknowledged that the Ansar al Khilafah presence consisted entirely of nonlocal people—fighters from elsewhere in the southern Philippines who moved around frequently and subsisted on criminal activity, especially extortion of local business.

That was the reason for this agricultural demonstration. I had come with Justin Richmond, head of a nongovernmental organization called the impl. project, which was trying to assess how development funders could help Butril without simply making the village a juicier target for Ansar al Khilafah or others. Richmond, thirty-seven, is a veteran of two great American expeditionary institutions, the U.S. Army's Special Operations and the missionary wing of the Church of Jesus Christ of Latter-day Saints. Now lapsed in his religion, he remains committed to his area of military expertise, which had been Islamist and criminal activity in the southern Philippines. He is one of the only foreigners, and probably the only American, who regularly travels in the unsettled hinterlands of Mindanao, which for most of the last twenty years has been known for local groups' proclivity for kidnapping white people and cutting their heads off. The two groups with the sharpest knives are Ansar al Khilafah and Abu Sayyaf, which operates from the more dangerous Sulu Archipelago, just to the southwest of Mindanao. Abu Sayyaf's leader, Abu Abdullah al Filibini, has pledged *bay'a,* and in June 2016 an official Islamic State video declared the existence of a proto-province of the Islamic State. They executed three men on camera in celebration.[4]

Richmond hoped that the donation of a solar dryer—a concrete slab for drying crops, to prevent rot—might stimulate the economy enough to strengthen the local community and make it work more closely with the government to resist the jihadists. "We see the pattern over and over," Richmond told me. "If you have prosperity, something that gives them work and opportunity, you address the communities' main vulnerability. If the livelihoods are strong enough, they get a community that is strong enough to band together again when they face a threat."[5]

The battle for Mosul would be fought with drones and tanks. But the next battle would be fought like this, village by village, with solar dryers and other farm equipment. Towns like these—not particularly interested in jihad, but vulnerable to annexation by those who were—would be next on the target list, as the Islamic State plotted to rise from the ashes of Mosul and Dabiq.

The jihad in the area around Butril is fragmented. That is just how the Islamic State likes it. A Marine officer informed us that Abu Sayyaf did have a presence—their confinement to Sulu had been exaggerated—and nearby, other groups maintained cells. If Ansar al Khilafah had a monopoly on all Islamist activity here, the Marines could control the beast by putting a collar on it. But this beast had many different heads, each requiring its own collar. Mindanao has for years been a center of Muslim grievance, in part due to federal policies that moved Christian populations, mostly Cebuano and Ilonggo, onto formerly Muslim land in the 1970s and 1980s. In addition to Abu Sayyaf were the Moro National Liberation Front (which cut a deal with the government in 1996), the Bangsamoro Islamic Freedom Fighters, the Moro Islamic Liberation Front, and other groups formerly part of it (now known by the wonderful name of "rogue MILF"). The jihadist cells made temporary alliances but also fought among themselves, and plundered villages as targets of opportunity. The island was a mess, Richmond admitted, and the only force of stability that could keep a solar dryer safe and its owners unextorted was the Philippine military.

The town elders were torn between wanting the solar dryer (no one will turn down free agricultural equipment) and knowing that closer ties with the Philippine government could mean more extortion, even reprisal, from Ansar al Khilafah, whose fighters were just a few hundred meters up the road. The Marines hadn't been here long, and there was no guarantee they'd remain. A lasting level of insecurity, on the other hand, was certain.

At the end of our meeting, Butril's mayor said he'd look forward to Richmond's next visit. Richmond agreed, but both were noncommittal. Richmond's NGO is a small outfit, and Mindanao has many hundreds of villages just as easy for local jihadis to victimize. No one, not even the Philippine government, could monitor them all and make sure the projects all built the communities up and conferred more jihad resistance. Everyone had his own priorities. (As we left, the mayor looked up askance, with the trace of a mischievous grin. "Maybe you'd like to give us a tractor, too?") Evidently the next stage in the generational war would be a complicated one.

Yahya encouraged Musa to travel to the *Dawlah,* but he stressed that the trip need not entail a risky (and, for the passport-free Musa, probably impossible) flight to Turkey and a furtive slide under barbed wire at the border. The *Dawlah* had provinces elsewhere, and though they were not in the blessed Sham, they still counted as lands of Islam. *Hijrah* was *hijrah.* Few doubt that the southern Philippines was Musa's intended destination. He had traveled there previously and maintained contacts. According to Australian media, he told the Sydney psychologist he spoke to before he left that jihadists in the Philippines had asked him to help them convict and execute a "spy" they had captured.[6]

If Musa was truly bound for the southern Philippines, what mystified me was the optimism that he must have brought to his journey— not just the survival at sea (martyrdom would have been its own reward) but the confidence that upon arrival his jihadist friends would welcome him as a colleague rather than, say, as a commodity that could be sold to a rival group. Kidnapping, after all, was the Philippines' single most lucrative jihadist industry, and far more profitable than shaking down coconut huskers. None of the groups, even the ones that pledged themselves openly to the Islamic State, had the scholarly aspect that Musa and Yahya thrived on. (The Marines told me that according to their intelligence, no one in the groups around Butril could read and understand Arabic.) Moreover, the groups were squabbling, and even if he found one that adopted and adored him, he would still be a bit player in a snake pit of mutual jihadi distrust. Was this the paradise he wanted, the dream to end all dreams? Among the many questions I would like to ask him—his lawyers, perhaps concerned with his impending trial, would not make him available—is if anyone went there as an outsider, how would that person's life look?

But no one ever got far analyzing the Islamic State by underestimating its ability to see the glory in a setback. I remembered, first of all, the line Musa quoted frequently about the importance of *khilafah*: that if a caliph ruled just a single road (let alone a few villages in Kunar, or a tropical island in the Pacific), then his caliphate remained in effect, and Muslims remained obliged to obey. "True defeat is the loss of willpower and desire to fight," 'Adnani said in his final address. "We would be defeated and you victorious only if you were able to remove the Quran from the Muslims' hearts."[7]

Again, the best way to understand the incomprehensible was to migrate mentally to the caliphate, to imagine oneself already in a fantasy of revival, where one's every action could, and should, mirror the virtuous acts of the earliest Muslims. I tried to see the Philippines through his eyes, and through the caliphate's. When Muhammad first preached monotheism to his fellow Quraysh in Mecca and they drummed him out of town, he went not to a place of harmony but to a place of discord. He fled to Medina—a city so riven with internal disputes that the southern Philippines' interjihadi, MILF-on-MILF violence might look tractable by comparison. *Hijrah* is a journey not to comfort but to other challenges. Until his trial takes place one cannot say whether or not Musa may have welcomed those challenges. The goal of the caliphate, and of his own revival of Dhahirism, was to unify Muslims under the most basic version of their faith. If Musa was really traveling to the Philippines, he could be the unifier and, although he was probably too shy to say it, the latter-day Muhammad of his own little corner of the world.

He had rejected the mosques of Australia, and been rejected by them. His best efforts on Egyptian television earned him rejection there, too. Perhaps, if he indeed intended to come to the Philippines, he saw the relative lack of religious knowledge among the jihadis not as a downside but as an opportunity—finally to be a figure of respect, the mufti of his own private island. That would have been a utopia of a kind.

The Islamic State, notably, has been defining utopia down. If Mosul falls, Raqqah will be next. Both reconquests will be bloody, and some of the blood might be Yahya's. But the strategy of the Islamic State is larger than either city, and extends beyond the desert foxholes in which its fighters will conceal themselves once they scurry out of town. The building of provinces thousands of miles from Raqqah was a parallel and simultaneous theory of expansion, an insurance policy for when the blitzkriegs in western Iraq stopped increasing the caliphate's territory. The theory involved finding places disturbed by unrest and criminality, then leveraging it to the Islamic State's ultimate advantage.

The military officers in Mindanao stressed that the local jihadis were exactly what Yahya and Musa were not—simple thugs. "They are just criminals," a senior officer said. "They don't care about religion."[8] To the caliphate, for all its intellectual pretensions, an atmosphere of thuggery—even secular thuggery—is a virtue. It is no surprise that the wreckage of Saddam Hussein's Iraq proved fertile soil for the Islamic State. When belief is laid low, it deputizes savagery to restore it to power. Like Leninists and Maoists before them, the Islamic State knows that people who live in intolerably violent conditions will seek salvation from anyone who credibly offers it. They accept salvation in this world, in the form of physical security, first. Then they learn to seek it from the same sources, for the next world.

Once their territorial control dissolves in Iraq and Syria, the diaspora activity will matter more. Lawlessness is a problem everywhere, as the Butril example shows. The Islamic State sees those conditions of chaos and knows that if it can offer security under its own brand, by unifying factions and employing extraordinary and unprecedented violence, it might find new footholds, using exactly the tactics that earned it such spectacular, if temporary, success in the Middle East.[9]

The same chaotic conditions allowed Boko Haram, the Islamic State's West African affiliate, to claim territory there. Rapid social change in the north of Nigeria left a Muslim population—once powerful and stable—upended and neglected by the national government. "It is a place that used to be rich but has become poor," Lamido Sanusi, the sultan of Kano, the largest northern Nigerian city, told me. He compared the pangs of social change to the intellectual dissonance that the philosopher Karl Popper cited as a source or sign of upheaval. "It is a typical Popperian moment, where you had a deep sense of instability where the North had lost economic and military power and then retreated into a Muslim identity."[10] And yet those who see religion's being exploited for political ends have it exactly backward. Boko Haram found disillusionment and misgovernment, then accelerated both to further a religious goal.[11] The believers and the thugs have worked in tandem, each using the other. In Syria and Iraq, the believers vanquished the thugs, purging any nonbeliever Baathists in their midst and any criminals unwilling to put their violence into the service of a theocratic state.

As its presence in Iraq and Syria becomes ever more precarious, the Islamic State's strategy is to forge similar partnerships worldwide. A look at a map of Muslim-majority countries, and a passing knowledge of the outrageous levels of misgovernment and criminality in many of them, shows that Mindanao and Nigeria are but two instances of a global problem. Any place with a history of unrest is a potential niche for the caliphate. In early 2015, the Islamic State dispatched half a dozen supporters to scout territory in the perennially war-torn eastern Congo.[12] A large menu of other locations exists in Africa, Asia, perhaps even South America. Wherever there is grievance, savagery can be sown. Wherever there is savagery, it can be used and exploited. Wherever it can be exploited, the nightmare can endure.

But the nightmare will end someday. After two years of listening to the group's followers, I have come to think of them as sick romantics, a visionary company whose longing for meaning was never matched by an ability to distinguish good from evil, or beauty from horror. They set high standards for themselves and sometimes have met them. It will not do to pretend that they believed in nothing, or that they believe weakly. Most people who subject themselves to such onerous standards eventually fall short, and they then revise their ideals and return to the society of mortals and more modest ambitions. The tragedy is that even those inverted visionaries who live to realize their error will never be able to undo the misery they have inflicted on so many others.

ACKNOWLEDGMENTS

I wrote this book as a visiting fellow at the Council on Foreign Relations. Janine Hill, Victoria Alekhine, and Richard N. Haass supported me there, and meetings with Council members and fellows clarified my thinking. Gabriella Meltzer provided valuable research assistance.

Greg Veis, former executive editor of *The New Republic,* commissioned my first two stories about the Islamic State and the first of my stories about Salafism. Don Peck, James Bennet (now of *The New York Times*), Yvonne Rolzhausen, and Scott Stossel recognized that there was more to be said, and edited my cover story on the Islamic State for the March 2015 *Atlantic.* My string of good luck in editors continued at Random House with Hilary Redmon and Mika Kasuga. I owe much to Jin Auh, James Pullen, and Andrew Wylie for their zealous representation.

Several audiences gave helpful comments. For the invitations to speak to them, I thank Robert Kerr of the U.S. Embassy in Abuja; R. Nicholas Burns of the Aspen Strategy Group; Fernando Cardoso of the 2nd Lisbon Conference; R. Scott Appleby, Ebrahim Moosa, and Atalia Omer of the University of Notre Dame's Keough School of Global Affairs; Thomas Sanderson of the Center for Strategic and International Studies; Isak Svensson of Uppsala University; Graham T. Allison and Niall Ferguson of the Harvard Kennedy School's Applied History Working Group; Francis X. Clooney, S.J., and Laura Thompson of the Harvard Divinity School's Center for World Religions; Stephen Sestanovich of Columbia University; Boston University; the University of Toronto's Munk School of Global Affairs; the University of Chicago's Pearson Institute for the Study and Resolution of Global Conflicts; the University of Lagos; Georgetown University; and Ahmadu Bello University.

Many people gave their time and wisdom freely. By saying that any remaining errors are mine, I am not engaging in the usual acknowledgments ritual of absolving them for mistakes. In some cases our disagreements are profound; indeed, some of those listed below believe that it is permissible to murder me. All have made the book better, though, and for that I thank them. Especially helpful were Bernard Haykel, Cole Bunzel, Will McCants, David Cook, Abdullah Pocius, Musa Cerantonio, Anjem Choudary, Mizanur Rahman, Ebrahim Moosa, Jon Hoover, Mia Bloom, Charlie Winter, Yasir Qadhi, Hamza Yusuf, Hesham El Ashry, Hassan Ko Nakata, Nelly Lahoud, Kecia Ali, Fred Donner, Jean-Pierre Filiu, Kévin Jackson, Pieter Van Ostaeyen, Shadi Hamid, Aymenn Jawad Al-Tamimi, Keith Lewinstein, Chase F. Robinson, Joas Wagemakers, Yahya Michot, Jacob Olidort, Shiraz Maher, Jacob Zenn, the ISIS-aligned indoor soccer team at RecWest Footscray, and others who have asked to remain anonymous.

I learned, too, from conversations and correspondence with Ali Sada, Andy Kim, Carool Kersten, Anna Grzymala-Busse, Richard Nielsen, Vartan Gregorian, Leon Wieseltier, Ryan Crocker, Peter R.

Neumann, Maajid Nawaz, Gregory Johnsen, Mark Juergensmeyer, Monica Duffy Toft, Rolf Mowatt-Larssen, Tariq Ramadan, David Ignatius, Richard Danzig, Jared Cohen, and Thomas Hegghammer. Also invaluable was the advice of my Yale colleagues Sigrun Kahl, Philip S. Gorski, Bruce Gordon, Zareena Grewal, and Frank Griffel.

In the course of writing and reporting this book, I enjoyed the hospitality and advice of dozens of friends. Kuba Wrzesniewski, Mauro De Lorenzo, Benjamin J. Dueholm, Benjamin Healy, Ryan Calder, and Thomas Rid read and commented on parts of the text. Others who contributed include Yasir al-Gabara, Osama Ali, Mohammed Munder, Hakimuddin Dawud, Annette Rid, Matthew Cordell and Erin Renner, Chantana and James Noel Ward, Nils Rosenberg and Karen-Sofie Aasgaard, Gudmund Aasgaard, E. Clark Copelin, Will Masters and Diane Asadorian, Toshiko and Kent Calder, Theodor Dunkelgrün, Graham Harman, Paul Warham and Eriko Yamazaki, Zac Unger and Shona Armstrong, Natasha and Jesse Weisz, Nathan F. Sayre, Geoffrey Gresh and Leigh Nolan, Reihan Salam, Gabrielle Revlock and John Mangin, Kinch Hoekstra, Adelaide Papazoglou, Hunter Keith, Christopher Kirchhoff, Aubrey Clayton and Melissa Goldman, Urs Naber, Alexandra Leichtman, Andreas Schafer, Tim Heffernan and Lindsay Goldwert, and Jennifer MacDonald. None of these people ever said no when I asked for their help. Some critiqued me harshly, and for that help I am especially grateful.

Davenport College
October 2016

NOTES

A NOTE ON TERMINOLOGY

1. See C. E. Bosworth et al., "al-Shām," *Encyclopaedia of Islam,* 2nd ed., ed. P. Bearman, Th. Bianquis, C. E. Bosworth, E. van Donzel, W. P. Heinrichs (2012).
2. For more on the names of the Islamic State—especially "Da ʿesh"—see Alice Guthrie's essay "Decoding Daesh: Why Is the New Name for ISIS So Hard to Understand?" *Free Word,* February 19, 2015.
3. See "The Rafida: From Ibn Saba' to Al Dajjal," *Dabiq* 13 (January 2016). Unlike Shia and other "apostates," Christians and Jews may submit to the Muslims and live as protected but subjugated citizens. There is one known exception to the Islamic State's general order to kill Shia, and that is the Zaydi sect of Yemen, which Islamic State scholars have designated as merely deviant and corrigible.
4. Koran 48:10.

PROLOGUE

1. "Jesus Christ's Return to Earth." Pew Research Center, July 14, 2010.
2. "From the Mannan Family in the Land of Khilafah," July 3, 2015, http://justpaste.it/m4sy.
3. Rachel Olding, "Australian Islamic State Doctor: Tareq Kamleh a 'Lazy Doctor Who Flirted with Patients,'" *Sydney Morning Herald,* April 29, 2015.
4. Tareq Kamleh, "My Reply to the Australian Health Practitioner Regulation Agency (AHPRA)," May 8, 2015, http://justpaste.it/l0ec.
5. Roger Ebert, *Pink Flamingos* review, *Chicago Sun-Times,* April 11, 1997.
6. Graeme Wood, "'What ISIS Really Wants': The Response," TheAtlantic.com, February 24, 2015.

THE CHOSEN SECT

1. The terms "Islamist" and "jihadist" are contested. By "Islamism," I refer to a broad spectrum of political persuasions united by a conviction that Islam should be a guiding principle in government. By "jihadism," I mean support for forms of Islamism that seek to establish Islam's dominance through force if necessary.

2. For more on Salafism, see Bernard Haykel, "On the Nature of Salafi Thought and Action," and other chapters in Roel Meijer, ed., *Global Salafism: Islam's New Religious Movement* (London: Hurst), 2009.

3. Another category of venerated early Muslims is the Companions [*sahaba*]. They and the pious forefathers [*salaf*] are overlapping but not identical categories. The former are restricted to the men and women whom Muhammad knew personally while they were Muslims, and who never apostatized.

4. Bukhari 6065, Muslim 2533.

5. The Koranic references most often marshaled against democracy include 6:116 ("If you obey most of those upon the earth, they will mislead you from the way of God") and 12:106 ("most [people] do not believe in God, except while attributing partners to him [i.e., polytheism]"). There are, however, several active Salafi democratic movements—most notably, Egypt's Nour Party. For a review of Salafi attitudes toward democracy, beyond the common view that it is haram, see Ovamir Anjum, "Salafis and Democracy: Doctrine and Context," *The Muslim World* 106:3, 2016.

6. Mary Anne Weaver, *A Portrait of Egypt: A Journey Through the World of Militant Islam* (New York: Farrar, Straus and Giroux, 2001), p. 94.

7. Ibn Hanbal's quietism is described in Michael Cook, *Commanding Right and Forbidding Wrong in Islamic Thought* (Cambridge, UK: Cambridge University Press, 2000), pp. 95–109.

8. For more on the biography of ʿUmar ʿAbd al Rahman, see Malika Zeghal, *Gardiens de l'Islam: Les oulemas d'Al Azhar dans l'Égypte contemporaine* (Paris: Presses de la Fondation Nationale des Sciences Politiques, 1996), pp. 336–358.

9. Sometimes Salafis will skirt this issue by saying they "reverted," rather than "converted," to Islam—irrespective of whether they were born Muslim and became observant, or were born non-Muslim and became Muslim.

   This nomenclature is not exclusive to Salafis. Muhammad said, "No baby is born except according to the *fitrah* [roughly, 'God's plan']; then his parents make him a Jew or a Christian" (Muslim 63/6426). Therefore everyone who finds his way to Islam really finds his way *back* to it.

10. It would be cheap to point out these lurid tortures without noting that Christendom, too, has excelled in the field of sadism (and indeed takes as its main symbol an instrument of torture). Less obvious, perhaps, is the secular world's equal titillation at gross human suffering. Have you seen *Hostel II*? As Wim Raven writes of a medieval Muslim text on the punishments of the damned:

    > It is easy enough for a modern person to dispose of this text as vulgar and sloppy . . . [But] when one tries to visualize hell from this text, the result is similar to present-day sadistic fantasies, horror films and underground comic strips: monsters with iron hooks in their claws, severed limbs spouting blood and pus, stripped-off skins, snakes and scorpions wriggling over naked bodies. Today, quite a number of people derive a mixture of fright and lust from such pictures or descriptions; would that have been so different in past centuries?

    See Wim Raven, "Hell in Popular Muslim Imagination: The Anonymous Kitāb al-ʿAẓama," in Christian Lange, ed., *Locating Hell in Islamic Traditions* (Leiden: Brill, 2016).

11. "Open Letter to Al-Baghdadi," http://lettertobaghdadi.com.

12. One of its pamphlets, about the practice of sex slavery, included this Q&A:

> *What is the reward for freeing a slave girl?*
> God the exalted said [in the Koran]: "And what can make you know what is [breaking through] the difficult pass [Hell]? It is the freeing of a slave." And [the Prophet Muhammad] said: "Whoever frees a believer God frees every organ of his body from hellfire."

"Questions and Answers on Taking Captives and Slaves," translated in part by MEMRI Jihad and Terrorism Threat Monitor, December 4, 2014.

13. Quoted in Ebrahim Moosa, "Overlooking Political Theologies: ISIS and Versions of Sunni Orthodoxy" (working paper). Moosa continues to say that ʿUthmani argues for a temporary modern ban on slavery, but solely on the grounds that Muslim countries have agreed not to take slaves. In the absence of those agreements, the enslavement could proceed. He goes on to name the Al Azhar sheikha Suad Salih and the Saudi Suad al-Ghayth as two other prominent scholars who have endorsed slavery as a living concept in Islam.

14. These reactions find close parallels in the treatment of slavery in the West, and particularly in the United States. Few Americans are willing to recognize how deeply ingrained slavery is in American life. Nor do most of us fully appreciate the monstrous irony that the same Enlightened, democratic thinkers who founded the country also enshrined its most un-Enlightened, anti-democratic practice into law. Thomas Jefferson's ownership of his sexual partners is rarely referred to as sex slavery, but it is exactly that—and the fact that he freed slaves as well as having sex with them would hardly be evidence that he tended toward abolitionism. Orlando Patterson has suggested that we scrap the pretense that slavery is the "peculiar institution" and instead call it "the embarrassing institution." See Orlando Patterson, *Slavery and Social Death* (Cambridge, MA: Harvard University Press, 1982), p. ix.

15. David Brion Davis, *The Problem of Slavery in Western Culture* (Ithaca, NY: Cornell University Press, 1966), pp. 31–32.

16. See Koran 74:20. Similar sentiments about the danger of cleverness can be found in the work of other great simplifiers of religion. Consider John Calvin's warning that the mind is "a perpetual forge of idols" ("Impiety of Attributing a Visible Form to God," in *The Institutes of the Christian Religion* [1536]); "the heart is deceitful above all things" (Jeremiah 17:9, a verse cherished by Evangelicals); Cardinal Newman's polemics against "private judgment" ("Faith and Private Judgement," from *Discourses Addressed to Mixed Congregations,* 1849); and the Alcoholics Anonymous/12-step inveighing against "stinkin' thinkin'."

17. Abu ʿAmr al Qaʿidi, *A Course in the Art of Recruitment.* The document is available online and is described by Brian Fishman and Abdullah Warius in "A Jihadist's Course in the Art of Recruitment," *CTC Sentinel,* February 2009.

18. Maajid Nawaz, email, October 2, 2012.

19. Koran 4:56.

20. See, for example, the spartan, icon-free interiors depicted in the paintings of Pieter Jansz Saenredam and Emanuel de Witte. Many of their churches are, to a squinting eye, indistinguishable from a certain kind of mosque.

21. Bukhari and Muslim.

22. Sherman Jackson, trans., *On the Boundaries of Theological Tolerance in Islam: Abū Ḥāmid Al-Ghāzalī's Fayṣal Al-Tafriqa Bayna Al-Islam Wa Al-Zandaqa* (Oxford: Oxford University Press, 2002), p. 112.

23. Others have suggested that only Muslims can blaspheme, because infidels' insults against the Prophet arise from ignorance. (If they were less ignorant, they would be Muslims.) The Koran indirectly supports this position in passing, while commanding Muslims not to insult false gods: "Revile not those whom they call upon besides God, lest they out of spite revile God in their ignorance" (6:108).

24. The classical version of this accusation appears in the writings of Ibn Battutah, the greatest of the Arab wayfarers, who met Ibn Taymiyyah in Damascus and wondered whether he "had a screw loose." Quoted in George Makdisi, "Ibn Taymiya: A Sufi of the Qadiriya Order," *The American Journal of Arabic Studies* I, 1973, p. 119.

25. Th. Emil Homerin, "Sufis and their Detractors in Mamluk Egypt," in Frederick de Jong and Bernd Radtke, eds., *Islamic Mysticism Contested* (Leiden: Brill, 1999), p. 233.

26. "Ibn Taymiyya," in Gerhard Bowering, ed., *Princeton Encyclopedia of Islamic Political Thought* (Princeton, NJ: Princeton University Press, 2012), p. 239.

27. Quoted in ʿAbd al Salam Faraj, *The Neglected Duty: The Creed of Sadat's Assassins*, trans. Johannes J. G. Jansen (New York: Macmillan, 1986 [1980]), p. 173.

28. For most of the period after his death and until the nineteenth century, Ibn Taymiyyah occupied only a minor place among Sunni scholars, particularly outside the Hanbali school prevalent in the Arabian Peninsula. See Khaled El-Rouayheb, "From Ibn Hajar al-Haytami (d. 1566) to Khayr al-Din al-Alusi (d. 1899): Changing Views of Ibn Taymiyya Among Non-Hanbali Sunni Scholars," in Yossef Rapoport and Shahab Ahmed (eds.), *Ibn Taymiyya and His Times* (Karachi: Oxford University Press, 2010), p. 270.

29. Ibid., p. 172.

30. Lawrence Wright, *Thirteen Days in September* (New York: Knopf, 2014), p. 16.

31. Bernard Haykel has noted the Salafi fetish for classical Arabic: "I have encountered Salafis in India, and elsewhere outside the Arab world, for whom the ability to speak fluently in classical Arabic is a major marker of being a true Salafi [. . .] Some have even argued that ideally all Muslims should speak Arabic as a mother tongue. This is not an easy feat to accomplish and its realisation is a mark of distinction and high status among the members of the movement." Haykel, "On the Nature of Salafi Thought and Action," p. 35, n. 5.

32. "There is no compulsion in [matters of] religion" (Koran 2:256). Some have interpreted this verse as applying only to Christians and Jews, since the Prophet compelled the idolaters of Mecca to abandon their faith, or have suggested that subsequent "sword" verses (such as 9:5 and 9:29) abrogate this verse. Discussion of this verse's abrogation in the context of the Islamic State appears in Ella Landau-Tasseron, "Delegitimizing ISIS on Islamic Grounds: Criticism of Abu Bakr Al-Baghdadi by Muslim Scholars," MEMRI Inquiry & Analysis, no. 1205, November 19, 2015, pp. 12–13.

MADNESS AND METHODOLOGY

1. In Jonathan Z. Smith, *Imagining Religion: From Babylon to Jonestown* (Chicago: University of Chicago Press, 1982), p. 108.

2. Cole Bunzel, "The Caliphate's Scholar-in-Arms," *Jihadica,* July 9, 2014.

3. "Treasury Sanctions Key ISIL Leaders and Facilitators Including a Senior Oil Official," United States Department of Treasury press release, February 11, 2016.

4. Cole Bunzel, "Binʿali Leaks: Revelations of the Silent Mufti," *Jihadica,* June 15, 2015.

5. Bernard Haykel, interview, New York, September 30, 2016.

6. The jihadist affection for poetry would astonish most non-Arabs. Many of the leadership statements from the Islamic State include verse (Baghdadi's are an exception), and since 2014, the Islamic State has had an official poetess, a Syrian named Ahlam al Nasr. See Robyn Creswell and Bernard Haykel, "Battle Lines," *The New Yorker*, June 8, 2015. Islamic State a cappella groups sing *nashid*s, a related poetic form, prolifically, and in December 2015 they issued their first *nashid* in Chinese ("Mujahid"). One of the most popular and oldest jihadist *nashid*s bears the familiar title "Strangers" (*Ghuraba'*). Portions of it consist solely of the word *ghuraba'*, repeated to exhaustion. For more on the jihadi poetry, see Elisabeth Kendall, "Jihadist Propaganda and Its Exploitation of the Arab Poetic Tradition," in Elisabeth Kendall and Ahmad Khan (eds.), *Reclaiming Islamic Tradition: Modern Interpretations of the Classical Heritage* (Edinburgh: Edinburgh University Press, 2016), chapter 9.

7. Cole Bunzel, interview, New York, November 4, 2015.
   I have encountered a bewilderingly incommensurable range of opinion on the fluency of

Baghdadi's classical Arabic. Zareena Grewal, a professor of religious studies at Yale, says his Arabic is "not impressive" (interview, April 29, 2015), and Hamza Yusuf (interview, May 10, 2015) was similarly underwhelmed. Haykel and Bunzel have noted Baghdadi's "mastery of classical Arabic" ("A New Caliphate?" Project Syndicate, July 10, 2014), and their opinion is echoed, grudgingly, by most Arabs I have asked. Since Baghdadi did doctoral work in Koranic recitation, it would be reasonable to expect facility with classical religious speech.

8. Reproduced by Aymenn Jawad Al-Tamimi on his blog at http://www.aymennjawad.org /2015/10/this-is-our-aqeeda-and-this-is-our-manhaj-islam, October 27, 2015.

9. Richard Nielsen, a political scientist at MIT, argues that jihadi ideological activity—writing fatwas and other scholarship in defense of jihadism—is often a response to rejection by mainstream Islamic institutions. (It may be the cause of that rejection as well.) His "blocked ambition" hypothesis suggests that being denied mainstream success creates massive chips on jihadist clerics' shoulders, which in turn lead to more energetic jihadism. Richard Nielsen, *Deadly Clerics: Blocked Ambition and the Turn to Violent Jihad* (New York: Cambridge University Press, forthcoming).

10. For more on Maqdisi, see Joby Warrick, *Black Flags: The Rise of ISIS* (New York: Doubleday, 2015), and Joas Wagemakers, *A Quietist Jihadi: The Ideology and Influence of Abu Muhammad al Maqdisi* (Cambridge, UK: Cambridge University Press, 2012).

11. Quoted in Eli Alshech, "The Doctrinal Crisis Within the Salafi-Jihadi Ranks and the Emergence of Neo-Takfirism," *Islamic Law and Society* 21, no. 4: 419–452.

12. Abū Muḥammad al-Maqdisī, *Waqafāt ma'a thamarāt al-jihād,* 23–4. Quoted in Alshech, "Doctrinal Crisis," p. 432.

13. Maqdisi distinguished between killing to inflict pain on the enemy [*qital al nikaya*] and killing to consolidate power [*qital al tamkin*], and favored the latter over the former. See Joas Wagemakers, "Protecting Jihad: The Sharia Council of the Minbar al-Tawhid wa-l-Jihad," *Middle East Policy* 18:2, 2011.

14. Wagemakers, in "Protecting Jihad," identifies Bin'ali as a member of Maqdisi's "Sharia Council," under the pseudonym Abu Humam Bakr ibn 'Abd al 'Aziz al Athari. Maqdisi felt particular affection for Bin'ali at that stage, according to Wagemakers, because of Bin'ali's rising to Maqdisi's defense in squabbles with other jihadist ideologues.

15. Hélène Sallon, "Abou Mohammed Al-Maqdissi, un théoricien du djihad contre l'organisation Etat islamique," *Le Monde,* September 23, 2016.

16. Joas Wagemakers, interview, Nijmegen, March 27, 2015.

17. Patrick Cockburn, "Middle East Leader of the Year? You'd Be Surprised . . . ," *The Independent,* December 21, 2013.

18. See Cole Bunzel, "Introducing the 'Islamic State of Iraq and Greater Syria.'" *Jihadica,* April 9, 2013. For a comprehensive description of this process and its relation to the larger Syrian civil war, see Charles Lister, *The Syrian Jihad: Al-Qaeda, the Islamic State and the Evolution of an Insurgency* (London: Hurst, 2016).

19. Will McCants, "The Believer," Brookings Essay, September 1, 2015.

20. Nelly Lahoud, interview, New York, April 10, 2015. See also Nelly Lahoud, "Metamorphosis: From al-Tawhid wa-al-Jihad to Dawlat al-Khilafa (2003–2014)," in Bryan Price, Dan Milton, Muhammad al-'Ubaydi, and Nelly Lahoud, *The Group That Calls Itself a State: Understanding the Evolution and Challenges of the Islamic State* (West Point, NY: Combating Terrorism Center, December 2014). Extended further, the analogy between Zarqawi and Nur al Din pays an even greater compliment to Baghdadi. Nur al Din's successor was Saladin, the Kurdish warrior who conquered Jerusalem.

21. Cole Bunzel, interview, Princeton, NJ, April 5, 2015.

22. Baghdadi is not the first to copy Abu Bakr al Siddiq. Here is Muhammad Morsi's speech upon winning the Egyptian presidency in 2012:

> O people of Egypt, you have bestowed upon me a heavy trust and great responsibility. I say to all of you, by the grace of [God] and your will, that I

have been entrusted with this and I am not best of you [. . .] I call upon you my people to support me as long as I establish justice and righteousness among you, and as long as I obey God in your affairs. If I don't do so, and I disobey God and I do not adhere to what I promised, you are not obliged to obey me.

(Translation by the Muslim Brotherhood and reproduced by *The Guardian,* June 25, 2012.)

23. See Fred Donner, *The Early Islamic Conquests* (Princeton, NJ: Princeton University Press, 1982), pp. 82–90, and *Muhammad and the Believers: At the Origins of Islam* (Cambridge, MA: Harvard University Press, 2010), pp. 100–102.

24. The global Muslim community rejected Baghdadi's jihad nearly as decisively as they rejected the last caliph's call. During the First World War, Sultan Mehmed V declared jihad against the Allies and specifically demanded that Muslims under British rule rise up against their government. Not only did British Muslims fail to revolt, but non-British Arabs joined the Allied cause, and the Ottoman Empire was carved up and disbanded.

25. Koran 50:16.

26. I have found no source for this folktale other than Hesham and posts on Facebook. Colin Imber, who wrote a study of Abu al Su'ud, reports no such story in standard sources.

27. H. A. R. Gibb, "The Fiscal Rescript of 'Umar II," *Arabica* (January 1955), pp. 4–5.

28. For an attempt to analyze *Dabiq*'s multiple audiences, see Brandon Colas, "What Does *Dabiq* Do? ISIS Hermeneutics and Organizational Fractures within *Dabiq* Magazine," *Studies in Conflict and Terrorism,* June 6, 2016.

29. A modern interpretation of the word "jihad" claims that it is not primarily a term related to violence or war. (For an example of this, see John L. Esposito, *The Islamic Threat: Myth or Reality* [New York: Oxford University Press, 1999], p. 30; and Reza Azlan, *No God but God: The Origins, Evolution and Future of Islam* [New York: Random House, 2005], pp. 81–82.)

These interpreters quote a saying of the Prophet, generally regarded as spurious by Muslim scholars, that refers to war as "lesser jihad" and to inward struggle for moral perfection as "greater jihad." "Jihad," while built from an Arabic verb *jahada* ["to struggle" or "to strive"]— the "holy" aspect is not semantically necessary—has historically referred to warfare in the service of God. For discussion of this topic, see David Cook, *Understanding Jihad* (Berkeley: University of California Press, 2005), pp. 35–44.

30. Ella Landau-Tasseron, "The Religious Foundations of Political Allegiance: A Study of Bay'a in Pre-modern Islam," Hudson Institute Research Monographs on the Muslim World, Series no. 2, Paper no. 4, May 2010, p. 1; Andrew Marsham, "Bay'a," *Encyclopaedia of Islam,* 3rd ed. (Leiden: Brill, 2014).

31. "Iraq: ISIS Execution Site Located," Human Rights Watch, June 26, 2014.

32. Virtually all social media platforms found themselves conscripted by their users into the Islamic State propaganda war, and YouTube was not the worst offender in hosting bloody and genocidal content. Twitter, Facebook, and YouTube have all screened for Islamic State content and deleted accounts when possible. Recent research has shown that those deletion campaigns have been somewhat effective, keeping the networks from growing and limiting the reach of celebrity jihadist tweeters. See J. M. Berger and Heather Perez, "The Islamic State's Diminishing Returns on Twitter: How Suspensions Are Limiting the Social Networks of English-Speaking ISIS Supporters," Program on Extremism Occasional Paper, George Washington University, February 2016.

One symptom of the success of these campaigns of deletion is migration to other less user-friendly or widely used platforms. Justpaste.it, a website run single-handedly by a young Pole, became a popular medium for photo galleries of the Islamic State, and as of late 2016, Telegram—an encryption-friendly messaging platform—is the easiest source of official information and videos. See Carmen Fishwick, "How a Polish Student's Website Became an Isis Propaganda Tool," *The Guardian,* August 14, 2014.

33. See Mehdi Hasan, "What the Jihadists Who Bought *Islam for Dummies* on Amazon Tell Us About Radicalisation," *New Statesman,* August 21, 2014.

34. Mona El-Naggar, "From Cairo Private School to Syria's Killing Fields," *New York Times,* February 19, 2015.

35. Posted in December 2014 at http://justpaste.it/IslamYaken0.

36. Twitter user @i_yaken, July 31 [account deleted].

37. Smith, *Imagining Religion,* p. 112.

38. See, for example, John Esposito's presentation at a Center for the Study of Islam and Democracy panel, August 28, 2014.

39. Kevin McDonald, "ISIS Jihadis Aren't Medieval—They Are Shaped by Modern Western Philosophy," *The Guardian,* September 14, 2014.

40. "There aren't any direct quotes in the speech from Maududi," McDonald wrote to me. "My piece was trying to argue that the sacralization of political power within contemporary Islamism has a western, rather than Muslim, origin." "[Baghdadi's] description of the role of the Calif is constructed in language that I believe comes directly from Maududi's *Islamic Way of Life.*" (Email, December 15, 2014.)

41. Liz Sly, "The Hidden Hand Behind the Islamic State Militants? Saddam Hussein's," *Washington Post,* April 4, 2015.

42. Aya Batrawy, Paisley Dodds, and Lori Hinnant, " 'Islam for Dummies': IS Recruits Have Poor Grasp of Faith," Associated Press, August 15, 2016.

43. "Tariq Ramadan: 'ISIL's Acts Are Un-Islamic,' " Al Jazeera, October 17, 2014.

44. I'm grateful to Kyle W. Orton and Craig A. Whiteside for their work establishing this timeline. See Kyle Orton, "Saddam's Former Loyalists Are Leading ISIS—as True Believers," *National Review,* July 20, 2015.

45. See the archive of documents amassed by Aymenn Jawad Al-Tamimi. These include many documents of a secular, religious, and hybrid nature. http://www.aymennjawad.org/2015/01/archive-of-islamic-state-administrative-documents.

46. Thomas Hegghammer, "Why Terrorists Weep." Paul Wilkinson Memorial Lecture, University of St. Andrews, April 16, 2015.

47. Thomas Hegghammer, interview, Stansted, UK, August 24, 2015.

48. Andrew F. March identifies an irony in the lack of interest Western scholars have paid to Islamic theology in general. Today, scholars who dwell on jihadist scripture and theology, to the exclusion of jihadist politics, demography, or sociology, should expect to be vilified by their colleagues as Orientalists—members of the long, sometimes disreputable tradition of Western academics who have fetishized or denigrated the East in the course of studying it. But prior to the 1990s, Orientalists were the ones who ignored or downplayed theology. They sidelined these scripturally focused intellectual activities in favor of the Greek-influenced *falsafa* [philosophy] traditions, which, as Tim Winter says, are not "obstructed by futile scriptural controls." Quoted in Andrew F. March, "Speaking About Muhammad, Speaking for Muslims," *Critical Inquiry* 37, Summer 2011, p. 808, n. 3.

49. Will McCants, *The ISIS Apocalypse: The History, Strategy, and Doomsday Vision of the Islamic State* (New York: St. Martin's Press, 2015).

50. Reuel Marc Gerecht, "The Last Orientalist," *Weekly Standard,* June 5, 2006.

51. Bernard Lewis, "The Significance of Heresy in Islam," *Studia Islamica* 1 (1953): 44.

The specter at this banquet of godless social science is Karl Marx. Marx famously wrote religion out of history by claiming analgesic properties ("the opium of the people") for it, and saying that it masked root causes related to iniquitous material conditions. The quest, often successful, to find these underlying material causes has animated a huge amount of the social science of religion. The assumption, however, that religion is *always* reducible to material explanation is nothing more than dogma.

52. Michael Cook, *Ancient Religions, Modern Politics* (Princeton, NJ: Princeton University Press, 2014), p. 270.

53. Ibid., p. xii.
54. For a sketch of Islamic liberal politics and their theoretical coherence with liberal states, see Andrew F. March, *Islam and Liberal Citizenship* (Oxford University Press, 2009).
55. A common characteristic of Bunzel's peer researchers is their youth. Aymenn J. Al-Tamimi of the Middle East Forum, Aaron Y. Zelin of the Washington Institute for Near East Policy, and Charlie Winter of King's College London are all in their twenties. The elders of the field—Peter R. Neumann and Shiraz Maher of King's College London, Thomas Hegghammer, Pieter Van Ostaeyen (an independent Belgian researcher), Will McCants of the Brookings Institution, and Pieter Nanninga of the University of Groningen—tend to be in their forties. Trust at your peril any Islamic State expert over the age of fifty.
56. Bunzel, "Introducing the 'Islamic State of Iraq and Greater Syria.'"
57. Cole Bunzel, "The Islamic State of Disobedience: al-Baghdadi Triumphant," *Jihadica*, October 5, 2013.
58. "Statement by the Council of Senior Ulama Supporting Actions Taken by the Leader Inviting Qualified Forces to Respond to the Aggression Against This Country," August 14, 1990.
59. Stanley Cohen, personal communication, February 5, 2015.
60. Ibid.
61. *Dabiq* 6 (December 2014), pp. 34–37. The reference in the title of the film *Although the Disbelievers Dislike It* is to Koran 61:8: "They want to extinguish the light of God with their mouths, but God will perfect His light, although the disbelievers dislike it."
62. Joas Wagemakers, "Maqdisi in the Middle," *Jihadica*, February 11, 2015.
63. A hadith states that fire is a punishment reserved only for God: "Atheists were brought to ʿAli, and he burnt them. The news of this event reached Ibn ʿAbbas who said, 'If I had been in his place, I would not have burnt them, as God's Messenger forbade it, saying, *Do not punish anybody with God's punishment (fire).*'" Bukhari 9:84:57.

The Islamic State's justification on the grounds of reciprocal punishment is clear from the choreography of the immolation video. The man who ignited the gas-soaked Kasasbeh was identified as the leader of a military unit whose men had been burned in an airstrike. As a coup de grâce, a front-end loader dropped a load of rubble on Kasasbeh's charred body—again because airstrikes had destroyed buildings and crushed Islamic State personnel with broken concrete.
64. Cole Bunzel, "Binʿali Leaks: Revelations of the Silent Mufti," *Jihadica*, June 15, 2015.

MUSA CERANTONIO

1. Michele Amari, *Biblioteca arabo-sicula* (Turin and Rome: Ermanno Loescher, 1880), p. 213; and *Storia dei musulmani di Sicilia* (Florence: Felice Le Monnier, 1858), pp. 79–80.
2. Joseph A. Carter, Shiraz Maher, and Peter R. Neumann. "#Greenbirds: Measuring Importance and Influence in Syrian Foreign Fighter Networks," International Centre for the Study of Radicalisation (ICSR), April 2014.
3. Peter R. Neumann, *Die neuen Dschihadisten: IS, Europa und die nächste Welle des Terrorismus* (Berlin: Econ, 2015), p. 156.
4. Indeed, in one case, a prominent disseminator turned out to be a Joshua Ryne Goldberg, a mentally unstable Jew living in his parents' Ocean Park, Florida, basement.
5. Peter R. Neumann, interview, London, November 21, 2014.
6. Horst Dickhäuser, interview, Dinslaken, March 27, 2015.
7. Andrew Higgins, "A French Town Linked to Jihad Asks Itself Why," *The New York Times*, January 17, 2015.
8. James Boswell, *The Life of Samuel Johnson* (Oxford: Oxford University Press, 2008 [1791]), p. 347.
9. Muslim 4562.
10. Like many things in early Islamic history and in the Koran, the usage and meaning of *khalifah* are still hotly debated. The Koran says that Adam, of Garden of Eden fame, was a *khalifah*

(2:31), as was David (38:26), and it uses variants on the word to speak of other "successors" or viceregents for God on earth.

That *khilafah* entails succession is clear. The Arabic word-root *khalafa* [to succeed or follow] is an antonym of *salafa* [to precede or come before]. The first produces the words *khilafah* and *khalifah* and the second *salaf* [predecessors or forefathers], the root of "Salafi." But the nature of the succession is not clear, since attempting to stand in for God would be blasphemous on its face, and claiming the mantle of Muhammad would not be much better. And in any case, during the "caliphates" of Adam and David, Muhammad hadn't been born, and God was, as usual, eternal (and therefore incapable of being "succeeded," in a temporal sense). At issue, in part, is whether the caliph should be considered plenipotentiary in religious affairs, or in politics only. The politics-only camp prevailed until 1986, when Patricia Crone and Martin Hinds complicated the picture by arguing that the caliphate began as a political *and* religious institution, with the caliph inheriting the spiritual and temporal authority of the Prophet. See Patricia Crone and Martin Hinds, *God's Caliph: Religious Authority in the First Centuries of Islam* (Cambridge, UK: Cambridge University Press, 1986).

The first caliphs may not have claimed the title at all. No records show the title's use by the first four caliphs, including Abu Bakr al Siddiq. They instead used the title *amir al mu'minin* [prince of the believers], which Abu Bakr al Baghdadi has also arrogated to himself. See Fred M. Donner, *Muhammad and the Believers: At the Origins of Islam* (Cambridge, MA: Harvard University Press, 2010), pp. 209–211.

11. Traditions about the Qurayshi criterion appear in standard collections. But over the centuries, caliphates—from the Abbasids (750–1517) to the Ottomans (1517–1924)—have flouted this criterion flagrantly, and many people have dubiously claimed Qurayshi blood. The surnames Qureshi or Kureishi, common among Muslims in South Asia, imply Qurayshi descent.

    Scripture warns that even the true Quraysh are bad as well as good. Recall that in 622, the Quraysh elite rejected Muhammad's teachings and forced him to flee to Medina. The Quraysh are, according to tradition, the leaders of good and wicked factions, and loved by God for their goodness as much as they are scorned for their wickedness.

12. Representative quotes about *Sham* include, from the hadith, "The angels have rested their wings upon *Sham*" and "belief and the time of turmoil are in *Sham*." In the Koran (17:1), God says he has "blessed the surroundings of the Aqsa Mosque," i.e., the Levant.

13. Enemies of the Islamic State will take Musa's quick rise as evidence of the organization's callowness. Salafis, however, tend to see virtue in a meritocratic religious order. They are, as Bernard Haykel has written, "open, even democratic" in their authority structures. See Haykel, "On the Nature of Salafi Thought and Action," p. 36.

14. John Safran, "Musa Cerantonio: Muslim Convert and Radical Supporter of Islamic State," *Sydney Morning Herald,* January 17, 2015.

15. Graeme Wood, "ISIS: A History of the Islamic State's New Caliphate in Syria and Iraq," *New Republic,* September 1, 2014.

16. See Cass Sunstein, "Why the Unconstitutional Conditions Doctrine Is an Anachronism," *Boston University Law Review* 70, no. 4 (1990): 597.

17. *Oz* purists will note that elements of his take on the story are lifted from Gregory Maguire's novel *Wicked* and the musical based on it.

18. Ibn Qayyim al-Jawziyya, *Madarij al-Salikin* (Beirut: Dar al-Kitab al-'Arabi, 2004), p. 186.

19. See Koran 9:107.

20. Will McCants reports that Baghdadi, too, was a star on the soccer field, known as "our Messi" to his fellow mosque-goers. (See "The Believer.") Note, too, that Bin Laden's radicalization took place partly in a soccer environment. See Lawrence Wright, *The Looming Tower: Al Qaeda and the Road to 9/11* (New York: Knopf, 2006), pp. 86–91.

21. Koran 5:44.

22. "Statement of Hudud," Islamic State, Aleppo Province, n.d. This notice and the one that fol-

lows were both collected and reproduced in Arabic by Aymenn J. Al-Tamimi. https://just paste.it/hududlistaleppo.

23. The Islamic State killed no fewer than twenty-seven men for the crime of sodomy between June 2014 and June 2016. See Aaron Y. Zelin and Jacob Olidort, "The Islamic State's Views on Homosexuality," Washington Institute for Near East Policy (Policywatch 2630), June 14, 2016.

　　The scriptural justification is a report that says Abu Bakr al Siddiq killed a homosexual in this manner. (Another report says he burned one at the stake, and still another says he toppled a heavy wall on one, crushing him. This last method was preferred by the Taliban.) The punishment for sodomy is derived from a hadith in which Muhammad prescribes death for "the one who does it and the one to whom it is done" (Abu Dawud 4462; Tirmidhi 1:152). According to a report by Ibn Taymiyyah, Muhammad was so concerned about the dangers of pederasty that he once told a boy to sit behind him, out of his view, to avoid tempting him. Ibn Taymiyyah, al Tafsir al Kabir, 5:348; quoted in Sara Omar, "From Semantics to Normative Law: Perceptions of Liwāṭ (Sodomy) and Siḥāq (Tribadism [Scissoring]) in Islamic Jurisprudence (8th–15th Century CE)," *Islamic Law and Society* 19 (2012): 223, n. 5. Muhammad is also quoted as saying that "the thing I fear most for my community is sodomy" (Tirmidhi 1457).

24. See W. Heffening, "Sāriḳ," in *Encyclopaedia of Islam,* 1st ed. (1913–1936), ed. M. Th. Houtsma, T. W. Arnold, R. Basset, and R. Hartmann.

25. Koran 24:2.

26. "Statement on the Hadd Punishment for Theft," Islamic State, Wilayat al Kheir, n.d. Trans. Aymenn Al-Tamimi and attributed to Bukhari and Muslim. https://justpaste.it/istheftdez.

27. Koran 24:2.

28. Quoted in Michael Cook, *Commanding Right and Forbidding Wrong in Islamic Thought* (Cambridge: Cambridge University Press, 2000), p. 81.

29. Abu Muhammad al ʿAdnani, "Indeed Your Lord Is Ever Watchful." September 29, 2014.

30. In the first two years of the caliphate's existence, Australia has suffered four attacks, with another eleven thwarted. Megan Palin, "The 11 'Imminent' Terror Attacks Australia Narrowly Escaped," news.com.au, October 15, 2016.

31. In his last major address before being obliterated by a drone near Aleppo on August 30, 2016, ʿAdnani told supporters to reverse the tide of hijrah:

> If the *tawaghit* [tyrants] have shut the door of *hijrah* in your faces, then open the door of jihad in theirs. Make your deed a source of their regret. Truly, the smallest act you do in their lands is more beloved to us than the biggest act done here; it is more effective for us and more harmful to them. If one of you wishes and strives to reach the lands of the Islamic State, then each of us wishes to be in your place to make examples of the crusaders, day and night, scaring them and terrorizing them, until every neighbor fears his neighbor.

Abu Muhammad al ʿAdnani, "That They Live by Proof." Al Hayat Media Center, May 2016.

32. See Abbottabad document SOCOM-2012-0000019-HT and Nelly Lahoud et al., "Letters from Abbottabad: Bin Ladin Sidelined?" Combating Terrorism Center, U.S. Military Academy (West Point), May 3, 2012.

33. Ayman al Zawahiri, "Letter to Abu Musʿab al Zarqawi." Dated July 9, 2005, and released by the Office of the Director of National Intelligence on October 11, 2005.

34. See Khaled Abou ElFadl, "Islamic Law and Muslim Minorities: The Juristic Discourse on Muslim Minorities from the Second/Eighth to the Eleventh/Seventeenth Centuries," *Islamic Law and Society* 1, no. 2 (1994): 142–163.

　　There is debate over the meaning of "Muslim territory." A recent survey by Feisal Abdul Rauf, for example, attempted to find the most Islamic government in existence, as measured by commitment to Islamic ideals concerning life, family, property, and honor. Scandinavian countries, which are frequent targets for Muslim immigration but not *hijrah* in the religious sense, ranked so high that Abdul Rauf excluded them from the index. See Imam Feisal Abdul Rauf, *Defining Islamic Statehood: Measuring and Indexing Contemporary Muslim States* (Basingstoke, UK: Palgrave Macmillan UK, 2015).

35. The fatwa is translated in Alan Verskin, *Oppressed in the Land? Fatwās on Muslims Living under Non-Muslim Rule from the Middle Ages to the Present* (Princeton, NJ: Markus Wiener, 2013), pp. 151–152.

36. James Dowling and Laura Banks, "Sydney Psychiatrist Allegedly Knew About Extremist Robert Cerantonio's Plan to Leave Australia to Fight Islamic State [*sic*]," *The Daily Telegraph* (Sydney), September 22, 2016.

37. Sahih Muslim 1915 a.

38. For more on Dhahiri jurisprudence, see Ignác Goldziher, *Die Zahiriten: Ihr Lehrsystem Und Ihre Geschichte* (Leipzig: Verlag Otto Schulze, 1884), translated into English as *The Zahiris* (Leiden: Brill, 2008); and Adam Sabra, "Ibn Hazm's Literalism: A Critique of Islamic Legal Theory," *Al-Qantara* 28:1, January/February 2007.

39. Maribel Fierro, interview (phone), October 1, 2016.

40. José Miguel Puerta Vílchez, "Abu Muhammad 'Ali Ibn Hazm: A Biographical Sketch." In Camilla Adang, Maribel Fierro, and Sabine Schmidtke (eds.), *Ibn Hazm of Cordoba: The Life and Works of a Controversial Thinker* (Leiden: Brill, 2013), pp. 3–25.

41. Some have translated *dhahir* as "literal," but Dhahiris resist the label of literalism. The distinction is a small but reasonable one. They do not reject metaphor; a strict "literal" reading might yield idiotic consequences that an apparent but figurative reading would avoid. If scripture says that a bird in the hand is worth two in the bush, it is not proposing a fixed rate of exchange for poultry. Dhahiris would say the "apparent" meaning is the metaphorical meaning, and the literal meaning is nonsense.

42. Koran 6:89, 16:89.

43. The only school of law that rivals Dhahirism in its hatred of "opinion" [*ra'y*] is Hanbalism—which is, not coincidentally, the legal school of Ibn Taymiyyah and Wahhabi Saudi Arabia. Ibn Hanbal declared that no one ever uses opinion "unless there lies in his heart some deepseated resentment. An unreliable narration is thus dearer to me than the use of reason." Quoted in Jonathan A. C. Brown, *Hadith: Muhammad's Legacy in the Medieval and Modern World* (Oxford: Oneworld, 2009), p. 17.

44. Dhahiris like to note that the founders of other legal schools frowned upon *qiyas* as well. Ahmad ibn Hanbal used it only narrowly (and Hanbalites make comparatively little use of it today), and Malik ibn Anas said he used *qiyas* only once, and regretted it.

45. Muslim 279, 280.

46. See Avner Giladi, *Infants, Parents and Wet Nurses: Medieval Islamic Views on Breastfeeding and Their Social Implications* (Leiden: Brill, 1999), p. 85; also Raymond Ibrahim, "New Fatwa Calls on Men to Drink Women's Breast-Milk," *Middle East Forum*, June 4, 2010.

47. Israfil Yilmaz, in a Tumblr post (since deleted).

48. "Open Letter to Al-Baghdadi," p. 17.

49. William McCants and Andrew March, "Experts Weigh In (Part 3): How Does ISIS Approach Islamic Scripture?" Brookings Institution (Markaz blog), May 5, 2015. https://www.brookings.edu/blog/markaz/2015/05/05/experts-weigh-in-part-3-how-does-isis-approach-islamic-scripture/.

50. Koran 4:29.

51. Dhahiris join the Hanafis (the legal school dominant in Turkey) in this opinion, and dissent from the imposition of capital punishment for sodomites by Malikis, Hanbalis, and (in some cases) Shafi'is. See Camilla Adang, "Ibn Hazm on Homosexuality: A Case Study of Zahiri Methodology," *Al-Qantara* 24:1, 2003, pp. 9–11, 21–23.

52. The Islamist ecumenicism of the Islamic State is underestimated. For a sense of the range of the influences it will accept, see Jacob Olidort, "Inside the Caliphate's Classroom: Textbooks, Guidance Literature and Indoctrination Methods of the Islamic State," Policy Focus 147, Washington Institute for Near East Policy, August 2016.

53. Ibn Hazm is far from the only source of a sense of urgency in the Islamic State's pantheon of scholars. Ibn Taymiyyah, for example, chided his fellow Muslims for taking a lazy attitude toward their religious obligations just because there was no caliphate, and he urged the caliphate's revival. See Mona Hassan, "Modern Interpretations and Misinterpretations of a Medieval Scholar: Apprehending the Political Thought of Ibn Taymiyya," in Yossef Rapoport and Shahab Ahmed (eds.), *Ibn Taymiyya and His Times* (Karachi: Oxford University Press, 2010), pp. 338–341.

YAHYA THE AMERICAN

1. Griff Witte, Sudarsan Raghavan, and James McAuley, "Flow of Foreign Fighters Plummets as Islamic State Loses Its Edge," *Washington Post,* September 9, 2016.

2. This account of his life is drawn from information posted on social media sites and his own sites by Yahya, by his wife, and by their online fans, and from my interviews with people who know Yahya and his family.

3. Frank Lindh, interview (phone), November 3, 2014.

4. Evan Thomas, "A Long, Strange Trip to the Taliban," *Newsweek,* December 16, 2001.

5. John Walker Lindh (letter), May 17, 2016.

6. John Walker Lindh (letter), June 15, 2016.

7. "Obituary: John George Georgelas," *Washington Post,* February 12, 2007.

8. This profile is widely and persuasively described in literature from social science as well as law enforcement. As Peter Bergen has written, the predictability of terrorists' upper-middle-class upbringing and above-average education is such that asking "Who becomes a terrorist?" is "a lot like asking, 'Who owns a Volvo?'" Peter Bergen, *United States of Jihad: Investigating America's Homegrown Terrorists* (New York: Crown, 2016). For a short summary of the literature on American terrorist profiles, see Mitchell D. Silber and Arvin Bhatt, *Radicalization in the West: A Homegrown Threat* (New York Police Department Intelligence Division, 2007).

9. To the surprise of no one who observes the personalities drawn to global jihad, the hypothesis that jihadists are overwhelmingly quantitative types has now been confirmed by social science. As many as sixty percent of Western jihadis have engineering backgrounds. The next most common subject of study is Islamic sciences. Very few become soldiers of the caliphate after studying arts or humanities. See Diego Gambetta and Steffen Hertog, *Engineers of Jihad: The Curious Connection Between Violent Extremism and Education* (Princeton, NJ: Princeton University Press, 2016).

10. Surveys of the most common genera of neurotropic mushrooms are incomplete, though at least one suggests they do not occur in Arabia. See Gaston Guzman, John W. Allen, and Jochen Gartz, "A Worldwide Geographical Distribution of the Neurotropic Fungi," *Ann. Mus. Civ. Rovereto* 14 (1998): 207. These mushrooms thrive on dung, and camel dung could be a growth medium, though the literature does not observe magic mushroom relatives growing on camel waste in Arabia. See Abdulkadir E. Elshafie, "Coprophilous mycobiota of Oman," *Mycotaxon* 93 (2005): 355–358. On the other hand, mycologists find magic mushrooms everywhere they look, and no one seems to have looked hard in the Arabian Peninsula, at least not since the *sahabah*. I thank Jack Murphy and Jochen Gartz for this information.

11. Koran 4:34. See also a hadith concerning Muhammad's favorite wife, Aisha, who requested permission to go with him to fight. In this hadith, quoted by Ibn Hazm, Muhammad does not forbid her but does say that "for you [women], the best jihad is a pilgrimage." Ibn Hazm, *Al Ihkam fi usul alahkam,* 1:344–346; translated by David Vishanoff.

12. Kévin Jackson, interview (phone), December 15, 2015.

13. Kévin Jackson, "The Forgotten Caliphate," *Jihadica,* December 14, 2014.

14. Some speculate that Baghdadi delayed his announcement of a caliphate until after Abu 'Issa's death, to avoid the possibility of dueling caliphates (although it's doubtful that anyone would seriously consider Abu 'Issa's a caliphate, given that he was not a free man during those final years).

In the early days of the Islamic State, several of Abu ʿIssa's old associates pledged allegiance to Baghdadi. The most prominent of these, Abu ʿUmar al Kuwaiti, was an acquaintance of Yahya and attended his public shaming in London. Abu ʿUmar later became prominent as leader of a subgroup (also called Jamaʿat al Muslimin) operating northwest of Aleppo. He became a judge in the Islamic State—only to be executed for his extremism. According to reports, he took *takfir* to new levels, pronouncing death sentences for apostasy on those who were ignorant of scripture—and then pronouncing *takfir* on those too reluctant to pronounce *takfir*. See Abdallah Suleiman Ali, "IS Disciplines Some Emirs to Avoid Losing Base," *Al Monitor*, September 2, 2014.

15. Thomas Jefferson, Letter to Judge William Johnson, June 12, 1823.
16. "Former Data Technician at Local Internet Hosting Company and Self-Admitted Supporter of Pro-Jihad Website Sentenced to 34 Months for Attempting to Cause Damage to a Protected Computer." U.S. Department of Justice press release, August 15, 2006.
17. Goldziher discusses this view, attributed to Ibn Hazm. See *The Zahiris,* pp. 142–143.
18. Koran 4:97–99.
19. Bukhari 3029; Muslim 58.
20. The roles of women in terror organizations are diverse, but certain generalities apply. In most cases they are not leaders, and in some cases they appear to be cannon fodder of sorts—such as in Kurdish terror groups and perhaps Boko Haram today. They are, however, useful for shock value, since global audiences to terror attacks associate women with nurturing behavior, and are therefore extra-shocked when they kill. See Mia Bloom, *Bombshell: Women and Terrorism* (Philadelphia: University of Pennsylvania Press, 2011), pp. 22–23, 136–137.

    In the case of the Islamic State, I have observed conversations on social media in which female recruits have expressed desire to kill—only to be disciplined by other women. "What do you think you can do on the battlefield that a brother cannot do better?" asked one. Instead they are shunted toward household and procreative duties. ("The position of women in the movement," as Stokely Carmichael once said, "is prone.") Some have taken roles in the Islamic State's media department, including Umm Sumayyah, a regular columnist for *Dabiq* on women's issues.

    Islamic State women continue to volunteer for violence anyway. Khadijah Dare, a twenty-two-year-old British convert, took to Twitter after the beheading of U.S. journalist James Foley to announce that "I wna b da 1st UK woman 2 kill a UK or US terorrist!" (Twitter user muhajirah fi Sham (@Ash_Shamiyyah), August 20, 2014.) See also Erin Marie Saltman and Melanie Smith, "'Till Martyrdom Do Us Part': Gender and the ISIS Phenomenon," Institute for Strategic Dialogue, 2015.
21. See "Kill the Imams of Kufr in the West," *Dabiq* 14, April 13, 2016.

    The reference to repentance may sound unexpectedly merciful. In fact, the Islamic State has made repentance from apostasy a cornerstone of its military strategy: anyone who repents and corrects his behavior is, according to the Islamic State's propaganda (and possibly its practice), "guaranteed amnesty, even if they had killed a million mujahedin."

    Yahya does not mention anywhere in the article the practice of formal repentance [*istitabah*], which Shariah judges have traditionally afforded apostates irrespective of whether they are apprehended in a state of apostasy. Serious thinkers in the Islamic tradition—most famously Ghazali—have argued against *istitabah*. Yahya may well have such an argument—perhaps noting that *istitabah* has no basis in revelation—but he does not offer it here.
22. "Contemplate the Creation," *Dabiq* 15, July 2016.

A DREAM DEFERRED

1. Two of Bakri's sons, Mohammed Omar Bakri Mohammed and Bilal Omar Bakri, have died recently in Syria and Iraq. Reports differ about whether the former was executed by the Islamic State for apostasy or blasphemy or was killed on the battlefield, fighting for the Islamic

State in Homs. Bilal died in Iraq's Salahuddin Province, fighting for the Islamic State. "Son of Radical Cleric Omar Bakri Believed Killed in Iraq Fighting for ISIS." Agence France-Presse, December 29, 2015.

2. Jytte Klausen, Eliane Tschaen Barbieri, Aaron Reichlin-Melnick, and Aaron Y. Zelin, "The YouTube Jihadists: A Social Network Analysis of Al-Muhajiroun's Propaganda Campaign," *Perspectives on Terrorism* 6, no. 1 (2012).

3. "God will raise for this community at the end of every hundred years the one who will renovate its religion for it." Abu Dawud, *Kitab Al-Malahim,* Book 37, Number 4278. See also Ella Landau-Tasseron, "The 'Cyclical Reform': A Study of the Mujaddid Tradition," *Studia Islamica* 70 (1989), pp. 79–117.

4. See Raffaello Pantucci, *"We Love Death as You Love Life": Britain's Suburban Mujahedeen* (London: Hurst, 2015).

5. Vikram Dodd and Jamie Grierson, "Revealed: How Anjem Choudary Influenced at Least 100 British Jihadis," *The Guardian,* August 16, 2016.

6. Koran 5:38.

7. In the case of sexual crimes, a guilty verdict requires either four credible eyewitnesses to the penetration, or a confession from the accused. Each witness must testify that he saw a penis in a vagina—as one sixteenth-century Egyptian scholar put it, "like a stylus into a kohl jar." (Moreover, false testimony is itself a *hadd* crime.) "Praise be to the One Who made the penalty of that obscene act so great," wrote Abu al Qasim al Qushayri, "then made it extremely onerous and burdensome to prove!" Quoted in Marion Holmes Katz, "The Hadd Penalty for Zina: Symbol or Deterrent," in Paul M. Cobb, ed., *The Lineaments of Islam: Studies in Honor of Fred McGraw Donner* (Leiden: Brill, 2012), p. 351.

8. Koran 6:80.

9. See Majid Khadduri, "Hudna," in *Encyclopaedia of Islam,* 2nd ed., ed. P. Bearman, Th. Bianquis, C. E. Bosworth, E. van Donzel, and W. P. Heinrichs.

10. The Islamic State is not the only jihadist group with this view of its role in personal moral development. Theo Padnos, a journalist who spent nearly two years as a captive of Jabhat al Nusra, told me something similar. His torturers insisted that their children participate in inflicting pain on him. The adults said they themselves were a generation polluted by life in a secular state. But their kids would be raised knowing no other life but Islam.

11. The Islamic State started its own health service, modeled on Britain's National Health Service. See "Health Services in the Islamic State—Wilāyat al-Raqqah," April 24, 2014. Confirmation of free hospital visits for *muhajir*s can be found in Azadeh Moaveni, "For ISIS Women, Fraught Choices," *New York Times,* November 22, 2015.

12. Jamie Hansen-Lewis and Jacob N. Shapiro, "Understanding the Daesh Economy," *Perspectives on Terrorism* 9:4, 2015.

13. Some data are on his side. More than half of the prisoners in U.S. jails report being drunk or high at the time of their offenses. Dylan Matthews, "Mark Kleiman on Why We Need to Solve Our Alcohol Problem to Solve Our Crime Problem," *Washington Post,* March 28, 2013.

14. Koran 23:6.

15. See Haroon Moghul, "Why It (Still) Makes Little Sense to Call ISIS Islamic," Religion Dispatches, August 24, 2015.

16. However, Muslims are bound to offer this option only when the Christians and Jews have not yet been vanquished. If they resist conquest, they may be enslaved.

17. In a separate issue, *Dabiq* published an article that took up the question of whether Yazidis (members of an ancient Kurdish sect that borrows elements of Islam and had come under attack from Islamic State forces in northern Iraq) are lapsed Muslims, and therefore marked for death, or merely pagans and therefore fair game for enslavement. A study group of Islamic State scholars had convened, on government orders, to resolve this issue. If they are pagans, the article's anonymous author wrote,

Yazidi women and children [are to be] divided according to the Shariah amongst the fighters of the Islamic State who participated in the Sinjar operations [in northern Iraq]. . . . Enslaving the families of the *kuffar* [infidels] and taking their women as concubines is a firmly established aspect of the Shariah that if one were to deny or mock, he would be denying or mocking the verses of the Koran and the narrations of the Prophet . . . and thereby apostatizing from Islam.

"The Revival of Slavery Before the Hour," *Dabiq* 4, October 2014.

18. The only evidence I have seen that the Islamic State is embarrassed by sex slavery is a general directive to fighters in Aleppo province that specifically forbids "uploading to the Internet photos of *sabaya* [sex slaves]." General notification, Aleppo Province, February/March 2015. https://justpaste.it/aleppogeneralnote. This document was found and translated by Aymenn J. Al-Tamimi.

19. "Report on the Protection of Civilians in the Armed Conflict in Iraq," UNAMI/OHCHR, January 11, 2016, p. 18, n. 37.

20. This "spirit of the laws" form of legal argument, appealing to the goals of Shariah [*maqasid al shari'ah*] rather than the letter of the law, is in obvious tension with the literalism insisted upon in other situations.

21. "Slave Girls or Prostitutes?" *Dabiq* 9, May 22, 2015.

22. Abu Baraa's defense echoed modern feminist theory: the master-slave relationship is inherently unequal, he acknowledged. But could we not say the same about all male-female relations? Consent is a fiction. Men are physically stronger than women. Yet women are capable of giving consent. "We don't say that Lois Lane can't consent to sex with Superman," he said, after I suggested the analogy.

23. " 'Claim Jobseeker's Allowance and Plan Holy War': Hate Preacher Pocketing £25,000 a Year in Benefits Calls On Fanatics to Live Off the State," *Daily Mail*, February 17, 2013.

24. Jürgen Todenhöfer, *Inside IS—10 Tage im "Islamischen Staat"* (Munich: C. Bertelsmann Verlag, 2015), p. 210; and on Todenhöfer's Facebook: https://www.facebook.com/video.php?v=10152723644955838&fref=nf.

25. See Michael Weiss, "Confessions of an ISIS Spy," *Daily Beast*, November 15, 2015; and Rukmini Callimachi, "A Global Network of Killers, Built by a Secretive Branch of ISIS," *New York Times*, August 4, 2016.

26. Peter R. Neumann, "Victims, Perpetrators, Assets: The Narratives of Islamic State Defectors," ICSR, October 12, 2015.

27. Horst Dickhäuser, interview, Dinslaken, March 27, 2015.

28. See Graeme Wood, "Wrestlemaniac," *The Atlantic*, July 2012.

29. 私はなぜイスラーム教徒になったのか [*Why I Became a Muslim*] (Tokyo: Ohta Shuppan, 2015).

30. That Hassan ate a valedictory slab of pork will be taken incorrectly as evidence that his conversion was halfhearted. But the literature of conversion is littered with cases of converts whose sayonara to their former religion is complicated, and who grant themselves a final indulgence. The most famous of these is Saint Augustine ("Give Me Chastity and Continence—but Not Just Yet!" *Confessions*, book 3, chapter 1).

I know an (eventual) Muslim convert who delayed conversion because of a self-described "love of bacon." If this sounds absurd—and I would not argue otherwise—consider the case of the Islamization of Sulawesi:

Pig-eating was a major obstacle to conversion in all the cases for which there is first-hand evidence. . . . A pious legend had one Makassarese chief threatened with jihad declare that he would not accept Islam even if rivers flowed with blood, as long as there were pigs to eat in the forests of Bulo-bulo. . . . Even when rulers were convinced of the need to convert, they often asked for a grace period during which they could have a mighty feast of all their domestic pigs.

Anthony Reid, "Continuity and Change in the Austronesian Transition to Islam and Christianity," in Peter Bellwood, James J. Fox, and Darrell Tryon, eds., *The Austronesians: Historical and Comparative Perspectives* (Canberra: Australian National University Press, 2006).

31. The great fourteenth-century historian and philosopher Ibn Khaldun argued that the caliph need not come from the Quraysh, because the term "Quraysh" was meant in scripture to refer to the strongest and most unified tribe, which would then have been the Quraysh but might be another tribe today. See Ibn Khaldun, *The Muqaddimah*, trans. Francis Rosenthal (Princeton, NJ: Princeton University Press, 1967), p. 397. Needless to say, Dhahiris and other sticklers do not accept this reading.

32. "The camp of sincerity gathered in the Levant and Iraq and spread to other corners of the earth, reviving thereby the Caliphate, which had been absent for centuries, since the collapse of the Abbasid state." The author of the article is "Abul Harith ath-Thaghri," a likely pseudonym for Yahya. "Contemplate the Creation," *Dabiq* 15, July 2016. Note, however, that other documents accept even the late (and definitely non-Qurayshi) Ottoman caliphate. One document, translated by Aymenn Jawad Al-Tamimi, refers to "the Caliphate state whose fortresses had fallen at the hands of global Zionism in al-Astana [Istanbul] 100 years ago." Abu Abdullah al-Masri, "Principles in the Administration of the Islamic State," *The Guardian*, December 7, 2015.

33. For more, see Suha Taji-Farouki, *A Fundamental Quest: Hizb Al-Tahrir and the Search for the Islamic Caliphate* (London: Grey Seal Books, 1996).

34. Hassan Ko Nakata, *The Mission of Islam in the Contemporary World: Aiming for the Liberation of the Earth Through Reestablishment of the Caliphate* (Kuala Lumpur: Sabah Islamic Media, 2009).

35. The Koranic authority for this ethic of privacy is at 49:12 (which also specifies the punishment—forced cannibalism—for speaking ill of absent company: "Do not spy [on] or backbite each other. Would one of you like to eat the flesh of his brother when dead? You would detest it"). Furthermore, Koran 2:189 forbids entering homes except through the front door, and Koran 24:27 forbids entering them "until you ascertain welcome and greet their inhabitants." Not all governments that seek to rule by Islam have interpreted these verses in privacy-protecting ways. See Intisar Rabb, *Doubt in Islamic Law: A History of Legal Maxims, Interpretation, and Islamic Criminal Law* (Cambridge, UK: Cambridge University Press, 2014), pp. 107–110; and Eli Alshech, " 'Do Not Enter Houses Other Than Your Own': The Evolution of a Notion of a Private Domestic Sphere in Early Sunni Islamic Thought," *Islamic Law and Society* 11, no. 3 (2004).

The Islamic State flagrantly disregards privacy. See, for example, the film *Men of the Hisbah* (Information Office of Raqqah Province, January 2015), which shows the invasion and search of the home of an alleged sorcerer. He is subsequently beheaded. It also opposes free movement across borders, when that movement is away from the caliphate.

36. David Thomson, *Les Français jihadistes* (Paris: Éditions Les Arènes, 2014), p. 205.

37. Antonio Slodkowski, "Radical Scholar Provided Japan with Channel to IS at Hostage Crisis Peak," *Reuters*, February 8, 2015.

DISSENT

1. Thomas Hegghammer, interview, Stansted, UK, August 22, 2015.

2. Aimen Dean, interview, Doha, June 2, 2015.

3. "The Extinction of the Grayzone," *Dabiq* 7, February 2015; "Apostates in the West," *Dabiq* 14, May 2016.

4. Yusuf advised Bush to scrap the name "Operation Infinite Justice," since infinite justice belongs to God alone. Yusuf later pointed out that the main thrust of his advice was to avoid unnecessary violence and war, and that Bush didn't listen.

5. Ask.fm posting by user "AskaDhahiri."

6. Hamza Yusuf, "The Plague Within," Facebook post, July 5, 2016.

7. Of course some Muslims will declare the Islamic State non-Muslim. But these declarations of excommunication nearly always come from lay Muslims unacquainted with the high stakes of *takfir*. Among Muslim scholars, the consensus that the Islamic State's followers are Muslim is broad and robust, encompassing everyone from Sufis to Madkhalis to the jihadist ideologue Abu Muhammad al Maqdisi. See Hélène Sallon, "Abou Mohammed Al-Maqdissi, un théoricien du djihad contre l'organisation Etat islamique," *Le Monde,* September 23, 2016.

8. On Westboro Baptist Church: Megan Phelps Roper, interview, March 1, 2015; on Mel Gibson: Peter J. Boyer, "The Jesus War," *The New Yorker,* September 15, 2003; on the 969 movement: Graeme Wood, "A Countryside of Concentration Camps," *The New Republic,* January 21, 2014.

   For sensible discussion of the question of whether the Islamic State is Islamic, see Amarnath Amarasingam and Aymenn Jawad Al-Tamimi, "Is ISIS Islamic, and Other 'Foolish' Debates," Jihadology.net, April 3, 2015.

9. How small a minority? According to a Pew survey, there are at least 50 to 70 million Muslims (out of 1.6 billion total Muslims in the world) who have a favorable view of the Islamic State. "Spring Survey 2015: Global Attitudes & Trends," Pew Research Center, June 23, 2015.

10. For further discussion of the danger of criticizing the Islamic State on the basis of its minority status, see Kecia Ali, *Sexual Ethics and Islam: Feminist Reflections on Qur'an, Hadith, and Jurisprudence,* 2nd ed. (London: Oneworld, 2015), pp. 67–68.

11. The figure most prominent in declaring the Islamic State "not Islamic" was Barack Obama. In his prime-time address on September 10, 2014, Obama said, "ISIL is not Islamic. No religion condones the killing of innocents." He was being politic. But he was also obviously wrong on both counts. Religions and religious people condone the killing of innocents all the time. Christians have had no difficulty, historically, condoning the Crusades. The God of the Hebrew Bible explicitly calls for the killing of innocents (1 Samuel 15:3: "both man and woman, infant and suckling") from among the Amalekites.

   By February 18, 2015, Obama had softened his position: "Al Qaida and ISIL [. . .] try to portray themselves as religious leaders, holy warriors in defense of Islam," he said, accurately. "We must never accept the premise that they put forward, because it is a lie. . . . [They] are not religious leaders—they're terrorists."

12. Abu Ammaar Yasir Qadhi, trans. and ed., *An Explanation of Muhammad ibn ʿAbd al Wahhab's Kashf al Shubuhat: A Critical Analysis of* Shirk (Birmingham, UK: Al Hidaayah, 2003).

13. Andrea Elliott, "A Marked Man in America," *New York Times Magazine,* March 20, 2011.

14. "I made some serious historical blunders," he wrote, seven years later. "Its [*sic*] been almost a decade since that one-time mistake; I admit it was an error and an incorrect 'fact' was propagated." Yasir Qadhi, "GPU 08 with Yasir Qadhi: When Islamophobia Meets Perceived Anti-Semitism," Muslimmatters.org, November 10, 2008.

15. Yasir Qadhi, "To Blair or Not to Blair?" Muslimmatters.org, February 4, 2009.

16. Yasir Qadhi and Daniel Haqiqatjou, "What Is 'Islamic'? A Muslim Response to ISIS and *The Atlantic,*" Muslimmatters.org, February 23, 2015.

17. Edward Gibbon, *History of the Decline and Fall of the Roman Empire,* vol. 3, ch. 50. Giorgio Levi Della Vida describes the specifics of the conspiracy as "almost certainly apocryphal," but since it's a good story and continues to be an element of the Kharijite mythos, I reproduce it here. See Giorgio Levi Della Vida, "Khāridjites," in *Encyclopaedia of Islam,* 2nd ed.

18. Keith Lewinstein, "Azāriqa," in *Encyclopaedia of Islam,* 3rd ed., ed. Kate Fleet, Gudrun Krämer, Denis Matringe, John Nawas, and Everett Rowson. On the contest over prayer times in early Islam, see Uri Rubin, "Morning and Evening Prayer in Early Islam," *Jerusalem Studies in Arabic and Islam* 10 (1987).

19. Only one sect that exists today can be seen as a remnant of Kharijism, and it is Ibadiyya, a branch of Islam practiced in Oman, Zanzibar, and pockets of North Africa. It is relatively benign, and more sinned against than sinning in its relations with other Muslim sects.

20. The association between Kharijites and the "Ethiopian slave" hadith is another case in which non-Kharijites have assumed the right to speak for their vanquished enemies. Patricia Crone argues that the hadith is not distinctively Kharijite, and indeed was used to polemicize against them. Patricia Crone, "'Even an Ethiopian Slave': The Transformation of a Sunni Tradition," *Bulletin of the School of Oriental and African Studies* 57.01 (1994), pp. 60–62.

21. There is dispute among Muslim scholars about whether the hadith stating that a Kharijite-like group will "exit Islam and not come back to it" means definitively that the Kharijites are not Muslim. The Saudi scholar ʿAbd al ʿAziz bin Baz states that the majority of jurists consider them Muslim, though he himself disagrees. See "Who Are the Khawarij, Are They Disbelievers or Muslims?" YouTube, uploaded November 25, 2014. https://www.youtube.com/watch?v=Bpw5Umi4EYQ.

22. Shaykh Abu Sufyan As Sulami, "Sind wir Khawarij?" Uploaded to YouTube by Al-Ghurabaa Media, July 25, 2013.

23. See Abu Ismael, "Are the Islamic State Khāwārij?" July 15, 2015.

24. Abu ʿUmar al Kuwaiti, the follower of Abu ʿIssa who joined the Islamic State and became a judge, was likely killed on these grounds. (See pp. 296–97, n. 14.)

25. For more on Yusuf and Qadhi, see Zareena Grewal, *Islam Is a Foreign Country: American Muslims and the Global Crisis of Authority* (New York: New York University Press, 2013).

26. See chapter 2.

27. Judged as argument, the "Letter to Baghdadi" is seriously deficient. Ella Landau Tasseron provides the best summary of objections in "Delegitimizing ISIS on Islamic Grounds: Criticism of Abu Bakr Al-Baghdadi by Muslim Scholars," MEMRI Inquiry and Analysis #1205, November 19, 2015. Landau Tasseron's analysis notes that many of the Koranic verses adduced by the letter's authors are, in fact, generally considered to have been superseded by other Koranic verses, and that the Islamic State's interpretations are often more in line with historical and scholarly readings than those of the authors of the letter.

    Kecia Ali has noted separately that the anti-slavery statement in the letter—which alleges a consensus of Muslim scholars against the current-day practice of slavery—relies on "historically ludicrous claims." Kecia Ali, *Sexual Ethics*, p. 71.

28. Saadia Gaon, *The Book of Beliefs and Opinions,* trans. Samuel Rosenblatt (New Haven, CT: Yale University Press, 1948), p. 5.

29. Hamza Yusuf, "The Plague Within," Facebook post, July 5, 2016.

30. For an attempt to rehabilitate Murjiʾiism, see Mustafa Akyol, "A Medieval Antidote to ISIS," *New York Times,* December 21, 2015. The task of reclaiming Murjiʾiism is heterodox, though, since the category has nearly always been considered a negative one. One might compare it to gays' appropriation of "queer."

31. Abdullah Pocius, interview, Philadelphia, November 20, 2014.

32. Khoder Soueid, July 22, 2016. http://invitetoislam.tumblr.com/post/147749122618/the-council-of-senior-scholars-in-saudi-arabia. As if to confirm the allegation of obtuse navel-gazing, Saudi religious authorities then released a statement denying that they had issued a new fatwa against the 2016 gaming hit Pokémon GO; however, a 2001 decree against the *card-based* game Pokémon was still in effect. "Saudi Arabia Denies Issuing New Fatwa Against Pokemon," Reuters, July 21, 2016.

33. Yahya Michot, interview, Hartford, CT, September 23, 2015.

34. Quoted in Michot, p. 77.

35. The Islamic State's supporters often ridicule *taqlid* as "blind following"—a phrase so obviously pejorative that one might wonder why anyone would defend the practice. But its virtues become more apparent upon inspection. Mohammad Fadel has described how *taqlid* introduced stability to the legal system, since the following of senior jurists' opinions reduced the chaos inherent in having each judge come to his own conclusion following his own reasoning. A pragmatic rather than ideal view of law might therefore favor a *taqlid*-heavy system. The Islamic State, however, is nothing if not idealist. Mohammad Fadel, "The Social Logic of Taqlid and the Rise of the Mukhatasar," *Islamic Law and Society* 3:2, 1996, pp. 193–198.

Simultaneously, though, Islamic tradition rewards the practice of *ijtihad:* a Prophetic saying promises reward even to a jurist who, after sincere and responsible effort, judges incorrectly. God doesn't penalize wrong answers, in other words—only guesses.

36. Conversation, Miami Beach, May 4, 2015. See also Jonathan Sacks, *Not in God's Name: Confronting Religious Violence* (New York: Schocken, 2015).

THE WAR OF THE END OF TIME

1. Jonathan D. Spence, *God's Chinese Son: The Taiping Heavenly Kingdom of Hong Xiuquan* (New York: Norton, 1996), pp. xxvii, 48, 191. The quotes from Hong are a mixture of his own poetry and official Taiping edicts, adapted by Spence.
2. See Stian Michalson, "Islamisme på norsk—Profetens Ummahs ideologiske utvikling," in Øystein Sørensen, Bernt Hagtvet, and Nik. Brandal, eds., *Islamisme: Ideologi og Trussel* (Oslo: Dreyer, 2016), pp. 282–285.
3. "A Selection of Military Operations," *Dabiq* 12, November 2015.
4. There are many popular and lavishly illustrated books cataloguing these signs. Two recent titles are Dr. Muhammad al-ʿAreefi, *The End of the World: Signs of the Hour Major and Minor* (Riyadh: Darussalam Publishers, 2014), and Muhammad bin Bayyumi, *Smaller Signs of the Day* (Riyadh: Darussalam Publishers, 2014).
5. Tony Ortega, "America's Most Prominent Muslim Says *The Atlantic* Is Doing PR for ISIS," RawStory.com, February 17, 2015.
6. See Jean-Pierre Filiu, *Apocalypse in Islam,* trans. M. B. DeBevoise (Berkeley: University of California Press, 2011), pp. 12–23. I have used Filiu's chronology to fill in gaps in the accounts of the apocalypse, as told by Islamic State supporters in their conversations with me.
7. Will McCants, interview, November 10, 2014. See also William McCants, *The ISIS Apocalypse: The History, Strategy, and Doomsday Vision of the Islamic State* (New York: St. Martin's Press, 2015).
8. There is evidence that Muhammad, like many other religious visionaries, believed the world would end soon—perhaps during his own time. He told his followers, "When I was sent, I and the Hour were thus—joining his two fingers, the middle finger and the one next to the thumb." "I and the Hour were sent together. It almost preceded me." *The History of Al Tabari,* v. 1, trans. Franz Rosenthal (Albany: SUNY Press, 2015), pp. 180–181. See also Stephen J. Shoemaker, *The Death of a Prophet: The End of Muhammad's Life and the Beginnings of Islam* (Philadelphia: University of Pennsylvania Press, 2012), ch. 3.
9. "No Respite," Al Hayat Media Center, December 2015.
10. Musa Cerantonio, "Which Nation Does Rum in the Ahadith of the Last Days Refer To?" Available online, February 2015.
11. See Filiu, *Apocalypse in Islam,* p. 15, and *Dabiq* 12, p. 66.
12. The Islamic State's own propaganda suggests that this will be the case, and that the confrontation between its forces and (Turkish-backed) rebel forces at Dabiq in October 2016 was not the prophesied battle.
13. Filiu, *Apocalypse in Islam,* p. 16.
14. The Islamic State refers frequently to the return of Jesus. In February 2015, when they recorded the beheading of almost two dozen Copts in Libya, the masked emcee of the bloodbath addressed the camera in North American English:

> Today, we are on the south of Rome, on the land of Islam, Libya, sending another message. "Oh Crusaders, safety for you will only be wishes, especially when you are fighting us all together. Therefore, we will fight you all together, until the war lays down its burdens and Jesus, peace be upon him, will descend, breaking the cross, killing the swine and abolishing jizya."

"A Message Signed with Blood to the Nation of the Cross," Al Hayat Media Center, February 15, 2015.

15. Quoted in Filiu, *Apocalypse in Islam*, p. 14.

16. Bernard Haykel, "The History and Ideology of the Islamic State," testimony delivered to the U.S. Senate Committee on Homeland Security and Governmental Affairs, January 20, 2016.

17. There is irony in the unwillingness of majority-Christian countries—and the United States in particular—to take the apocalyptic currents in the Islamic State's support seriously. It was President George W. Bush, not Abu Bakr al Baghdadi, who informed Jacques Chirac that "Biblical prophecies are being fulfilled," and that "Gog and Magog are at work in the Middle East." (Chirac asked his aides: "Do any of you know what he is talking about?") See Kurt Eichenwald, *500 Days: Secrets and Lies in the Terror Wars* (New York: Touchstone, 2013), p. 459.

18. See "On the Great Slaughter of Dabiq," *Al-Naba* magazine, 12 Muharram 1437 (October 13, 2016).

19. Jürgen Todenhöfer, interview (phone), August 18, 2015.

20. Abu Bakr al Baghdadi, "March Forth Whether Light or Heavy," Al Furqan Media, May 14, 2015.

21. Musnad Ahmad 12491.

22. This essay is partially translated in McCants, pp. 179–181.

23. *Although the Disbelievers Dislike It*, November 16, 2014.

24. "No Respite," November 24, 2015. The title is from the Koran 10:71, a call by Noah urging his enemies to attack him. "So resolve upon your plan and [call upon] your associates. Then let not your plan be obscure to you. Then carry it out upon me and do not give me respite."

25. "Donald J. Trump Response to the Pope," February 18, 2016. https://www.donaldjtrump .com/press-releases/donald-j.-trump-response-to-the-pope. See also Graeme Wood, "Is Donald Trump Right About ISIS?" TheAtlantic.com, February 22, 2016.

26. See Will McCants, "ISIS and Israel," *Jihadica*, November 6, 2015.

27. Christopher Dickey, "Behind the Copenhagen Killings, the ISIS Vision of Apocalypse," *Daily Beast*, February 19, 2015.

28. Norman Cohn, *The Pursuit of the Millennium*, 2nd ed. (New York: Harper Torchbooks, 1961), p. 74.

29. See Yaroslav Trofimov, *The Siege of Mecca* (New York: Anchor, 2008), and Lawrence Wright's *The Looming Tower*, pp. 88–94, for details on the Grand Mosque seizure and its aftermath; and Thomas Hegghammer and Stéphane Lacroix, "Rejectionist Islam in Saudi Arabia: The Story of Juhayman al-'Utaybi Revisited," *International Journal of Middle East Studies* 39 (2007), for the history and goals of the group.

30. Millenarians love round numbers. Jalal al Din al Suyuti, an Egyptian scholar of the fifteenth century, predicted the end of the world in the year 1500 of the Islamic Hijrah calendar. That's A.D. 2076.

31. Cole Bunzel, interviews and a lecture at Boston University, May 3, 2015.

32. Wagemakers, *A Quietist Jihadi*, pp. 167–169.

33. Yasir Qadhi, "1979: When the Ka'bah Was Hijacked by the Fake Mahdi," Lecture in Oslo, April 12, 2014.

34. Facebook comment, November 20, 2015.

35. Leon Festinger, Henry Riecken, and Stanley Schachter, *When Prophecy Fails: A Social and Psychological Study of a Modern Group That Predicted the Destruction of the World* (Minneapolis: University of Minnesota Press, 1956), p. 4. For an update and survey of efforts to replicate the theory, see Lorne Dawson, "Prophetic Failure and Millennial Movements," in Catherine Wessinger, ed., *Oxford Handbook of Millennialism* (New York: Oxford University Press, 2011), pp. 150–170.

36. See Cole Bunzel, "The Islamic State of Decline: Anticipating the Paper Caliphate," *Jihadica*, June 15, 2016.

37. Mario Vargas Llosa, "Antonio Consejero." In *Contra viento y marea*, vol. 2 (Barcelona: Seix Barral, 1983), p. 185.

AFTERLIFE

1. Timothy Snyder, *Black Earth: The Holocaust as History and Warning* (New York: Tim Duggan Books, 2015), p. 158.
2. Abu Bakr al Baghdadi, "So Wait, Indeed We, Along with You, Are Waiting," December 2015.
3. Abu Muhammad al ʿAdnani, "That They Live by Proof," Al Hayat Media Center, May 2016.
4. "The Solid Edifice," Al Bunyan al Marsus, June 21, 2016.
5. Interview with Justin Richmond, Mamasapano, Philippines, October 7, 2016.
6. James Dowling and Laura Banks, "Sydney Psychiatrist Allegedly Knew About Extremist Robert Cerantonio's Plan to Leave Australia to Fight Islamic State [*sic*]," *The Daily Telegraph* (Sydney), September 22, 2016.
7. ʿAdnani, "That They Live by Proof."
8. Interview, Palimbang, Philippines, October 6, 2016.
9. The classic statement of this strategy is by Abu Bakr Naji, *The Management of Savagery: The Most Critical Phase Through Which the Islamic Nation Will Pass,* which was published online in the mid-2000s and translated by William McCants (John M. Olin Institute for Strategic Studies, May 23, 2006). Naji claimed that to triumph, Al Qaida would not need to defeat other Islamist factions, only to manufacture support among Muslims worldwide, through war and exploitation of youth:

> On the assumption that we need half a million mujahedin for our long battle until it ends as we wish (by the permission of God), the possibility of adding this number from a nation of one billion people is easier than adding them from the youth of the Islamist movements who are already polluted by the doubts of the evil sheikhs. The youth of the nation are closer to the innate nature of humans on account of the rebelliousness within them.

   Hassan Hassan has reported widespread distribution of the book within the Islamic State. See Hassan Hassan, "ISIS Has Reached New Depths of Depravity. But There Is a Brutal Logic Behind It," *The Guardian*, February 8, 2015. The strategy has clearly been adopted, though the text is rarely cited in the Islamic State's propaganda.
10. Interview with Lamido Sanusi, London, November 13, 2015.
11. In Boko Haram's case, one of the key figures is Uthman Dan Fodio, the nineteenth-century sheikh whose writings affirm many of the Islamic State's positions about living in Muslim lands. Many analyses of Boko Haram sell its ideological claims short, but its statements have been largely orthodox, from the perspective of broader Islamic State ideology. Here is Ahmed Shekau, at the time the group's leader:

> I am the leader of [Boko Haram] in that country called "Nigeria" (a name in which we do not believe, but are forced to address as such because it has no better name). For there is nothing like Nigeria but the Islamic caliphate. . . . We still have the magnanimity of asking you to repent, because you will never succeed in this way by the grace of God, and I swear by God that we will never stop killing you. If we pity and spare you, one day you will become infidels; so to us, having pity on you is an act of disbelief.

   Quoted in David Cook, "Boko Haram: A New Islamic State in Nigeria" (Baker Institute for Public Policy, December 11, 2014). For general information on the ideology of Boko Haram, see Abdulbasit Kassim, "Defining and Understanding the Religious Philosophy of jihādī-Salafism and the Ideology of Boko Haram," *Politics, Religion & Ideology,* September 1, 2015.
12. Rwandan security official, Kigali, August 7, 2015.

INDEX

ABOUT THE AUTHOR

GRAEME WOOD is a national correspondent for *The Atlantic*. He has written for *The New Republic, The New Yorker, Bloomberg Businessweek, The American Scholar, The Wall Street Journal, The New York Times*, and many other publications. He was the 2014–2015 Edward R. Murrow Press Fellow at the Council on Foreign Relations, and he teaches in the political science department at Yale University.

gcaw.net

@gcaw

ABOUT THE TYPE

This book was set in Minion, a 1990 Adobe Originals typeface by Robert Slimbach (b. 1956). Minion is inspired by classical, old-style typefaces of the late Renaissance, a period of elegant, beautiful, and highly readable type designs. Created primarily for text setting, Minion combines the aesthetic and functional qualities that make text type highly readable with the versatility of digital technology.